it's **not** what
you think

chris evans
it's not what you think

HarperCollins*Publishers*

HarperCollins*Publishers*
77–85 Fulham Palace Road,
Hammersmith, London W6 8JB

www.harpercollins.co.uk

First published by HarperCollins*Publishers* 2009

3

All photos courtesy of the author except for
plate section pages 9 (top), 10, 11 © Big Pictures;
15 (top) © Virgin Radio; 16 © Rankin.

Illustration on page 255 reproduced by
kind permission of Private Eye magazine.

A catalogue record of this book is
available from the British Library

HB ISBN 978-0-00-732721-8
TPB ISBN 978-0-00-732722-5

Printed and bound in Great Britain by
Clays Ltd, St Ives plc

dedication

To everyone that's ever helped me, tolerated me, loved me, laughed with me, cried with me, created with me and forgiven me at any time, anywhere. Thank you.

contents

acknowledgements   x
a book about christopher evans   xi
note to reader   xiv
preface   xv

part one mum, dad and a girl called tina

Top Ten ...

Basic Facts about Christopher Evans   3
Things I Remember about My Dad   6
Best Things about Mrs Evans Senior   11
Double Acts   14
Resounding Memories of Primary-school Life   17
Tastes, C. Evans, 1966–86   20
First Memories of Going to School   22
Weird Things about Teachers from a Kid's Point of View 25
Deaths   32
Favourite Jobs (Other than Showbiz)   38
Bosses I've Worked For   45
Treats   51
Girls – Actually Women – I Thought about Before I Had
   My First Girlfriend   53
Schoolboy Errors   59
Things I'm Rubbish at   67
Things that Freak Me Out   74
Things I Remember from School Lessons   77

part two **the piccadilly years**

Top Ten ...

Best DJs I Have Ever Heard	83
First Commercial Radio Stations in the UK	86
Most Significant Cars in My Life	89
Items of Technology in the Evans Household, circa 1983	96
Things to Consider When Attempting to Make a Move in Your Career	101
Things a Boss Should Never Do	105
Things to Do When the Cards Are Stacked Against You	111
Business Names I Have Been Involved in	114
Dance Floor Fillers for Mobile DJ C. Evans circa 1985	117
Memories of the great Piccadilly Radio exponential learning curve	122
Things that Will Happen to You and that You Will Have to Accept	127
Genuine Names of 80s Nightclubs in the North West of England	134
Stars Recognised by a Single Name	137
Records I remember from My Piccadilly Radio Days	144
Things Never to Joke about on the Air	150
Christmas Presents	153

part three **fame, shame and automobiles**

Top Ten ...

Things No One Tells You about London	161
Legends I Have Worked With	167
Books that Have Inspired Me and at Times Kept Me Sane	173
Jobs at a Radio Station – in My Very Biased Opinion	177
Pivotal Moments in My Career	181
Things that Make a Successful Radio Show (the type of shows I do, that is)	183

Seminal Items of Technology that Had the World Aghast   188

Pads   192

Things to Take to a Meeting if You Think You are Going
to get Shafted   196

Memories of *The Big Breakfast*   202

Female Pop Stars   205

Things to Consider When You Split Up with Someone   210

Songs Regularly Murdered at Karaoke   215

TV Shows   222

Expletives   224

Great Questions to be Asked   229

Reasons to Stay Friends with Your Ex   234

Memories of Radio 1   239

Bands on Radio 1 During Our Watch   242

TFI Moments   245

Things that are True about Showbiz   248

Signs You Are Losing the Plot   251

Things a Celeb Should Never Do   254

Things I Think About – Other than My Wife and Family   260

Offers I Have Declined   265

Best Bits of Advice   274

Most Useless States of Mind   278

Things that Help Get a Deal Done   285

Mantras   290

Things People Put Off   293

Reasons Why I Presume Capital Never Took Us Seriously   301

Human Responses I Experienced Leading Up To the Deal   309

Houses I Have Found Myself In For One Reason
Or Another   312

preview prologue of the next book: top ten stories
still to come …   319

appendix: it is what you think … notes from the cast   320

acknowledgements

I would like to thank my agent Michael Foster for making me sign a contract which meant I had to write this book otherwise I would be put in jail.

I would like to thank Belinda Budge, my publisher at HarperCollins, for being so enthusiastic and supportive, right from the off.

Most of all I would like to thank Natalie Jerome, my editor, who has been incredibly dedicated to this cause. She even stayed at our house for a whole week – overnight bag and all. Nat, you are the best. (I told her she definitely wasn't allowed to edit this bit.)

a book about
christopher evans

My first autobiography, aged 6, complete with original artwork.

My Family   Chris Evans

Mum Dad David   Diane   me

I like my mum best of all because
she gives me alot of coffees and
never shouts at me. Her main
job is gardening. My baby's Golf
My dad is ok his main job is he
proper work is a clark.
A Our Davids job is a deputy at
Winick he thinks alot of himself
Our Diane goes to...   My House

My House is Semi-detached It is
made out of eh jagged stone it has
two gardens one at the front and
one at the back. My house has
a loft. me and my sister Keep
our toys there but we can not
play up there because the floor
boards are too weak to stand on
My house is the middle house it has ventilators

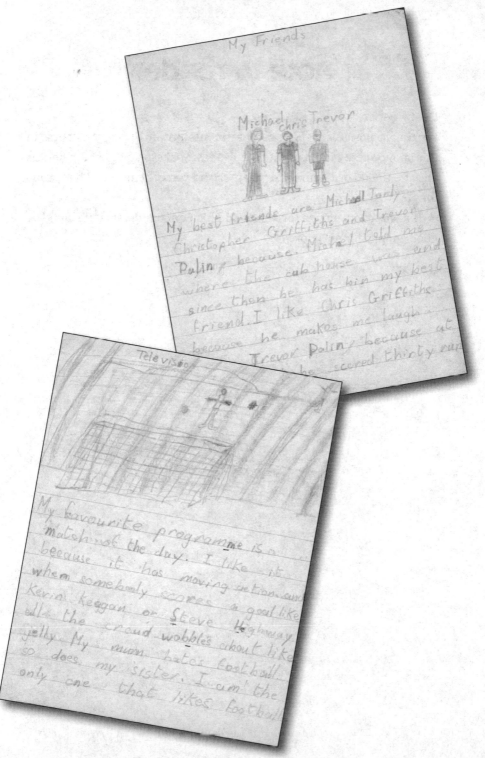

My Friends

Michael Chris Trevor

My best friends are Michael Tanly,
Christopher Griffiths and Trevor
Paliny because. Michael told me
where the cub house was and
since then he has bin my best
friend. I like Chris Griffiths
because he makes me laugh
Trevor Paliny because at
he scored thirty run

Television

My favourite programme is a
match of the day. I like it
because it has moving action and
when somebody scores a goal like
Kevin Keegan or Steve Highway
all the croud wobbles about like
jelly. My mum hates football
so does my sister. I am the
only one that likes football

note to reader

Dear Reader,

For the purposes of bespoke compartmentalisation during the course of this book, where Dickens went for episodes, Shakespeare went for stanzas and the Good Lord himself for chapter and verse, being a DJ I have gone for Top 10s.

If it was good enough for Moses and his Commandments, it should be good enough for my book.

CE

preface

top
10 Tabloid Newspaper Descriptions of Me

10 <u>GENIUS</u>
9 <u>WHIZZ KID</u>
8 <u>MOGUL</u>
7 <u>MOTORMOUTH</u>
6 <u>UGLY</u>
5 <u>MEGLOMANIAC</u>
4 <u>DRUNKARD</u>
3 <u>TYRANT</u>
2 <u>LIAR</u>
1 <u>TOSSER</u>

As you can see there have been countless occasions when I have done myself few favours in the public eye. After some deep thought and consideration on the road back to the real world, I can only conclude that this was because I reached the top of a mountain I never even expected to climb. Once there it's obvious to me now that I didn't have the first clue what to do next – so I jumped off.

'Far more fun than merely walking back down and having a rest before setting off in search of the next one,' I thought.

Wrong!

As a thirteen-year-old paperboy I never for a second imagined the tabloids I was then delivering would one day take me into their beloved bosom and splash me on their front covers with such regularity and for such varying reasons. Some good, some bad, some true, some fittingly published, but that's all part of the deal. Anyone that complains about it – famous people that is – have to realise they can't have their cake and eat it. The fatal mistake is to moan – if you don't like the bright lights and everything that comes with them, get off the stage.

For years, as the song went, I did it my way; for years I thought I was bomb-proof; for years I was just plain lucky when I thought I was being a wise guy. Of course I got things wrong from time to time, but I put that down to being part of life's rich tapestry – after all, few of us set out to get things wrong on purpose.

In the first half of my life – at least I hope it's only been the first half of my life – I achieved everything I ever aspired to. I performed a job that I loved, I punched way above my weight when it came to dating the opposite sex, I worked with and met some of the most talented and exciting people on the planet, I bought cars and houses that were to die for and at one time I was co-owner of a company that was worth over a billion pounds. Yet here I am, sat back in front of the keyboard with a cup of tea, wondering just how on earth any of this happened.

Was there a plan? Not that I'm aware of, but then again I suppose there must have been – surely a story like this couldn't occur by chance? Or maybe that's what life is: just one big accident from start to finish and what comes round the corner to hit us depends on which road we're on at the time.

Ultimately I look back and see a minefield of huge risks and high stakes in all aspects of my life, some of which went my way, some of which did not, but most of which I didn't have to take in the first place, yet I still felt compelled to do so. Barring physical, mental and social disadvantages, I think this is the single most common theme that links people who might be more likely to exceed their so-called 'expectations' as opposed to those who don't.

I am constantly intrigued by this existence of ours and why we are here at all in the first place and therefore, as a result, I am fascinated as to just how far we can take things before we are asked to leave. I also don't want to leave; I love being alive and here and breathing and laughing and crying and loving and feeling, and so I have tried to grab every day by the scruff of the neck and wring it out for all it is worth. (Often to the detriment of my own well-being as well as to the exasperation of those around me.) But I'm sorry, I just can't help it: that's the way I am. Anyone who has a half-decent life and doesn't wonder on a daily basis about the magnificence and irony of being a human being I simply cannot comprehend. Life is too fantastic to ignore.

Along this path of frustration and wonderment I have been lucky enough to achieve what many consider to be a reasonable level of success in my professional life (if not in my personal life) – or at least that's what I thought. I have since come to realise that real success is about the long term. There is no better way to prove yourself than to get better at what you do every day you do it.

There is no question I have made at least as many bad decisions as good ones, probably many more, and there's plenty of evidence to prove it – losing a bunch of money for a start – £67 million at the last count (not that I had much to start with, so let's not dwell on that). But I have also learnt that it only takes one good break to turn your life around and launch you into a stratosphere you never even dared dream of.

If I had to sum up the difference between the good times and the bad, the bottom line is that when I have put the effort in I have reaped the rewards, and when I have failed to do so my life has stalled – on several occasions going into a complete flat spin. It really is as simple as that.

As far as I can see, life is one big bank account and the best philosophy is just to keep on making deposits whenever you can; be they financial, emotional, occupational, or otherwise. This is the absolute number one way to reduce the risk of disappointment, unhappiness, poverty and loneliness. By rights, I'm not at all sure I should even still be here to tell my tale, but by the grace of God I am, so here goes.

part one

mum, dad and a girl called tina

top 10

Basic Facts about Christopher Evans

10 Born 1 April 1966

9 In Warrington in the north-west of England

8 Mother Minnie (nurse)

7 Father Martin (wages clerk, former bookie)

6 Brother David (twelve years older – nursing professional)

5 Sister Diane (four years older – teaching professional)

4 Very bright

3 Reluctant student

2 Needed glasses but nobody knew for the first seven years of his life, which meant I couldn't see a bloody thing at school (presuming this is what the world actually looked like)

1 Had fantastically red hair

Life for me growing up was no great shakes one way or the other. We were an average working-class family with an average working-class life. We weren't poor but, looking back, we were much less well off than I had realised.

I was nought to start off with, but I quickly began to age and lived with my loving mum and dad, Minnie and Martin, and my elder brother and sister, David and Diane. Our house at the time was both a home and a business. We had a proper old-fashioned corner shop like the ones you see on the end of a terraced row of houses, just like in *Coronation Street,* some of which had those over-shiny red bricks that looked more like indoor tiles. This is my first memory of one-upmanship: we never had those bricks but what we did have was a thriving retail outlet. Our shop sold almost everything – at least that's what my mum says – not like Harrods sell almost everything, like elephants and tigers and miniature Ferraris, but like a general store might sell almost everything, like chickens, shoelaces, cigarettes and liquorice.

I don't remember the shop at all, to be honest, but I do remember the tin bath that we all shared on a Sunday night in the living room behind where the shop was. It was a heavy, old, silvery grey thing, rusty in parts, which was ceremonially plonked in front of the fire (for heat retention

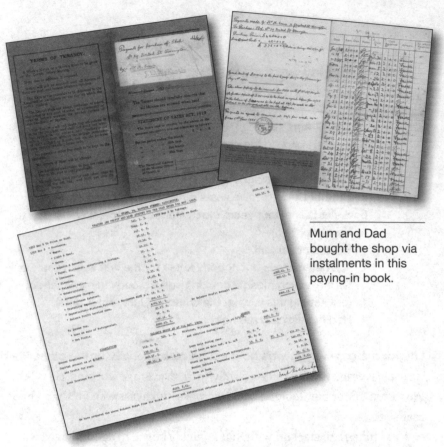

Mum and Dad bought the shop via instalments in this paying-in book.

purposes, I assume) before being filled by hand with scalding-hot water from the kettle boiled on the stove. This was then topped up with cold water via a big white jug, after which we took our turns bathing *en famille*.

I remember the outside toilet, the coal shed, Mr Simpson the greengrocer, and the rag and bone man – who I was a bit scared of – but if I'm honest that's just about it, apart from how upset my mum was when the Council made a compulsory purchase, not only on our house and our shop, but on our whole street, not to mention hundreds of other houses around where we lived, to make way for something so instantly forgettable I've actually forgotten what it was.

As a result of this compulsory order we were forced to move to council housing and another part of town some three miles away, which for a working-class family was tantamount to emigrating to Australia. Although many years later my brother did emigrate to Australia and he assured me it was not the same at all.

For my part I wanted to break out of the council estate which we were forced to call home and where I was brought up mostly. From day one I felt compelled to escape those grey concrete clouds of depression.

The house we lived in was of no particular design, in fact it was of no particular anything. It was more nothing than something. In short, it was not the product of passion. Council estates don't do passion, they just do numbers.

The estate I lived on didn't even do bricks. Huge great slabs of pebble-dashed prison walls had been slotted together in rows of mediocrity as an excuse for housing. Housing for people with more pride in the tip of their little finger than the whole of the town planners' hearts put together. People like my mum, who had survived the war as a young girl whilst simultaneously being robbed of her youth by having to work in a munitions factory. People like my dad and my uncle who had fought overseas to protect us from other kinds of Nazis.

How dare they 'home' these fine people in such an unnecessary hell?

It was waking up to this backdrop of pessimism and injustice every day that made my childhood blood boil. It was like the whole place had been designed to make you want to kill yourself. A curtain of gloom against a drama of doom. I hated the unfairness of it all.

Why did some people, for example, who lived not more than half a mile away, have a detached or semi-detached house that looked like someone may have actually cared about how it turned out? How come they had nice drives and nice cars and a pretty garden at the front and the back?

Not that I begrudged the owners of such places, or rather palaces as they appeared to me, on the contrary – good for them. I just thought things should be the same for my family.

The apathy of it all also drove me crazy. Why did people who lived on these estates all over Great Britain accept this as their lot? Why did mums and dads bother going to work each day to be able to pay the rent for these shitholes? The authorities should have been paying them to live there, with a bonus if they managed to make it all the way through to death.

So there you have it, that's where my initial drive came from. It wasn't that I was bullied at school or the early death of my dad, or any of the other predictable psychobabble reasons often wheeled out to explain success. It was purely and simply that I wanted a better life.

top
10 Things I Remember about My Dad

10 The back of his neck creasing up on the top of his shirt collar
9 The fact that he never took me to a football match
8 His belly, which went all the way in if I pressed it with my finger
7 His vest-and-braces look
6 The smell of Brylcreem
5 His snooker-cue case
4 His handwriting (which was beautiful)*
3 His smile
2 His voice
1 How much my mum loved him

Dad is, sadly, a faint and distant memory for me.

Although he was around for the first thirteen years of my life, I only have a few vivid recollections of him as a personality. I remember him mostly as being just a great dad. What else does a dad need to be?

He was, however, relatively old for a dad, especially in those days, and to be honest I wish he had been a bit younger. Having said that, I'm only a

---

*

couple of years ahead of him now where my own son is concerned and if my wife and I are lucky enough to pop out another little sprog or sprogette any time soon, I will more likely than not be almost exactly the same age to our second child as my dad was to me.

But Dad was also older in his ways. He was a proud guy from a proud time who met my mum at a dance. Dancing was the speed-dating of its era, something we might want to learn from today.

Mum still says, 'You can tell all you need to know about a man if you dance with him – proper dancing that is.' And as the dance halls have disappeared while divorce rates have gone up, it looks like she may well have a point – she usually does.

Whatever Dad did on the dance floor that night, he obviously did it very much to my mum's liking, as from that day onwards, right up until now, some thirty years after he passed away, my mum's heart is still the sole property of one Mr Martin Joseph Evans.

My sister and I were once stupid enough to ask Mum if she had ever considered remarrying. She looked at us as if we had lost our minds – brilliant, beautiful and hilarious all at the same time.

Martin Joseph was a straight up and down suit and tie man for the majority of his waking hours. He was also a handsome bugger with a permanent tan which Mum insisted he received as a reward for serving with the RAF in Egypt during the war. I believed her – it was a cool story.

Dad worked hard every day except Sunday, leaving at the same time every morning and always arriving home at the same time every evening – a quarter past five, more than a minute or two after that and Mum would start getting worried whilst Dad's tea would start getting cold.

He played snooker once a week, where he apparently enjoyed a pint and a half of bitter, but other than that, unless he had a secret life none of us knew about, that was him.

Except, of course, for the gee gees.

Ah, now, there you have him. Dad loved the horses.

There's a famous phrase that goes something like: when you want to know who wins on the horses you need to bear something in mind: the bookmakers have several paying-in windows but only one paying-out window. That should tell you all you need to know about where most of the money goes.

Not that this should have concerned Dad as he was indeed a bookie; he was the enemy and his betting story is the strangest I've ever heard. My dad's entire bookmaking career both started and finished before I was born.

He set up his 'bookies' shop in the fifties with a pal of his, and by all accounts, particularly their own, they did pretty swift business – as most bookmakers do.

Warrington was a typical working-class town in those days, and many an honest man's one and only indulgence was a flutter on the nags once or twice a week. Dad and his partner were happy to facilitate such flights of fancy – until, that is, one day when the frost came down.

This was no normal frost, however, but an almighty frost – a frost that would last not for days or weeks but for months. Four months, to be precise. All racing came to a halt and consequently all wagering. It was the steeplechase season, the favoured genre of the northern man, but the race courses fell silent, the jumps remained unchallenged, the stands stood empty.

Every morning, day in day out, bookies and punters alike, would wake up and draw back the curtains, hoping and praying for a break in the weather, but for weeks on end to no avail.

Eventually, when the break did come, the respective members of both parties could not wait to get back to the business of backing. With news of a change in the weather rumoured the night before, there was a palpable excitement in the air. The horses would soon be free to commence battle once again – as would the punters and the bookies.

Dad, eager to return to business, was up and out the next morning way before dawn; his shop would be the first in town to open that day. The early bird catches the worm, as they say, but little did Dad know this worm had ideas of his own.

There was a man, you see, a man who liked to bet, an honest man, a working-class man, the type of man of whom I have already made mention. This particular man used to walk the three miles or so to work every day. He worked in a factory making soap powder. It wasn't the greatest job in the world, but since the war it was all he'd ever known; it was a wage and for him that was enough.

He would pass Dad's betting shop every morning on his way to work, but it would never be open as it was too early and although he bet with

Dad at the weekends, during the week he always placed his bets at the next betting shop on his journey, just before his work.

However, this morning, Dad's shop, as I said, was the first to open in town that day.

The man, not unlike the horses, was chomping at the bit to get back into the action, so when he saw Dad's shop with the blinds up and the open sign hung on the door, he had no hesitation in entering.

'Morning, Martin.'

'Morning, Fred.'

'Am I the first?'

'You are indeed and a pleasure to do some midweek business with you at last.'

'Well, what an honour. Let's have a look then, shall we?'

'Please go ahead.'

And with that, good old Fred started to study the form from racing pages Dad had pinned to the walls of his establishment half an hour previously.

Fred mused for a while, casting his eye over the various 'opportunities', before finally plumping for a choice. He placed his usual style of bet. It was a forecast – that's the way Fred always betted, and lots of people used to bet that way. The chances of winning were next to nothing but it was a lot of excitement for very little risk, not dissimilar from how the lottery is today. However, if a forecast did come in, there would be no need for any more shifts at the soap factory, that's for sure.

And that is exactly what happened. The frost had thawed, the horses had been saddled, Britain was racing again and Fred went and picked a string of winners.

The bet wiped Dad out. He was the only bookie I have ever heard of that was taken to the cleaners by a punter.

The win was so huge, he couldn't afford to pay Fred straight off, but he was a man of his word and vowed to return him every penny that was owed. Unlike his partner, who would have nothing to do with the whole affair. He reasoned that Dad should never have taken on such a bet without first laying it off, something he himself would have insisted upon doing.

Why hadn't Dad done this? In truth, who knows?

Maybe it was because he didn't have the time to do so with business being so brisk and all – on the first day back after the longest forced break in jump racing since the war. Maybe he was too excited and had simply forgotten. But maybe it was also because he took a chance.

Maybe he took a chance that the odds were massively stacked in his favour and massively stacked against Fred, and as a man who knew his maths well and his racing odds even better, he thought it was a risk worth taking – a safe bet, if you like. But as we all know, there is no such thing.

From that day onwards Dad's wealth would never be financial, but that doesn't mean to say he would never be rich. He had a woman he adored and who adored him back and he was the head of a loving family. 'It's not what you've got in your life, it's who you've got in your life,' he used to say. Now there's a wise man. A very wise man indeed.

top 10
Best Things about Mrs Evans Senior

10 Her name, Minnie. She was named after a horse but it suits her perfectly
9 Her obsession with death and anything or anyone dying
8 Her art for telling stories for hours on end and hardly ever repeating herself
7 Her magic hotpot from the war recipe, hardly any meat but oh so meaty*!
6 Her directness – second only to her vivid imagination
5 Her vivid imagination
4 Her rapier wit
3 Her wicked laugh
2 Her selflessness
1 Her love for my dad

My mum is a formidable piece of work, simple as.

When she had her cataracts done on her eyes, for example, she was well into her sixties and she requested only a local anaesthetic – this was so she could stay awake during the operation and see what was going on. Not an easy thing generally, but especially as this particular operation involves the popping out of the eyeball and the resting of it on one's cheek, while the back is then duly sawn off ready for a new, artificially improved lens to be attached.

Upon hearing a patient had requested such a thing and for such reasons, the consultant surgeon was at first a little shocked before becoming aware of the prospect of a rare opportunity. He wondered if he could also make the most of the situation with a request of his own. He asked my mum if it would be alright for him to invite some students in to watch the procedure and, if she could bring herself to bear it, would it be permissible for them to ask her questions as it took place? Mum was over

---

* I asked my mum for this recipe on countless occasions for the book. She kept fobbing me off for weeks until I informed her the deadline was imminent and it was now or never, at which point she merely replied: 'Time and patience!'

the moon, she couldn't get enough – apparently she had the students in stitches the whole time she was being operated on.

Before we were born Mum was many things, but for most of my childhood, she was a state-registered nurse.

Mum was one of the original night nurses. She started off working in psychiatric care at a place called Winwick Hospital, notorious in the area for being the local nuthouse. Looming large off the A49, it was set back in glorious green parkland and looked exactly like a Victorian prison, though it never had been. This was a proper insane asylum, designed and built solely for that purpose. At one time my dad, my brother and my mum all worked there. As a consequence of this I had been through the infamous heavy black iron gates many times. I even had the pleasure of wheeling the odd harmless 'patient' down some of its eight miles of corridors.

After several years of diligent service with the loonies (she said it was exactly like *One Flew Over the Cuckoo's Nest*, still her favourite film) Mum went on to work at Warrington General Hospital. She always worked nights so she could be with us, her children and her husband, to whom she always referred as Dad, in the day. Her hours were shiftwork, always 10–6, usually three nights on, four nights off, alternating with four nights on, three nights off.

Now of course this was all well and good, but it doesn't take a genius to figure out this meant she would be getting very little sleep. Here's one of Mum's work days:

Finish at 6 a.m., picked up by Dad, home soon after, where she would grab a quick half-hour's shut-eye 'in the chair'. She would then make Dad his breckie, get my sister and me up and ready for school, feed us and then see us out of the house just before nine. Next she would start on the housework and go to bed just before lunchtime where she would languish until three o'clock before having to get up to prepare for the family's return. After making our tea and washing up, she would have another quick half-hour's shut-eye 'in the chair' before getting herself washed and dressed for work and ready for Dad to run her back to the hospital for her next night shift. By my reckoning that's no more than three hours' sleep a day!

During all the years she did this, I never heard her complain once. In fact she only ever laughed about the crazy episodes she and her colleagues came across while the rest of us were in the land of nod. Like the Christmas

Eve that Mr Jolly died whilst on the loo: she thought this was hilarious and seeing as it was she and her pals who had to get his trousers back up around his bottom and hump him back to his bed, they felt a little laughter was the least they were allowed.

After Dad passed away Mum was forced to take on the one remaining role she'd been spared thus far.

Never the greatest at maths, my mum now had to handle the family accounts.

I remember distinctly her sitting us down and telling us the score. She told us she'd sold Dad's car for eighty pounds and that was it.

'That was what?' we wondered.

'That was it,' she repeated, 'that's what we, as a family, are now worth.'

Our house was rented from the council and we didn't own anything else. Mum had resisted selling Dad's car before he died as a mark of respect and so the neighbours wouldn't talk, but now he was gone, so was the Vauxhall.

'OK, fine,' we thought nonchalantly. We didn't really understand what a big deal it was to have so little money and as far as we were concerned things had always been alright anyway. Until Dad became bedridden we'd always had days out and a week away in the summer and nice Christmas presents and sweets at the weekend.

My mum went back to work immediately, although probably as a magician rather than a nurse, as a few years later we had a family bank account with some proper 'rainy day' money in it, added to which somehow she'd managed to buy our house! Alright, it was only a couple of thousand pounds, but nevertheless.

Maybe there was something Dad hadn't been telling us. Mum was a fox with the finances.

top
10 Double Acts

10 Little and Large (I don't care, I loved them)
 9 Abbott and Costello (Saturday mornings, there was little else on television)
 8 Bodie and Doyle (the kings of cool)
 7 Pixie and Dixie (left-field, and nowhere near as predictable as Tom & Jerry)
 6 Ernie and Bert (I wanted to be Ernie but fear I will end up becoming Bert)
 5 Morecambe and Wise (of course)
 4 Zig and Zag (… more later)
 3 Lennon and McCartney (they wrote the only songs I really know)
 2 Tom and Max (my cousins, both international rugby players and top boys all round)
 1 Mum and Dad (a loving but lethal combination)

Dad never once hit me – he didn't have to, I was scared enough of him as it was, not all the time, just when he wanted me to be. Is that what good parenting is all about? Scaring your kids half to death at precisely the right point for precisely the right amount of time – selective scaremongering at will, if you like? Is this how parents get their kids to behave? With the threat, tacit or otherwise, of physical violence? It definitely worked in our house.

In Dad's case the simple raising of his voice or the odd glare in my direction was enough to instil the fear of God into me – I don't know what I feared, I just did. I wasn't scared of my mum at all but I didn't have to be, she had figured out the genius and infallible Mum and Dad combo threat. How about this …

Mum (if I had done something wrong sometime in the afternoon):

'You mark my words (another one of those phrases I've never really understood) your father is going to want to hear about this when he gets home.'

My goodness me, those words still send shivers down my spine even today. The Mum and Dad dreaded combo – just the threat of the man who never hit me was enough to make me conform.

I remember waiting and listening when Dad arrived home after such an episode to see if Mum would carry out her threat and tell him. More often than not it looked like she hadn't, as the evening would continue as normal, first around the dinner table and then another relatively uneventful family night around the telly. With each passing minute I would become slightly more relaxed about the fact that I was probably in the clear. The thing was, though, I never knew for sure, not even the next day, whether I was definitely off the hook or not. This was the master stroke.

Had Mum told Dad? Had Mum told Dad and Dad had decided to let it go? Had Mum told Dad so he knew what had happened and then Dad told Mum that he would pretend he didn't know what had happened; making her look more compassionate in the process?

Whatever the scenario, it worked like a dream. I remember Mum would often sit there for the rest of the night and every time I glanced her way she would give me one of those motherly knowing looks, the count-yourself-lucky look. She would then also go on to benefit from several days of me loving her even more for not grassing me up to the big guy.

Our dinner, or tea as we referred to it, was often prefixed with the phrase, 'Your tea's on the table!'

And it would be, literally. We would join the dinner table at the last possible minute where we would remain for not a second longer than it took to wolf our food down. We were not a family who sat and chatted, at least not over tea, not much over anything to be honest. My poor mum would make a proper full-on meal every night and we would all reward her by sitting down for no more than seven or eight minutes before leaving her as quickly as we'd arrived with the ingratitude of a huge heap of dirty plates and pans to wash up. No wonder she's never been that impressed when I cook her a meal!

I don't know when Mum and Dad did their chatting – if they ever chatted at all. I'm guessing they did, but maybe not – my sister and I were pretty much around all day, every day, and I can never remember them having any private time whatsoever to speak of. I never heard them argue, that's for sure – not the once. Maybe there wasn't that much to discuss or argue about. We were a simple family unit with simple family needs. Maybe they really were the happiest couple in the world or maybe Dad did have a secret life and thought the less he said about anything the better.

When it came to 'S-E-X', for example, the mere suggestion of any of our family talking to each other about such a subject would have caused us all to flee the house screaming. Most families that I knew were the same.

All of my friends and I, without exception, had absolutely no formal training in the science or art of anything to do with what goes on between a boy and a girl down below from any of our parents. Now, I really loved Mum and Dad, but come on guys, you have to tell your kids about the thrills, the spills and ultimately the pills that surround the desires of the flesh.

I didn't get the information from my parents, I didn't get it from my elder sister or brother and I didn't get even get it from school – well, not really. I had to fumble around and figure the whole tawdry affair out for myself. I'm not saying it wasn't fun or exciting, but a guiding hand would not have gone amiss. If you'll forgive the expression.

top 10 Resounding Memories of Primary-school Life

10 Mr Warburton, the school caretaker, who looked like he'd been cast from *Grange Hill*. He was perfect: brown overall, flat cap, pipe, black plastic specs, the works

9 Mr Antrobus, our headmaster, saying, 'If you can't say anything good about a person don't say anything at all'

8 Going swimming once a week on a big red Routemaster bus, never having enough time to get dried properly afterwards and wondering how come the other kids didn't seem to have this problem – did they have special quick drying skin?

7 The hot chocolate from the vending machine after swimming

6 The first day I told my dad it would probably be a good idea if he stopped kissing me goodbye outside the school gates when he dropped me off

5 Making plasticine puppets that took me ages to produce and then performing a play with them on a stage constructed out of a crisp box (they'd fall to pieces before the end of the first page of dialogue)

4 The kid who thought it was hilarious to defecate anywhere but in the toilet cubicles – his tour de force was to do it in the pool when we were swimming

3 Competitions to see who could keep their hand on the hot radiators longest

2 Amanda, my first kiss

1 My packed lunch

School is in many ways the beginning of those shark-infested waters we call real life – when people, young innocent children in this instance, are hauled out of the utopia that is the family unit, hopefully full of love and warmth and protection, to be thrust instead into a whole other world where they are instantly told what they are and are not good at, who's better than them and why they need to change immediately.

What a particularly stupid idea. Within days, the humiliation begins. There are sports team selections that you do or don't make, the latter always being the case where I was concerned. Immediately you're made to

Much better than I ever remember.

ST. MARGARET'S CHURCH OF ENGLAND JUNIOR SCHOOL

ANNUAL REPORT

1974.

Name... Christopher Evans

Class... 1S

Class position... 1 =   Attendance... A

Age range of class... 7-8 yrs   Number of children in class... 36

Subject	Mark or Grade	Max: Mark	Class Posi- tion.	Subject	Mark or Grade	Max: Mark
English Studies	93¾	100	2=	Religious Education	22½	25
Mathematics	96	100	3=	Creative Activities	A	
Geography	19	25		Music	B	
History	21	25		Physical Education	B	
Nature Study and Science	22	25				

... Mrs M. C. Johnson ... Class Teacher.

... Headmaster.

The grades indicate:-   A - Very Good
                         B - Good
                         C - Satisfactory
                         D - Weak
                         E - Very weak

feel like a loser and maybe, like me, then start to consider the rounders team as an option as long as it means you might get picked.

Then there's the endless giving out of gold and silver stars and house points and merits and the ticks and the crosses and all manner of other things that start suddenly coming at you. All designed to let you know whether you are currently a chump or a champ – so many things that can cause a kid to become paralysed as the first pangs of the fear of failure begin to set in. How many self-help books have been written on the self-same subject? Yet it's something that's bred into us almost from the word go. And how about the poor kids who never get a mention?

How often do we hear of a professional sportsman who suffers career-threatening dips in confidence because of a run of poor results? Think about the poor little kiddies peeing their pants waiting for the humiliation of another set of spelling test results.

Then there's the social aspect of the pecking order, evident nowhere more than at lunchtime.

- There's the kids that go home for lunch – does this mean their parents love them more than yours love you?
- The kids that bring packed lunches – does this mean their folks can't afford school dinners?
- The kids who receive free school dinners – surely this should be kept a secret?!
- The kids who go back for seconds – is this the only meal of the day they're getting?
- The kids whose mum is a dinner lady and get extra chips as a result. (Not that we ever had chips at our school, not once – we had scooped mash that tasted strange, nothing resembling any other mash I've tasted before or since!)

For the record I was a packed-lunch child, not for any other reason than that I didn't like school dinners. My packed lunch was without doubt the pinnacle of my school day, it truly was manna from heaven and the thought of it was one of the few things that kept me going through the interminable hours that made up my morning lessons. Cold toast was included for break, an item of fruit, a choccie bar, usually a Breakaway but sometimes a Kit-Kat, a Blue Riband or a Penguin, a flask of soup* and the unquestionable stars of the show: two pasties for lunch that Mum had cooked from frozen in the morning and then opened up so she could fill them with ketchup before resealing them again. Absolutely mouthwatering.

---

* My flask was always under great threat as we used our bags for goalposts when playing footy at break or lunchtime – during which, if the ball happened to hit the post (i.e. pile of bags) hard enough, this would be heralded with the sound of several flasks simultaneously smashing from within. The only thing left to do with a flask after such a catastrophe was use it as a maraca for the rest of the day before getting shouted at when you arrived home.

top 10

Tastes, C. Evans, 1966–86

10 Chips and Tyne-brand tinned stewed steak with heaps of mint sauce and tinned peas

9 Bovril crisps dipped in tea or tomato soup

8 Ham on over-buttered floured baps from Greggs the bakers

7 Tinned toms and bacon with as many rounds of white bread and butter as it will stretch to – minimum five

6 Soggy tinned salmon sandwiches on white bread with white pepper and too much vinegar, hence the 'soggy'

5 Meat and potato pie sandwiches with ketchup – making my mouth water now as I think about them

4 Beans on toast, plain and simple, no poncey Worcestershire sauce or anything like that

3 Fish, chips and gravy – gravy on chips (it's a Northern thing)

2 Dad's gravy dip chip butties – sublime

1 Mum's hotpot from the war, again, with added miracle margarine pastry* – there is no better thing to put in your mouth on planet Earth

When you're a kid, there are hierarchies and *lowerarchies* (a word that doesn't exist but common sense says it should) springing up everywhere you look. Who's hanging out with whom in the sandpit? Who's always at the top of the climbing frame? Who's on their own in the corner of the playground?

The argument that all this is a good idea, I suppose, is that these are the situations that will help prepare children for similar environments they may encounter when they are re-released into the free world. Well, how about the fact that the future adult environments may only exist because of the creation of former childhood ones? Sure, it may have always been thus in the past, in caveman times, but shouldn't we be doing something to change that now instead of perpetuating them – at least honour the worst kids with something if only to stop the tears. Awards for one, awards for all, that's what I say. We're all good at something; it's up to the schools to prise out of us what that may be.

---

* This is a magic pastry that takes 15 minutes from bagged to baked, all brown and crusty. None of this resting it in the fridge for four hours wrapped in cellophane nonsense. Again, any attempt by me to get the recipe for this fell on conveniently deaf ears.

My infant/junior school was St Margaret's – absolutely run of the mill. Old Victorian classrooms complete with ornate, rain-echoing verandas somehow linked clumsily to a new unimaginative square concrete building that looked like it had fallen out of the sky and landed there by mistake.

From the off we had the good teachers and the bad teachers as most schools do, those that could and those that could not when it came to communicating. There was Mrs Clark, the old Ena Sharples battleaxe type who would scare the living daylights out of us – although I can't remember exactly how. There was the glamorous Mrs Johnson who looked like she should have been on one of those ever so slightly risqué *Top of The Pops* album covers and there was Mrs Smith who always reminded me of Virginia Wade for some reason. But my favourite was a supply teacher we had called Mr Hillditch. He was born to teach and took us to the Robinson's bread factory one afternoon where he used to work. When his two weeks of deputising came to an end I remember being genuinely sad that he was leaving. I even wrote him a song and stood up in class to sing it to him.

> *Mr Hillditch we think that thee*
> *Is no good at being referee.*
> *The only thing you're good at is baking bread*
> *Also we'd like to thank you*
> *For giving us such a lot to do*
> *Mr Hillditch we love you*
> *And go-od bye.*

(I was also pretty pleased with the tune I came up with for this ditty – on the audio book I will give it plenty, don't you worry.)

During breaks it was conkers, the climbing frame, a game of footy, or British bulldog, or you could, if you wanted, while away the hours clinging to the school fence, pretending to be a prisoner, dreaming of freedom and rueing the crime that put you inside. I did this quite a lot.

Prizegiving was one of the few highlights, as was sports day, mostly because it meant no lessons. Rarely did I feature in either of these annual events – from the first year it was obvious which three or four kids would rule the roost in both categories and after that the rest of us were demoted to mere bit-part players in the predictable soap opera of typical primary school education.

top 10 First Memories of Going to School

10 First desk
9 First school friend
8 First sports team not selected for
7 First hardest kid
6 First sportiest kid
5 First weird kid
4 First smelly kid
3 First mean teacher
2 First test
1 First exam

One of the unavoidable dividers in school (there are many, most of them unfair and upsetting) is the school test – you know, marks out of twenty. I always did OK in these but imagine if you were one of the kids who couldn't get out of single figures – poor souls. And then the teacher reads out all the results, just in case anyone might not quite have grasped just how dense you are.

Tests were bad enough but then along came another phenomenon – the 'exam'. Exactly when does a test become an exam? They must be different, I suppose, because they have different names. The thing is, for the first few years nobody tells you – or even gives you warning of their existence. You spend years having tests, spelling tests, maths tests, all sorts of tests and then one day the teacher says, 'And in a few weeks' time you will be having your first *exam*.'

Exam! Hang on a minute, what are you talking about exam? What the blinkin' bloomin' whatsit is an exam? Whatever it is, it sounds scary and it must be – otherwise why are we being warned about it several 'weeks' in advance like the potential of a nuclear strike? Kids don't do several weeks in advance. I remember thinking, 'Crikey, this must be really something.'

Even the word exam sounds big and dangerous. Test is a far more flighty word, a far more friendly word – test is light and trips off the tongue. Whereas exam is a deep and heavy word, its gravitas forcing your voice to go down when you say it: EX – AM.

It's a word that resonates in your head, like the hammer clanging in a bell – E X A M A A M A M A M A M.

'This is not a test, it's an exam!'

This phrase brought on another first for me – nerves. Early childhood is relatively free of nerves. What is there to be nervous about? Your job is to be a kid, no problem there, all you have to do is get up every morning, be fairly well behaved and go to bed again the next night. Nerves, I have deduced, all have one thing in common, they are generally brought on by 'expectation'.

Ah now, expectation, a dreaded thing if ever there was one. Expectation – similar to exams – suddenly turns up on the scene out of nowhere, coming into play and throwing up a whole host of other factors that previously did not exist. Expectation for me was a direct result of the past performances of my elder brother and sister – David and Diane. They were both pretty much top of the class, especially my big sis; I was from the same family and therefore I would be 'expected' to continue this tradition of achievement.

All the above could be encapsulated in the ominous ...

ELEVEN PLUS ENTRANCE EXAM *(dramatic music here)*

Fortunately I passed my Eleven Plus with flying colours, which meant for now at least I had fulfilled my expectations: I had overcome my peer pressure, avoided any kind of judgement that might have befallen me and in the process unknowingly scratched the first hairs on the back of those troublesome beasts that go by the names of pride and ego.

As a result of my recent success I was now qualified and officially brainy enough to attend the grandest of all grammar schools for the duration of the next five long years – or at least that's what was supposed to happen.

I was happy to accept the fact that it was now time to hop on the bus with the big boys, but not before Karen with the big boobies had taken me and a few other pals over to the park for a final farewell and a benevolent insight into why those big boys from the senior schools were already knocking on her door.

Why is it some people are just set apart right from the start? Karen was in a different class to the rest of the girls – not literally, of course, but generally, she was the first girl of my age to show any signs of sexiness and everyone knew it. All the girls wanted to be in her gang and all the boys just wanted to be … well, you know. But Karen didn't have a gang – she was a one-woman show and the only audience she was interested in was that of the male species. She was confidence personified. Even those girls who claimed not to be intrigued by Karen's 'powers' had to admit they wanted to know what it was like to be her and to know what she knew, which, compared to the rest of us, was pretty much everything.

I remember seeing Karen a few years later when she couldn't have been more than fifteen. She looked like a bloody supermodel. I have no idea what's happened to her since but I hope she's happy. She certainly deserves to be – goodness knows she spread enough happiness around herself.

top
10
Weird Things about Teachers from a Kid's Point of View

10 Their names
9 Their hair
8 Their clothes
7 Their shoes
6 Their moustaches
5 Their cars
4 Their bags
3 The way they walk
2 The way they breathe
1 Their obsession with punishment

My grammar school was a boys-only, stand-up-when-a-teacher-comes-in-the-class kind of establishment with all pupils having to pass the aforementioned Eleven Plus entry examination to get in.

Though now a subject of much controversy, the streaming system did undoubtedly work – for the clever kids at least. As a result no one in any of our classes was really that 'thick'; consequently learning was relatively swift and even.

While most of the teachers at my last school had been grey by comparison, most of the teachers at this new school were 'colourful', to say the least. This was an old-style school with old-style values and as excellent as the standard of education and learning was – the standard of discipline was formidable.

Good order was kept almost exclusively by the use of fear and violence; and boy did it work. Almost all the teachers were happy, actually more than happy, to dish out physical punishment. At the time it was the norm, but looking back now, it was highly questionable behaviour at best, more likely criminal. It's hard to believe that in all the time I was there not a single dad turned up to give one of the masters a good thump.

Almost all the teachers took great pride in their choice of weapon to beat us with, all feeling a perverted need to continue their academic theme.

Our chemistry teacher would beat us with a length of Bunsen burner rubber tubing, Normally brown, his length had blackened with age –

apparently he'd had it for years. At first we didn't believe it was real: we thought it was just a ruse told to us by the older boys to frighten the life out of us freshers, but one day we pushed our teacher too far and discovered we were wrong, the notorious whip did indeed exist.

This particular master was nicknamed after a cartoon character. We even had a song about him, sung to the juggling tune they use at circuses:

> *Here comes Sir with his Bunsen burner,*
> *Better watch out 'cos he's a learner.*

Our chemistry teacher hid his terror at the bottom of his battered old brown briefcase and when he decided to use it he would physically start shaking with a worrying mixture of anger and excitement. This would cause him to scatter the contents of his briefcase all over the place in the frenzy to dig out his whip. Even his comb-over came to life.

The offending malcontent would hear his name called out, followed by the instruction to come to the master's desk – or bench as it was in the chemistry lab. By the time the poor quivering pupil had arrived, 'Sir' was armed, winding up and getting ready to let rip.

He would first tell you to hold your non-writing hand out and then proceed to lash you on your outstretched palm. If the required degree of remorse was not forthcoming he would next make you bend over across his bench before ceremoniously lifting the flap of your school blazer up and over your buttocks and giving you a good few thrashes across your pert young arse.

Some of the tougher boys would not let him see their pain; for them it was a game, a game that often made 'the master' cry before they did. This was most humorous for the rest of us as he would continue to hit them bleating, 'Why are you making me do this, this is wrong, I don't want to hit you [now sobbing but still of course thrashing away] I don't ... want ... to ... hit ... you.'

Needless to say, he was a confirmed bachelor.

The sports teacher hit us with a plimsoll, the maths teacher with a yardstick. There was one teacher who ran the chess team, so he decided to bring an extra-curricular theme into his choice of weapon of mini destruction; he used to thrash us with a folded-up chessboard. This guy was seriously warped: he used to suck in the air on the back swing of his stroke and exhale triumphantly on the follow through. He was a truly evil man.

He was also king of the board-duster throwers. This was a sport several masters indulged in and one rumoured to have its own league table pasted on the wall of the staff room. The basic premise was: if you weren't paying attention in class, i.e. you were looking out of the window and wondering why most of your teachers weren't in jail, you were considered fair game to have a great heavy wooden blackboard duster hurled at your head. Not only would this scare the shit out of you but it could also cause serious injury – blood and concussion, to name just two.

The really unfair thing was when a master missed their intended target and hit someone else who was innocent instead. This used to happen all the time, especially if they went for someone at the back of the class.

To overcompensate for their obvious embarrassment and evident lack of skill, with the kid who'd done nothing wrong now on the floor screaming in agony, the master would often call out the original offender and give him an almighty whack, much harder than they would have normally, as if it was his fault somehow that they had missed in the first place.

Meanwhile, 'Get yourself off to the nurse lad, it's only a bump on the head,' would be the only sympathy offered to the half-dead boy still writhing around on the floor.

Absolute wankers, the lot of them.

I think I experienced almost all these various methods of sadism during my days at the grammar school – with maybe the exception of the yardstick and the strap, both of which looked too menacing to risk any misbehaviour. No thank you. Another reason I escaped their wrath perhaps was simply because I didn't stick around at the school long enough – we ended up parting company before my fourth year.

One afternoon we were attempting to survive a physics lesson. It was a sunny pleasant day outside and we were stuck in a classroom which looked out over the school playing fields, past the cricket pavilion and on to the railway line in the distance.

I hated school generally but I really hated physics, I was sure I would have absolutely no use for it at any point ever again in my life. I was permanently angry that my time was being wasted learning something I would have no use for. I also thought my physics teacher was a serious nut job.

He was an old, wizened, twisted and bitter man who had forgotten how to smile; all he could do nowadays was contort. I often wondered what might have happened to him in the past to cause him to turn out this way. It was almost impossible to imagine he'd ever been young at all and somewhere along the line he'd turned into the kind of person who gives old people a bad name.

I had long since drifted off far away from whatever it was we were supposed to be studying that day and had taken instead to writing on my desk. I know this is wrong and I shouldn't have been doing it, but as wrong as it was I didn't deserve what was about to happen next.

Unbeknownst to me, the physics master had been stood behind me silently for the last few minutes, for the duration of my 'vandalism', watching me scrape and scratch away at the wooden lid of my desk. He waited for a while before choosing the moment to begin his attack.

He then proceeded with a slow and determined diatribe of disgust at what the hell I thought I was playing at.

He began calmly – certainly.

'Evans, what-are-you-doing?'

It was one of those annoying questions when it was obvious what I was doing; he knew it and I knew it, he just wanted me to say it out loud, all perverts want you to say it out loud.

'What does it look like I'm doing? I'm bored out of my brains because you are a useless teacher and I hate physics anyway and I want to kill you but I know that is against the law, so now I am considering suicide which is also against the law but it means I'll be the only one dead, so that's alright in my book and at least I'll be out of here and away from you and your warped idea of existence – you miserable old ...'

Of course this is what I wanted to say and this is what all my classmates wanted me to say, but as it happened I didn't say anything.

He repeated his question, this time so perplexed and through such gritted teeth I could barely understand what he was saying. The veins in his neck were standing out like a penis with an erection, his mouth foaming at the sides.

'Evans ... what ... are ... you ... doing?'

This time I did manage to utter something, albeit very reluctantly. 'Writing on the desk, sir.'

This reply immediately had my classmates in fits: they were clasping their hands over their mouths to suppress the laughter. It was obvious I was for the chop and when you're at school, as long as it's not you, that's the funniest thing ever.

The sniggering and snorting was doing nothing to help my cause. It only added to making a mockery of the whole situation, something that thrust old Nutjob into hyper rage. He was furious by now, his ire consuming him. But what he hadn't yet seen was exactly what I was writing on the desk, I was praying to God he wouldn't.

'And ... *what* ... are you writing?'

Well now, here's the thing, you see, I was writing his name and my impression of his preferred sexuality.

'Oh fuck,' I thought.

'Oh fuck, fuck, fuck.'

'Fucking hell.'

'Fuck me.'

'I'm *fucked*.'

And I was.

'Come on Evans, WHAT DOES IT SAY?' he screamed.

Now he still hadn't seen what it said and was waiting for me to read it out, something I wasn't prepared to do because whatever he thought it said, I bet he didn't think it said what it did.

He asked me three more times but I just sat there. He couldn't understand why I was being so defiant. The rest of the class couldn't understand why either. Their sniggering had stopped, the room was now filled with an overwhelming air of tension, as if they were just urging me to get it over with. It was obvious I was going to get the whacks anyway. Why didn't I just say whatever it was that was written on the bloody desk?

Some of them even began to mouth: 'J U S T – T E L L – H I M.'

But I couldn't, I had decided that the only thing worse than writing those words was then to vocalise them in front of a class of thirty-odd boys and a man who was now the most insane man on Planet Earth.

'Alright Evans, then I will read it out. What *does* it say?'

'*Shit a fucking brick,*' I thought, 'here it comes ...'

And with that, his eyes widened as his brain engaged with the four simple single-syllable words that lay before him. There was a rumbling, like a volcano about to erupt, and then he screamed, 'SIR ... IS ... A ... QUEER!'

That was it, that's what I had written, the fact that, in my ill-informed schoolboy brain, he was indeed a queer. The rest of the lads were immediately back in hysterics.

This was bad, very bad, and made worse by the fact that I had declared that he was a queer in front of a class of boys who all had supposed he might well be for some time now.

He ordered me to stand up. I was reluctant to do so. He ordered me again. Petrified, I slowly rose to my feet.

He looked at me as if he wanted to kill me.

He then punched me as hard as he could, not in the face but in the chest.

There was shock all around the room. My classmates sat open-mouthed in amazement as I was thrown backwards down the aisle where I hit the wall before slumping to the ground, completely winded.

What in Christ's name did this psycho think he was doing?

I was a thirteen-year-old boy and, yes, I had been naughty, very naughty, but you don't punch a kid, no matter what he's done. My own father had never once raised a hand to me over anything and now here was a man whom I barely knew striking me with the full force of his adult strength.

I will never forget what I did next. There is a difference between bravery and fearlessness; I think bravery is more contemplated whereas fearlessness is more of a reaction to a situation, the consequences of which are not an issue. This is exactly how I was feeling.

Incredulous as to what had happened, I raised myself up off the floor, scrambled back to my desk, picked up my chair and smashed it over his head as hard as I could – at least I think I did, that's how it felt at the time anyway. It probably wasn't quite as dramatic as that but I was so angry.

I do remember for sure him looking up at me and visibly cowering; suddenly his whole demeanour had changed: he looked like he was scared to death. The coward had shown himself for what he really was – a sorry and pathetic bully who had been stripped of his so-called might. I threw down the chair and walked out.

As the big heavy classroom door thud shut behind me with the help of one of those big brass cantilever arms that no one ever knows the name of, I found myself transported from chaos and calamity to calmness and serenity. I was suddenly alone. The corridors, often so busy during changeover and break times, were now deathly quiet.

It was all very poignant.

I took one last look inside the classroom at the scene of bewilderment. *You can have that,* I thought.

I was by no means a model student, but nor was I one of the bad lads and I certainly didn't deserve what had just happened to me.

I turned and started to walk, the hollow sound of my own footsteps reminding me to keep on going. I can still picture it now, like a perfectly framed shot from a Luc Besson movie – the long, highly polished expanse of dark parquet flooring stretching out into the infinite distance, leading to a white light of hope, in my case the two huge main school doors which I was about to exit for the very last time, never to return.

When I woke up that morning I had no idea that by the end of the day, something would have taken place that would change my life for ever.

I would now need to find a new school, and the next school in question would have the added bonus of having girls – and one girl in particular.

But first let's get death out of the way.

top
10 Deaths

10 Elvis Presley
 9 Princess Diana (sorry, but it's true*)
 8 My dog Max
 7 My friend Ronnie
 6 Uncle Harry
 5 John Lennon
 4 My friend James
 3 My dog Rita
 2 My dog Enzo
 1 My dad

And so to the early death of my father – Martin Joseph Evans.

First of all let me I apologise for using the term 'early death' as I'm not quite sure whether that's right, it's just something we've always said about Dad. None of us know when we are supposed to die in the first place; therefore how can anyone's passing really be declared 'early'. Surely we are all meant to die when we do die and that's why it happens when it does. The reason I suppose we refer to Dad's death as being early is because he was relatively young, still in his fifties, when he was plucked out for promotion to that higher office in the sky.

Dad, like Mum, smoked twenty cigarettes a day – at least. Woodbines, evil non-tipped things. I often had a go on his dog-ends when he wasn't looking. Enough to put anyone off smoking for life – not that it did. Martin J was also marginally overweight, maybe a tad more than marginally if I'm brutally honest. He had a marvellous squishy belly that my finger used to disappear into whenever I would check it out. (I have one of those bellies

---

* Danny Baker phoned me up on the Sunday morning: 'Have you heard about Diana?' 'No,' I replied, still half asleep. 'She's been killed along with Dodi.' I immediately jumped out of bed and went downstairs to put the telly on. Fifteen minutes later I was outside the gates of Kensington Palace on my motorbike. When I arrived there was only a single bunch of flowers at the gate, later to become the famous sea of flowers, of course. I don't know why I went there that morning, I'd never even met Diana. I just felt drawn to go.

now.) My inspection of Dad's belly would usually take place while I was draped over him on the sofa, using it as a pillow. Another feature of this experience is that I would be able to hear his breathing loudly up against my ear. He always had a whistling wheeze at the end of each breath, like the last puffs of air faintly draining from a set of bagpipes.

When it came to Dad's diet, it wasn't the best in the world but by no means was it the worst either. He did, however, lead what was for the majority of his days a sedentary lifestyle, which couldn't have been good for him. He was either sat in his car driving to and from work, sat at home in his favourite chair or sat at work doing his sums as a wages clerk for the local health authority.

On the face of it, maybe not such a healthy existence, but then again he didn't drink, he went to bed at 10.30 every night, he led a nine to five existence which seemed pretty stress-free, and he enjoyed a steadfastly sound and happy marriage.

In short, I think the things he did do that were bad for him were counteracted by countless other things that he didn't do that could have been bad for him. I'm guessing he might have expected to make his early seventies at least.

Smoking is obviously the main suspect when it comes to the demise of people like Dad and can be merciless, but when my father died the docs said he had the lungs of a non-smoker – a fact Mum loves to reel out to anyone who will listen. She has a library of such facts from her life that she never wants us to forget, but this is perhaps her favourite.

Dad was hardly ever ill. In fact I only ever recall him being ill twice. Once with the thing that eventually killed him and the other time when he had earache.

I remember the occasion when he had earache as if it were yesterday. I was attending the grammar school when out of nowhere one morning, Dad said he would be able to give me a lift, something he had not been able to do since my leaving the juniors. I usually took the bus.

He had taken the morning off work to go to the doctors and found himself with half an hour to spare. This was another one of those all-round cool situations – a total win–win, it meant I got to be with Dad for an extra fifteen minutes, plus it spared me the bus fare, which gave me extra sweet purchasing power – whoopee!

Dad drove us both proudly on our journey in our usual car mode of near silence. We didn't talk much. For my part I didn't feel we needed to. I have no idea of Dad's thoughts on the matter. Was I the quiet one or was I quiet because he was quiet? Dad didn't do car radios either – 'They only attract attention,' he would say – hilarious!

Three miles later and there we were pulling up outside the main gates of the grammar school in our big, old, navy blue Vauxhall Victor. What a fine motor car that was – there's nothing like the smell of vinyl in the morning.

After bidding each other farewell, Dad drove off to his doctor's appointment while my mind turned to focusing on the far more important task of sweet selection with the spare cash I now had in my pocket.

The doctor duly examined both Dad and his ear but to no avail, he could find nothing wrong with either. Consequently he did what most doctors do in such circumstances and ordered a series of 'tests', a phrase I learnt to dread. It was the same doctor who would fail to spot Dad's bowel cancer.

Mum had noticed Dad was acting a little strangely, especially when it came to his private business. She confronted him one day, at first he was embarrassed, but being a nurse she persisted and discovered that things were not at all as they should be.

Dad said he'd been to see his doctor, something that Mum was furious about as he had not told her this until now. They were a couple that had few, if any, secrets and this revelation did not go down well. Dad went on to tell Mum that he had been sent for more tests but the results had proved inconclusive. His doctor's prognosis therefore was simply that Dad had an irritable stomach and so was prescribed Epsom salts.

This last piece of news sent my mum into apoplexy. She was more than aware of how easily things could go wrong as the result of a misdiagnosis, having seen such episodes at work. She ordered Dad to go and see her doctor immediately.

Mum and Dad had always had different doctors. It was the one thing I never understood about them. All us kids went to Mum's doctor as in her opinion he was the best in town; now it was Dad's turn.

Our doctor referred Dad straight away. As a result he was admitted to hospital. Upon further examination it transpired that Dad was riddled with cancer and there was nothing anyone could do to help him.

Had he been diagnosed in time, there was a good chance he could have been saved.

Mum was absolutely livid. She was told in no uncertain terms that within six to eight weeks, the man she had loved for her entire adult life would no longer be alive.

She is still justifiably very angry about it to this day.

Dad was a good man, a saint in her eyes. He had never wronged anyone, he had always put his family first and now here he was lying in a hospital bed unaware that he was dying.

Mum wanted him home. She wanted him home and she wanted him home now. The first night Dad had been admitted to the hospital the man in the next bed had died. As they wheeled away his body one of the porters gestured to Dad, who he thought was asleep, and whispered, 'He'll be next.'

This broke Mum's heart, she could see that for the first time since she had known him, her husband was frightened.

Dad did come home and somehow Mum managed to turn those six to eight weeks into eighteen months, that's how long Dad lasted with her tender love and care.

The irony of it all was that Mum and Dad never discussed the seriousness of his condition. Mum thinks Dad knew it was terminal but she can't be certain. She says that the only time he ever alluded to the fact that he might not be around for much longer was when he once told her, 'If anything happens to either of us, we will always be there for the other in the eyes of our children.' Still one of the most beautiful things I have ever heard.

As much as Mum didn't discuss the inevitability of his condition with Dad, nor did she discuss it with either my sister or brother and me. As far as we knew Dad was very sick, of that there was little doubt, but we had no idea he was so sick he was going to die.

Dad had been ill for over a year when one evening Mum, who had just finished attending to him, came down to the kitchen, which I was currently using as a workshop for my bike. It was a dark night and cold and wet outside so Mum said I could tinker indoors. My bike now upside down, I was busy cleaning the spokes, oiling the chain, and carrying out other vital maintenance when she came in.

'Oh hi, Mum,' I said, still focused on what I was doing.

'Hello luv.' She sounded down, really down. I looked up to see she was absolutely shattered. Not only that but there was something else wrong. She closed the door behind her, leant against it and looked up towards the ceiling, half as if to plead for some kind of intervention and half to stop the tears, which were now clearly visible welling up in her eyes.

Immediately I began to feel both panic and fear. I had never seen Mum even come close to crying before.

'What's up?' I asked in that kind of uncertain, nervous way a kid asks when he hopes the answer is going to be 'nothing'.

'It's your dad.'

'What about him?'

'He's just so ill, love.'

Well, we knew he was so ill, very very ill, but ill people get better – that's something we also knew, that's what had always been the case. Other less fortunate people died but they weren't ill, they were dying – our dad was not one of those.

'I know he's ill, Mum, but he's going to get better, don't worry.' I said.

The tears were now streaming down Mum's cheeks as if trying to speak on her behalf. There was something she was going to have to tell me, something she had been dreading. She walked over to where I was kneeling down, still next to my bike. She put her hand on my head and started to stroke my hair before whispering.

'He's not going to get better luv. He's never going to get better.'

At this point she completely broke down.

This was the worst moment of my life. Nothing since has come even close to it. When I first heard those words come out of Mum's mouth, I couldn't compute what she meant, it had sounded for all the world as if she had said Dad was no longer going to get better – and then of course I began to realise that's exactly what she had said.

Dad was now in that other category of very sick people: he was no longer ill, he was dying.

Life over the next few months or so – up until Dad's final passing – was much as it had been before, except now we were all much sadder and everything seemed to become much quieter. Dad's disease and everything that came with it continued to happen but now with more frequency and for longer.

The sooner any human being is spared the indignity of such a living hell the better – I don't care what anyone says.

In our minds, now that we knew there was no longer hope, it became more and more evident that our dad – once a big, burly, jolly, intelligent man – had long since left us. The frail old gentleman upstairs was little more than a stranger.

In many ways this made things easier, of course the old gentleman was still a welcome guest and to my mum a worthy patient, but our dad, as we knew him, had now very much gone. My sister, brother and I continued to visit the upstairs room to see the old gentleman every day, chatting about what we were up to at school, but we had already laid my real dad to rest. Secretly we had said our goodbyes, our pillows long since dry from the tears.

The old gentleman battled on but the slope was becoming ever steeper. I hope you never have to experience the silent killer, but as cancer grows everything else diminishes. It's truly awful. We prayed he would be free soon.

The crazy thing is, even when someone is dying, the rest of life has to go on, and so it was with us during those last few weeks. We carried on doing the things we were expected to do. You can't have time off just because your dad's dying – a bizarre state of affairs. Besides, to be honest, no one outside the immediate family knew Dad was so gravely ill. Mum had asked us to keep it between ourselves. I never told any of my friends and they were never interested enough to ask. Kids don't care about illness unless it's their own.

The night Dad died I was cycling home from school. Taking my bike to school instead of the bus was something I had begun to do more of late. I had around a quarter of a mile left to go when I came to the last roundabout just before you turned into our road. There was an ambulance coming the other way. Its lights were flashing but there was no siren. I knew it was him.

As the ambulance passed me on my right-hand side, I felt peace more than anything.

There were no tears, just relief. It was over.

top
10 Favourite Jobs
(Other than Showbiz)

10 Windscreen fitter
 9 Hi-fi salesman
 8 Seafood salesman
 7 Golf shop assistant (for about a week)
 6 Supermarket assistant (trolley boy)
 5 Tarzanagram
 4 Private detective
 3 Market stallholder
 2 Mobile DJ
 1 Newsagent

I would begin work as soon as life allowed me to, although ironically it was death that gave me the green light to start work in the first place.

My father's death when I was thirteen – although obviously devastating for a young boy who loved and respected his dad – did mean that I could, for the first time in my life, take on a paper round. Had my dad still been alive he would never have allowed such a thing.

'Slave labour! No child of mine is working for a pittance like that,' I can hear him saying it now. What Dad failed to realise was the fact that a paper round would elevate a kid of my current financial standing, i.e. almost zero (except for my pocket money), to relatively millionaire status.

My first job was for a newsagent called Ralph. He had an innate talent for impatience and was the sternest man I had come across thus far in my life, much more so than Mum or Dad or any of my teachers.

Ralph had just the one shop but if you ran it like he did, one shop was all you needed. It yielded enough for him to have one of the swellest houses in town – pretty damn large.

Chez Ralph and Mrs Ralph, whom I never met in all the years I knew him, was located in a place called Grappenhall, which is an area close to Warrington on the other side of the Manchester Ship Canal. To get there you have to cross one of two mighty bridges, the first being a huge clumping swing bridge, the second a towering cantilever bridge, both breathtakingly impressive for their time.

Grappenhall was generally accepted as the posh part of town, probably because they had their own cricket team and something akin to a village green, as well as lots of houses like Ralph's, of course. Ralph's grand pile, a testament to Victorian splendour, had both a drive *in* as well as *out* plus a vast stepped lawn at the rear.

One newsagent shop equals one very big, nice house, I made a mental note.

Ralph was firm but fair, something I have never had a problem with, but he could also be a real old grump – a 'misery guts' as they might say, usually at the expense of his own happiness. Don't grumpy people realise it's mostly them who lose out as a result of their moodiness?

And why would anyone do grumpy in the first place? Is it because they think it means the rest of us will take them more seriously, be less likely to try and take them for a ride perhaps? I have no idea why a person would choose to adopt such a posture. Surely it can't be worth it, no matter what the upside. Surely they don't enjoy being grumpy every day. It must be such a draining way to exist. I have never understood such grumps.

I still know people like Ralph today and it still bemuses me. What's wrong with these guys? Have they never read *A Christmas Carol* and thought to do something about themselves before it's all too late and the grim reaper comes a-knocking? Have they never watched *It's A Wonderful Life* and realised we all want to be George Bailey because he's a good guy and everyone loves him and we all want to be loved because it feels great?

Ralph's emotional misgivings, however, although observed, were of little matter to me. Ralph had a paper round up for grabs and I was very much up for grabbing a paper round. He needed someone like me and I needed someone like him.

Alright, so having a paper round would mean having to get out of bed while most of the rest of the country was still asleep, but I was only lying in bed waiting to grow up anyway. I might as well grow up on the move and get paid for it into the bargain, then come the weekend I would be able to afford things! I would be able to buy almost anything I wanted, pasties from the pie shop, sweets and pop, tickets to the pictures, space invaders from the arcade – my mind began reeling with the endless possibilities.

I was still only a kid but as far as I could see I would soon be almost completely financially independent. Although I suppose in a way I was already financially independent – it was just that I didn't have any money to be independent with.

All things considered I couldn't wait to step up to the employment plate for the first time.

Ralph's shop was the model of efficiency. A huge glass window at the front was full of children's toys, most of which had been there so long they had faded in the sunlight. As you entered his hallowed premises, to the left there were four substantial greetings card stands, whilst to the right was a beaten up old ice-cream freezer which flanked the sweet counter. The sweet counter itself was myriad plate-glass shelves laden with sixty or seventy jars of loose sweets. There were crisp boxes stacked high in the corner, chocolate bars and penny mix items at the front. Next to a simple wooden drawer which was used as a till were the weighing scales and numerous different-sized white paper bags tied together with string, hung from a series of hooks.

There were two further counters Ralph had managed to pack into his tiny square footage, each a little goldmine of its own. Opposite the sweet counter was a full-time post office, consisting of two teller positions safeguarded behind double-thick glass screens, which were busy for most of the day. Finally there was Ralph's stage: the mighty newspaper and cigarette counter. This is where the serious money was taken, buoyed by the additional revenue stream of the legendary football pools.

It was in front of Ralph's counter that I would ask for my first ever job.

'I've come about the paper round.'

Ralph looked down at me, I looked up at him; that's when I first noticed how miserable he was. My natural reaction was to smile, but this instantly made him feel uncomfortable. He quickly looked to the side before grumbling, 'Come in seven o'clock sharp tomorrow. Don't be late, one week's trial without pay.'

'Ah, I see,' a miserable man, a tough man and now most probably a mean man – often the three go together, Dickens had it right. Surely one day of delivering papers would be trial enough. If I couldn't do it after that, what difference would another several days of 'trial' make?

Of course this was simply Ralph's way of getting a free week out of a new boy but, as I suspected then and as I know for sure now, one should never allow the terms of a small contract to get in the way of a much bigger one down the line – without the rungs at the bottom of the ladder you'll never reach those that lead to the top.

Besides, if you feel like you're really being stung, there's always the potential for renegotiation in the future but not until after you've proved your worth. This is when you will have something to bargain with. At the beginning of such situations all the Ralphs of this world hold all the cards, but if you're any good, from day one, this balance immediately begins to shift your way.

My 'trial' week duly came and went, and I presumed I passed as nobody thought to tell me otherwise or asked me to leave. This, I surmised, meant I had got the job and poor old Ralph would now have to revert to his rather reluctant stance of paying another small boy very little, to make a grown man quite a lot.

I took to the world of employment like a duck to water and I especially enjoyed the quiet of the early morning, the stillness of the air which allowed sounds to carry much further than they did during the day. I marvelled at the absolute calm of everything before the rest of the neighbourhood decided to wake up. I realised for the first time what creatures of ridiculous habit we human beings are. I wondered why more people didn't seize the day earlier and set about their business when there was no one to get in the way or put them off.

In the summer I would have the sunrises all to myself; in the winter the snow was mine to step in first. I would often witness the best weather of the day. It's spooky how the elements often started off favourably and then grew a little more disgruntled the more people they had to deal with. 'The world only likes people who like the world,' I thought.

Back at the shop, I soon discovered that the earlier you turned up in the morning, the more quickly you were likely to get your paper round made up and hence be out of the door and on the road. This was because most of the boys were still in love with their sleep and left it till the last possible moment before they arrived. In their minds this also meant that they could go straight on to school afterwards without having to go home, if they wore their school uniform that is.

Potentially this may have seemed like a good plan, but apart from having to wear stinky, sweaty clothes for the rest of the day, as delivering papers was no walk in the park, these boys often ended up having to wait for their rounds because they all showed up at the same time – a complete false economy as far as I could see. If, on the other hand, you told the manager you would be in early he would try to make sure your round was ready for you. Bosses like employees who turn up on time, even better if they're early; they also like employees who make their lives easier.

It wasn't long before I was finishing my round before most of the rest of the boys had even started theirs, and it wasn't long before I was promoted to the heady heights of 'spare boy'.

The roll of spare boy was to be both my first promotion and the first position for which I would be retained. Spare boy was paid an additional weekly fee for coming back after his round every morning in case someone hadn't turned up. If this happened to be the case, spare boy would rush to the rescue like a paper boy superhero to save the day, all for a bonus payment of course.

There were occasions when I would end up doing not one extra round but two or three in all. If a boy was a no show, I would take on his round and see if I could do it quicker than him. I would sometimes run my rounds – the quicker I delivered, the lighter my bag would be; the lighter my bag, the quicker still I could go. It all made perfect sense to me. I would see other boys trudging their rounds, hating every second, where was their logic? If you don't like something, either don't do it in the first place, or get it over with as soon as possible, don't drag it out, for heaven's sake.

When old paper boys left, new paper boys replaced them and they in turn would have to be taught their rounds. This was another aspect of the spare boy's role. In time, I came to know all sixteen of our rounds, something that would stand me in great stead for the future.

The next step up the employment ladder was to get a collecting round. Not only were some people too lazy to get their own newspapers in the morning but some of them, it transpired, couldn't even be bothered to go and pay their bill once a week.

I found this incredible, I could hardly believe such goofballs existed but more fool them and more money for me. Their lethargy was my lolly.

Being given a collecting round was the first outstretched finger of trust from Ralph to one of his boys. The boys who held the lofty position of collector were considered very much senior to those who did not. Every

Friday, after school, the collecting cognoscenti would chase down the same paper rounds as we did in the mornings but this time free of our bulging bags and armed instead with book, biro and a pocket full of jangling coins.

We were each given a two-pound float to take with us in case any customers needed change. Upon our return, we then had to add up our receipts, count out our money, subtract our float from the total and hence, hopefully, balance our books. This was my first encounter with simple but highly effective early business practice. This is how business worked. What could be more straightforward?

The pay for collecting was 10 per cent of whatever you collected, which often turned out to be more than you would get for a whole week of delivering. This was easy street in comparison to the delivery rounds, but you had to deliver to get to collect and the better you delivered the better collecting round you were rewarded with. Ralph was a disaster at social intercourse but he sure knew how to get the best out of his boys. He was like a cross between Scrooge and Fagin.

So, what with my morning round, the hallowed position of spare boy, the collecting round, plus additional evening and the Saturday Pink Final rounds (the Pink Finals were sport result sheets, prepared to arrive half an hour after the final scores had come in), I was bringing home easily over a tenner, more towards fifteen quid a week!

Doing the maths, I figured this meant in six weeks I would have close to a hundred pounds. A hundred pounds to my mind was a small fortune – it was enough to buy a brand new bike and still have fifty quid left. It took my mum a whole year to buy my last bike. On this kind of money I could even afford a secondhand motorcycle, or even, at a stretch ... an old car! Not that I had any use for one as I was still three years away from being eligible to drive.

This was simply amazing to me, the concrete of the council estate where I lived was still all around but its greyness was beginning to fade. As I had suspected, working worked.

Some of the houses where I collected from on a Friday were also the 'nice' houses. I could see into their living rooms as I stood by the door waiting for someone to come and pay. These houses had a different smell, they had a different energy, there was more going on. The women who answered the doors seemed to smile more, they were prettier, kinder, they even looked younger. What was it with these people?

Then one day I realised. They were happier.

I made another mental note: bigger, nicer house, equals happier – usually, unless you were Ralph or one of the other grumblies.

top
10

Bosses I've
Worked For

10 Richard Branson (Virgin Radio)
9 Michael Grade (Channel 4)
8 Andrea Wonfor (Channel 4)
7 Don Atyeo (The Power Station)
6 Timmy Mallett (Piccadilly Radio)
5 Charlie Parsons (*The Big Breakfast*)
4 Waheed Alli (*The Big Breakfast*)
3 Matthew Bannister (Greater London Radio)
2 Lesley Douglas (Radio 2)
1 Mike Hibbett (Ralph's Newsagents)

My newsagency career continued to blossom and with it my bank account. It wasn't long before I saw my next promotion. Forget the army, there are more ranks to the hierarchical structure of a newsagents than most international organisations.

My next stripe on the arm was a biggy: I was to be elevated to the much-envied post of 'marker-up'.

The marker-up was the boy who arrived at the same time as Mike the manager. Mike was dead cool, he was forty, which I thought was pretty old at the time but not that old – not in his case at least. To my mind there are young forty year olds and there are old forty year olds, and Mike was definitely one of the former. He loved to play squash, had been a pretty handy footballer in his day and still kept himself fit by going for a run three or four times a week. He was also one of life's good guys.

Mike is still in the top three bosses I've ever had. He was the type of guy that you just did things for, he was always really kind to me. I remember he had a son who I thought was so lucky to have a dad like him.

Mike worked hard and always had a smile on his face, especially when the two girls from the chemist came in for their fags. The girls from the chemist were hot – and I mean really hot. I can still picture them perfectly today. They had huge big smiles, the kind that can take you away to another place. Both of them were brunettes, with bunches of gorgeous shiny hair cascading down over their shoulders and they always came in wearing their white coats, almost always giggling.

Please don't tell me – anyone who's reading this – that they ever got any older. Girls like that should be preserved for ever, just as you remember them. One was called Jill, the small one, she was the one I really fancied, but I never found out the name of the other one – I just called them Jill and Thrill.

Obviously I was far too young to stand a chance with either – they were in their twenties and I was only thirteen – but I could fantasise. Boy, could I fantasise.

Meeting and talking to women that I would never otherwise have come into contact with was another big bonus of working in the shop. I could see what made them laugh, what made them sad, how they were so different to the men that came in. Experience that undoubtedly helped me in the rest of my life when it came to getting on with the opposite sex.

If you think about it, boys of a certain age usually only get to talk to girls roughly the same age – their only other female interaction being with members of their family and their mum's mates or maybe their mates' mums. This is why so many young boys end up fancying such ladies, it's a question of needs must. These women are often the only other 'real women' young boys come into contact with.

Perhaps this is also why so many mums also fancy their sons' mates or their mates' sons. Both parties have an equally limited circle of opportunity; both sides are vulnerable and there is a common thirst to be quenched. Drink up everyone!

My job as marker-up meant I had to arrive at the shop just before 5 a.m. The newspapers having already been delivered in their bundles in the doorway, it was my first task of the day to haul them in off the step, cut them open and count them all out to make sure there was none missing – twenty-five to a quire, eight quires to a bundle, if you were any copies short, you'd make a note and then call and ask for the van to come back later to drop off replacements.

Next we would dress the counter, stacking each brand of paper in order of their popularity, the most popular nearest to hand for efficiency. In our shop it was the *Daily Mirror* first, the *Sun* second, then the *Daily Mail*, the *Star* and the *Express*; we hardly sold any broadsheets, maybe ten each of the *Telegraph* and *The Times* – and no *Guardians* at all! Once this was done we would be set to start, both Mike and I now barely visible surrounded by mini skyscrapers of newspapers.

It was always a competition as to who could finish marking up their rounds first, pistols at dawn, Bic biros at the ready. Each paper round had a corresponding marking up book. The marking up books were handwritten elaborate affairs, not unlike a cricket scorebook in their intricacy and precise beauty. The drawing up of these books was a delicate and painstaking process and one which Ralph had reputedly evolved over the years. No one was particularly clear exactly how or why his system worked but work it did. If there had been a fire there is little doubt the stack of marking up books would have been the thing that Ralph would risk his life to save, certainly way ahead of any of us paperboys.

Mike and I would split the books, eight rounds each and then get to work. The key to speed was getting used to where each brand of paper was without having to look up from the book and losing your place, like a drummer with a drumkit. Once a paper had been slid from the top of its pile, a fast firm fold was then required to make it behave as it was stacked on top of the round, having been marked somewhere in the right-hand margin of the front page with the number of the house to which it was destined. The first paper for each new street also bore the street name.

It sounds like a laborious process – and I suppose it was – but it could be carried out with relative alacrity. Once a rhythm was achieved you could really get into the swing, I loved it. You could almost make the papers crack if you folded them sharply.

My workstation was based behind the infamous post office counter while Mike would work from the main cigarette counter. He was so fast, the fastest, he would almost always beat me hands down, finishing his half of the rounds a good round or two before me. This was even more impressive considering he was serving customers as well as joking and laughing with them at the same time.

The best thing about getting the job of marker-up was that you then didn't have to do a paper round at all. Sure you had to get up even earlier than before, which some of the lads just couldn't comprehend, but then again you got paid *so much more*. The financial gain curve was exponential.

Marking up was also an officially recognised shop job which therefore meant it carried a compulsory hourly rate. This translated into me now being paid more an hour for working in a nice warm shop than the paper boys were being paid for a whole week of delivering newspapers, whatever the weather. Again, it baffled me why on earth they couldn't see the bigger picture.

Working behind the counter was the real deal for me: it was recognition, it was respect, it was civilised and with the marking up complete, it was a cup of coffee for Mike and tea for me. We would take turns brewing up before I took over the shop and Mike went 'in the back'. I never really knew what Mike did when he went 'in the back' – he was probably thinking about Jill and Thrill and the countdown to their fag run, not that I cared, I was out front performing my first ever breakfast show.

'Good morning, how are you today, what can I do you for?'

Real adults handing over hard cash. I used to pride myself on knowing the customers' different orders. Some would leave their car engines running outside while they popped in to pick up their paper and a half an ounce of tobacco. Others would announce their arrival with a glorious exhibition of uncontrollable coughing and spluttering.

Once these guys started to cough and splutter there was no telling how long it might last, it could go on for minutes and the noises that they used to make were extraordinary – exclusive only to the serious early morning smoker: chesty rumblings, throats sounding like they were gargling with broken glass, coughing so hard their faces would turn a violent shade of purple. Often they would have to excuse themselves as they found the need to go back out of the shop 'mid-order' to spit out a huge pavement-cracking greeny. A typical order would be:

'*Daily Mirror* please, sixty Senior Service and a box of Swan Vestas.'

Sixty cigarettes! And non-filtered Senior Service! A day!

Shit, man, that was serious, these guys were hard core. Do you have any idea what just one of these cigarettes would do to the average human lung? Maybe with the exception of Capstan full strength, which were just insane, Senior Service were the strongest cigarettes known to mankind. They would make the 'Lights' of today seem like fresh mountain air in comparison. It was incredible the men who smoked these coffin nails were still breathing, let alone going to work every day and asking for more.

Then there were the 'silents', a strange breed who only ever pointed to what they wanted and always had exactly the right money so they didn't have to speak to you. What was all that about?

As the morning developed, the shop would go through peaks and troughs of patronage with the clientele changing according to the schedule of the day. The shift workers would cough their way into the shop either side of six o'clock, depending on whether they were just starting or just finishing.

There would then be a bit of a lull between 6.30 and 7.30 when we'd try to get most of the boys loaded and on their way – if they had turned up by then that is – and then the school kids would start to come in at around a quarter to eight.

Eight till nine would see a procession of younger pupils stocking up on their daily supply of sweets and snacks, and as the big hand headed towards nine, in would come the young mums with their little bundles of joy off to playschool. Finally, the pensioners would begin to assemble on parade ready to descend upon the post office for their various benefits and other requirements.

The OAPs often arrived much earlier than they needed to. They used to meet their pals for a chinwag but Ralph made them queue up outside so as not to clog up the shop – even in the rain, even in the snow in the middle of winter. I suppose he had a point but it just seemed so wrong. These people were elderly, often infirm, and most of them had served in one if not both of the wars so we could still have a bloody post office in the first place.

I vowed that, whatever else I did in my life, I had to make enough money never to have to queue up in the rain for my pension. That's the least well off I ever wanted to be.

As my time behind the counter progressed I would stay on at the shop for as long as I could until the last possible minute before I had to leave to go to school. The shop was now my life, whereas school was quickly becoming the villain of the piece, a place I attended just because I had to, a mere interruption to my busy working day.

As far as I was concerned I was learning more of what I needed to know about life and how to get on at the shop every weekday morning and evening, all day Saturday as well as Sunday up until lunchtime, than I ever could from my lessons. If I could have left school there and then I would have done. School had taught me all it could by now and in my opinion had taken up far too much of my time in the process.

top
10 Treats*

10 Mint cracknel
9 Ice Breaker
8 Cough candy
7 Cola cubes
6 Refreshers
5 Black Jacks/Fruit Salad mix
4 Texan
3 Merry Maids chocolate caramels
2 Lyons midget gems
1 Curlywurly

After walking out of the grammar school that day, after my altercation with Nutjob the physics teacher, I just carried on walking, I walked all the way home.

For the first mile or so, I was still shaking with adrenaline, I felt no anger or fear, I was satisfied that my actions were justified. I kept going over in my mind what had happened and how crazy it was that one's circumstances could change so quickly. Soon it was like it had happened to someone else, and as my journey continued, my mind began to clear and it wasn't long before I found myself thinking about other things.

I had undertaken this three-and-a-bit-mile journey on foot several times before but usually in the summer when I had chosen to spend my bus fare on a bag of fizz bombs or a can of Lilt instead. I had a feeling this might be the last time I might have to consider such a dilemma.

When I arrived home, much earlier than expected, another Curlywurly had bitten the dust. (Who came up with the Curlywurly, by the way? Not only the concept of the funky lattice-shaped bar but the name Curlywurly – it has to be the coolest name in the world of confectionery.)

'How come you're home so early, love, has something happened?' Mum asked, naturally surprised to see me.

---

*Most of them courtesy of Dad on Saturday afternoons.

A design classic.

I managed to explain as honestly as I could what had taken place at school that day and that I knew I'd done wrong but that I didn't think a grown man should be allowed to hit a child in such a way. She listened intently, without saying a word. After she'd heard what I had to say, she congratulated me on my decisive action and said she would enquire about a new school the very next day. Her exact words were: 'You're not going back there, over my dead body.'

Mum is a very no-nonsense person and once a chapter is closed that's it – it's time to move on. Though she has never admitted it, I believe she went back to the grammar school soon after to give the headmaster a piece of her mind and to set the record straight.

Her enquiries as to a new school resulted in my being much nearer to home, albeit at a comprehensive school. Not that I had a problem with comprehensives, but they were generally considered inferior to the much grander grammar schools. Comprehensive schools were where you went if you couldn't get in anywhere else.

This school was a bit special though. It was a brand new school, where my year, the fourth year, were the eldest – there was no fifth form or sixth form yet. The school was so new that in fact half of it was still being built – hence its reduced capacity and the additional need for Portakabins as classrooms.

This new school was also an altogether much more civilised affair. The classrooms were much brighter, the teachers called you by your first name and their teaching methods were far less draconian, with not a cane nor a slipper in sight – and there were girls!

top

10 Girls – Actually Women – I Thought about Before I Had My First Girlfriend

10 Sabrina from *Charlie's Angels*
 9 Debbie Harry
 8 Sally James
 7 Both girls from *Man About the House*
 6 Jill from the chemists
 5 Mrs Johnson (teacher)
 4 Mrs Tranter (neighbour)
 3 Miss Leavesley (French teacher)
 2 Kim Wilde
 1 Karen with the big boobies

Padgate County High School was the school attended by the incredible Tina Yardley. Tina was to be my first love, deep and genuine and proper and innocent. I still love her now, I always will.

I met her when I was partnered with her as part of the school production of *Oliver!*. She was the girl I would have to link arms with for the opening few lines of the song, 'Let's All Go Down The Strand', one of those annoying cockney songs that not even cockneys like.

Tina was an experienced performer and a general all-round star pupil. She was so confident and smiley – the kind of smile only genuinely good people are allowed to have. She was also vibrant, full of life and, even though she was in the year below me, she was easily as tall as any of the girls in my year – and she smelt amazing.

What is it about girls and their smells? You can't be with someone you don't like the smell of. I don't mean if they stink of B.O. (although in the right circumstances I even find this a turn-on), or unfortunately if they have bad breath. What I'm talking about is their own smell, the smell that is them. I have loved everything about some girls I've met, the way they move, what they talk about, their hair, their eyes and then, wham bam, one whiff of their natural scent and it's 'No Way José' – this is never going to work. Sometimes you don't get down to their real smell until the morning after the night before, that is the worst-case scenario.

I have a friend, now blissfully happily married, who, in a similar vein, says she used to be able to tell when she was falling out of love with someone because she would begin to start to hate the way they used to eat – so much so it would begin to make her want to throw up.

I think this emotion comes from the same source – inexplicable but un-ignorable.

Suffice to say I immediately fell in love with Tina's smell, soon after which I fell in love with Tina herself.

I had seen Tina many times before, not only at school but because she also lived directly opposite my best mate in one of those big houses in the nicer parts of town with a drive and a nice garden at the front and the back. My best mate lived in a similar although slightly smaller house right over the road. He also lived two doors down from Tina's boyfriend!

Not that I knew about this until a couple of days before the opening night of our production when I was riding home on my bike from my best mate's house. I pulled out of his drive and, having pedalled no more than a few yards, I was punched full in the face by a very hard fist which seemed to appear out of nowhere.

The force of the blow, a superb direct hit, knocked me clean off my bike, smashed my glasses and bloodied my nose – a pretty comprehensive result all in all. I didn't have a blinkin' clue what was going on, nor did I know the identity of my assailant, let alone any likely motive behind such an unprovoked attack.

There is nothing like the 'bang' of a punch to shock a kid into bewilderment. Our heads weren't designed to be punched. I suppose that's why it hurts so much and this punch hurt as much as any I'd ever felt before – even the one from Loony Tunes back at the grammar school.

It turned out that this latest fist belonged to Tina's boyfriend. He was eighteen, three years older than me and four years older than Tina.

'That's what you get for messing around with another bloke's girl, you specky four-eyed ginger twat,' he said, as I scrabbled around on the floor looking for what might be left of my glasses.

'Not very nice,' I thought, but who was I to argue? If he was nearly able to decapitate me with one punch, what might he have done if I'd riled him into dishing out a few more?

May I also point out here that I had not 'messed around with another bloke's girlfriend' – I had merely linked Tina's arm several times in rehearsal as the script instructed me to. As far as I was aware she had no idea that I even liked her.

Several minutes later I was back at my mate's house where his mum, who I fancied by the way, was tending my wounds while my mate was trying not to laugh. Not that this bothered me, I would have thought the same if it had happened to him and besides I was privately getting my own back by imagining me and his mum getting married one day and him having to call me Dad.

His mum was livid and insisted on going over the road to tell Tina and her parents what had happened and ask her what such a wonderful girl like her was doing with an animal like 'Shit for Brains'.

My mate's dad – not my biggest fan; perhaps he knew about me and his wife – ended up 'having' to give me a lift home after being convinced that I really couldn't see anything without my specs.

He reluctantly went to get his keys and coat, but before he did so he looked at the state of me and audibly laughed.

'Thanks for that,' I thought. 'Please die soon.'

The next day at school I had to wear my old specs again, a far cry from the Reactolite Rapides that had said farewell the night before – these were altogether much more NHS. The weird kid with ginger hair from the grammar school had just got a little weirder.

We had rehearsals for *Oliver!* scheduled again later that day and all I could think about was what was going to happen when I saw Tina. I couldn't concentrate on my first lesson, I felt like such a loser. The only thing I knew for sure was that I must learn to fight – but first I had to endure breaktime.

I wandered off into a corner of the playground and was in that frame of mind where nothing matters, nothing that has gone before, nothing that exists now and nothing that may exist in the future. I was numb to the core and also really confused. I had done nothing wrong, had been nearly half killed by an idiot and his big knuckles, yet it was me who felt like the schmuck.

My poor old swollen nose was an inch away from the school wall. I was staring at a brick now, hoping breaktime would never end. If I had to stare at this wall for the rest of eternity I wouldn't mind as long as I didn't have to face Tina again.

It was one of those moments like when you climb into a bath and can put life on hold until you decide to climb out again. I recognised I was both at peace and yet totally fucked at the same time, but as long as I didn't move from the exact position I was in – ever – I would be fine. For anything else I would need a miracle. Which was, in fact, what was about to happen.

'Er, Chris ... hi.'

It couldn't be.

'Are you alright?'

It was Tina.

Slowly I turned around and sure enough the rest of the world was still there and in the middle of it all, larger than life with the sweetest, most benevolent expression on her face, framed perfectly, was Tina.

'Yeah, I'm OK thanks – just checking out the wall.'

'I know, I've been watching you for the last few minutes. I'd been trying to find you since break started and then I saw you over here.'

'Oh ...' (Brilliant reply, Chris, simply brilliant. That's how you get your girl, with a weak and pathetic 'Oh.')

'I heard what happened last night and I'm really sorry, he's such an idiot.'

'Oh ...' (I was getting good at this 'oh' business.)

'He's not my boyfriend, you know, at least definitely not now. I was sort of seeing him but not really, I mean, we hadn't ever done anything.'

'Er ... I see.' (Hey, look at that, I was evolving, like prehistoric man – only slower.)

She was still smiling, she really did have the greatest smile and she had more to say.

'So now he's not my boyfriend, that means we could go out together ... if you liked?'

If – I – liked?

IF I LIKED?

Of course I liked. Tina, I was in love with you.

'But ...'

Here's a little tip, whenever anyone gives you or offers you something you want, something you have longed for, something you have only ever been able to dream about before – *do not* – *whatever you do* – *start your next sentence with the word ... but.*

It's pointless, there is no need, it's not heroic or grateful sounding. To be meek at these times serves absolutely no purpose whatsoever. It just sounds wet and feeble, it introduces tedium into the proceedings and, above all, it's completely and altogether stupid.

'... but ...' (*Aggggghhhhh!!! Shut up, you cock.*)

'But what?'

But *nothing*, you prick. Say – 'But nothing.'

(The only word that should ever really follow 'but' is the word 'nothing', then the world would be a better place and we would all get more things done and there would be less wars.) Tell her you love her and you love her smell and you always have and you always will and that you would walk over hot coals just to be able to get her back her rough book.

'But ...' and then it came, the most ridiculous self-pitying, crap line of all time, '... why would you want to go out with me?'

Genius.

'I always have, ever since we first met. I think you're really nice and funny. I was going to ask you anyway. I just had to sort out the thing with Shit For Brains.'

'Ha ha, that's what I call him.'

'Ha ha – see, we already have something in common ... So what do you think?'

'I think yeah, absolutely.' This was more like it. Acceptance is everything on most occasions.

'Brill, so I'll wait for you at home time by the gates then. You can walk me back to ours.'

Wow bloody wee. She was amazing, different class, she had sealed the deal – almost.

'Alright,' I said, 'I would love to do that.'

'I would love you to do that.'

'Great,' I said.

'Fab,' she said.

'Fine,' I said.

'Well ...' she said.

'What?' I said.

'Aren't you going to kiss your new girlfriend?'

Oh my goodness, this girl was the tops, the nuts, it didn't get any better than this and if it did I didn't want it.

'Yes,' I said, 'I would love to do that.'

'I would love you to do that.'

And then we kissed – briefly but softly and beautifully. We pulled apart and smiled.

'Should we do it again?' I asked.

'Yehhhh,' said Tina enthusiastically.

This time we went for it, a full-on playground snog and it was earth-shattering. Tina was totally into it, I was totally into it. Unfortunately the teacher on duty at the time was not so much into it.

'Can you please stop that kissing, you two?' said the master in question.

When we pulled apart I remember him being visibly shocked to see who it was. As I said before, Tina was a model pupil.

'And Tina, you should know better.'

Without missing a beat, she replied, 'Sorry sir, we weren't really kissing, we were practising for later.'

And with that, the coolest girl ever to walk Planet Earth grabbed me by the tie and said, 'Come on Chrissy, this way.'

Shit the bed, I had a girlfriend and she was the greatest woman in the world.

top
10 Schoolboy Errors

10 Setting my pyjamas on fire whilst playing with matches.
   I was still in them at the time
9 Not being grateful for my first big bike one Christmas
   morning (I went on to love it)
8 Not going to see Queen at the Liverpool Empire (big big big
   mistake)
7 Smashing my toy garage up with a hammer in a make-
   believe bombing raid
6 Playing willy guitar and getting caught by my mum
5 Lending my Scalextric to Andy next door and never asking
   for it back
4 Thinking Mrs Tranter wanted to go out with me even
   though she was married with two children and I was
   only twelve
3 Thinking Jill from the chemist ever even noticed me at all
2 Listening to Mandy S. in the playground that day
1 Succumbing to the allure of the dreaded netball skirt

Tina and I were to enjoy the most idyllic of teenage courtships – sexless but beautiful. Maybe it was beautiful because it was sexless, I don't know. Sure we messed around a bit but no more than that. What we did do, however, was love each other madly – twenty-four hours a day madly, seven days a week madly. Madly, madly, madly.

What is it about 'first love' that makes it so incredibly special? It should be bottleable. (And while we're at it – why doesn't the word bottleable exist? We need to be able to bottle more good things in life, what with all the terrible things that are going on. But how do we stand a chance, when the word that defines its very possibility is not even in our language? If things that can be negotiated are negotiable and things that can be done are doable, why can't things that can be bottled be bottleable?)

Anyway I digress – I used to see Tina *all the time*. Before school, during all breaks and lunchtime, after school, every evening – usually at hers, and then every weekend. And when I wasn't seeing her I was thinking about her. She consumed my mind, my heart, my soul, my very spirit, my whole being. I couldn't get enough of her and she couldn't get enough of me. We did everything together – except the rude stuff, as I've just mentioned but for some reason felt the need to mention again. And we kissed, boy did we kiss, we kissed all the time. We couldn't imagine ever not kissing and ever being without each other. We were going to die together and we didn't care if that day was tomorrow or the next, as long as we were side by side.

I remember one night Tina had to go off to Manchester to watch a play with her class as part of her English literature coursework. As I walked her to the coach, we were both in floods of tears at the thought of being parted for even just a few hours. It was as if one of us was going off to war never to return. We were inseparable yet we were being separated. Who had dared dream up this cruel fate?

Who had thought to deny us our usual evening round at 'hers' snogging furiously on the bean bag in her parents' spare room, listening to Queen's *Greatest Hits* and Meat Loaf's *Bat Out of Hell* as well as, for some strange reason, an old King's Singers album! These three vinyl wonders were the soundtrack to our very own love story.

Tina was so sophisticated and clever and funny and energetic; her completeness was her beauty. And again that smile, so big and warm and welcoming. Her joy and abandon were infectious, she was naughty, too, cheeky and fruity in a way. I was sure this naughty side of her was only ever revealed to me – I used to think about that a lot, especially when we were at school and she was being the darling of the classroom. Little did they know what could also make Tina tick. They thought they knew but they didn't – that was our secret. God, I loved her.

I loved her so much that I went above and beyond the requirements of a normal teenage romance by bestowing upon her the lofty position of becoming the subject of my first ever padded greetings card purchase.

Padded greetings cards were a mysterious but wonderful phenomenon. They could always be found sat majestically on the top shelves of the greetings cards sections in most newsagents or stationers. Maybe they still can, I don't know. I have long since stopped looking for them. By the time I left school I was all padded out.

Ridiculously big – even the small ones – they were made of shimmery silk-like material, usually consisting of a garish floral design, though what they were actually padded with I never found out – I suspect it was highly flammable. I wonder how many house fires in the late Seventies and early Eighties were down to the accidental setting alight of a massive padded card during some kind of revelry or other. 'Here darling, here's a magnificent padded card, cost me an arm and a leg it did. Happy birthday and make the most of it. It could be your last if Auntie May's fag ash gets too close to it later on.'

These great padded cards came in big flat white boxes instead of envelopes and they were expensive, like, really expensive – maybe a fiver or more! But Tina was worth it, every penny. I bought her several of the monstrosities – I wonder if she still has them. I have a feeling she might, along with a smoke alarm, I hope.

So how does such a perfect, unblemished relationship come to an end? We'd never argued, we'd never stopped wanting to be together, we were the bestest of friendly friends and we still hadn't done the real rude stuff.

It's simple and predictable and the answer is …

Temptation.

The Bible may be dodgy in all sorts of other areas but it's pretty much bang on the money when it comes to explaining the evil that is temptation and the devastation it can cause.

The destruction of peoples, nations and in this case, as far as I was concerned, the most beautiful love affair the world had ever seen.

The apple is there – don't eat the apple. But more importantly don't even think about eating the apple. Basically, just forget apples exist and preferably as quickly as possible.

The infection with temptation is perpetuated by the dreaded 'thought'. One spends far too much time in this life of ours thinking about what we haven't got as opposed to enjoying what we have got. What's that about? I've been doing it for years, I still do! It's like a disease.

Temptation for me came in the form of the netball captain. Her name was Karen. Not the Karen from the junior school that took us to the park but another, more sporty, Karen – out of nowhere came Karen II.

Here's what happened.

Tina and I were happily insulated in our bubble full of love and loveliness and then one breaktime I was left on my own in the playground as Tina had some extra work to catch up on – I was alone, I was vulnerable and as far as temptation was concerned I was the ripest cherry on the tree. The netball captain and her ridiculously short netball skirt were waiting to pounce.

One of Karen's 'friends' approached me.

'Where's Tina?' she said.

'Oh she's doing some extra work,' I replied.

'Oh right, so you're still with her then?'

'Yes.'

'Only ... you know Karen fancies you.'

'What?'

'Karen, captain of the netball team, she fancies you. None of us get why but she says she thinks you're cute and if anything ever happened to you and Tina, she would definitely go out with you.'

And with that she was off.

Little did I know what had just happened: the wind of change had visited me, silently and deftly.

I was both rocked and shocked. The Karen in question – Karen II – although captain of the netball team, was actually quite modest and quiet in comparison to the rest of the female jocks in the main gang. They liked her because she was good at sport, by far and away better than anyone else. Sport was her ticket to the back seat of the bus and the big girls were more than glad to have her on board. She also had the most spectacular thighs.

This was the first sign of foreboding, I should have known. I hadn't thought about Karen's thighs ever before, but now the mere mention of her name instantly conjured up a snapshot of those muscly and impressive haunches, so adept at springing her forth, up and high to net another victorious goal.

I started to notice her and her thighs around more, like when you buy a car and suddenly you see them everywhere. I would smile at her and she would smile back. What was I doing? To smile at the enemy is to sleep with the enemy, you fool. And although Karen II wasn't a bad person, she was the enemy. She threatened everything I loved, everything that brought me joy – Tina, her smell, her mouth, her mum and dad's spare room – her mum and dad themselves, our beloved bean bag, Queen's *Greatest Hits*, *Bat Out of Hell* and even The King's Singers.

I was infected – the sickness had taken hold. All the symptoms I now recognise started to fall into place, lining up obediently, one behind the other, like a well-organised army getting ready to attack. I was surrounded by my inevitable doom. It was only a matter of time before I committed my first true act of betrayal – I began to compare!

I began to compare my beautiful Tina with the imposter that was Karen II, skipper of the netball team. What a lowly and despicable thing to do.

And even worse, I began to look for areas where Tina might be weak and Karen might be strong – rarely was it the other way round. When I was with Tina, I would almost wait for her to do something that suggested a chink in her armour, all the while looking for future reasons for us to split up, all the time comparing her against countless shiny images of Karen II gliding through the air in that damned navy-blue pleated PE skirt. Thinking about it now makes my stomach churn. This is not the behaviour of a decent person, a loving boyfriend, a doting partner. What a total loser! What were you thinking? Be grateful for what you've got, you fool. In fact, more than that, get down on your knees and thank God you've got the greatest girlfriend a boy could wish for. But it was not to be. I had become blind to the perfection that was our love and I was hellbent on tearing it apart.

Tina's heart was pure and true. She had given me everything and I had never been happier, but I was completely infatuated with the thighs of another. And this is what people do, especially blokes: they see a new nest and start to create an agenda that will justify them leaving their current one, even though if they were to stop for a second, they would realise there's no better place in the universe than where they are now.

The final act of the whole sorry tale began with a secret note and talk of, 'If you don't tell anyone I won't.' Karen II wasn't as backwards at coming forwards as I had first imagined. Her mum and dad were going away for the weekend and she had invited me to come round and check out their living room carpet in their absence. After a whole night of rolling around on some of the finest shagpile, there was no going back.

I was now with Karen II.

I had moved on and my first true love was over.

You only get one mum and you only get one first love and the passing of the relationship I had with Tina is a thing of gargantuan sadness. What can I say? I broke her heart and to this day I wish I never had.

Tina and Chris: The Epilogue

Two days later, Karen II dumped me.

Not five, or four, or three but two! Two days!!

I suppose it could have been worse, like one or none. (I wonder if anyone has ever dumped anyone in no days.) Karen II said she'd made a dreadful mistake and that she was sorry and that she thought I should try to get back with Tina.

'Well, thanks for that astute piece of advice, Karen, but I think you may just have ruined my life!'

For the record, I think the real reason she dumped me was more because she found me a terrible kisser.

I'm not bragging but the thing was, I knew I wasn't. I couldn't have been because Tina and myself had been getting off and on each other's lips with great success for the best part of the last twelve months. I think it was more the case that Karen and I together were terrible kissers, dreadful in fact – just awful.

It takes two to tango and it takes two to play tonsil tennis, but preferably two tongues on the same wavelength.

I heard a great story about wavelength once from a man sat by a swimming pool in a hotel in Los Angeles. He claimed that we are all basically electric and that we operate on varying frequencies. He said it was completely natural for someone to literally be operating on a similar or very different wavelength to someone else, and that often when we meet others and feel an instant attraction to them it's because their wavelength is similar to, or maybe even sometimes exactly the same as, our own. Adversely, when we feel an instant uneasiness towards someone and often for no apparent reason, the opposite may be true. It's nothing either person may have done particularly, it's simply that we are each operating on different frequencies too far apart to gel.

Well, whatever it was, Karen II and I were never going to get it together on any front, least of all when it came to kissing. I didn't understand her method and she didn't understand mine. Whereas Tina had teased and nibbled and tugged her way around my face, ears and eyes for the last year, Karen II kissed in a much more industrial manner. There was no journey, there was no gear change, it was foot down, full throttle and off we go.

Overnight, I had gone from a beautiful, perfectly balanced open-topped tourer on the Côte d'Azur straight to a stripped-down dragster at the Santapod raceway, exhausts flaring, tyres smoking, just desperate to get over the finish line.

I suppose that's the difference between the darling of the drama group and the captain of the netball team. I had gone against type, always a mistake – opposites attract, my arse.

For the first time in my life, I felt like a total dick. During the last twelve months I had been walking on air and living the kind of life that good people live, the kind of life when you know deep down inside that what you're doing is wholesome, the very foundation of decency. The kind of life all mums and dads wish for their children. The kind of life that makes you feel like you don't need to do the lottery.

Tina and I were never going to set the world alight but that's probably because we would have been too busy looking after and loving each other. How many great scientists, artists, musicians and writers have been lost to such happiness? And more power to them. The most deserving audience is always at home; anyone who saves their best performance for strangers is the most suspicious of characters.

So there I was, left feeling like the man who built his own private Idaho and then in a moment of typical male ego-fuelled madness, took a match to it and razed it to the ground.

Of course I made overtures to try to win back my lost love but Tina was having none of it – her mum even less. Mrs Y. even tracked me down to tell me what an idiot I had been for throwing away the chance to be with her wonderful daughter. She was entirely right.

Tina did agree to see me several weeks later and expressed her genuine desire to get back together, but in the end she decided ultimately for her own sake that this was not the most sensible approach to take in life towards the first man she had given her heart to. She had done so sincerely and fully and I had repaid her by scarpering at the mere sniff of a new testosterone-filled adventure. Oh if only all the girls of the world were half as wise. Tina was never going to be a loser and nor was she going to allow herself to be with one. She was made of far stronger stuff than her now ex boyfriend. She owed him nothing. He had told her that he would love her for ever and yet he had not been able to love her for little more than a year. He had lied, plain and simple.

From this moment school was still school but no longer as I'd known it: it was now Tina-less, the biggest reason yet to get it over and done with once and for all.

top 10 Things I'm Rubbish at

10 Skiing (I have been over thirty times, had lessons, the lot:
complete waste of time)
9 Snowboarding (even worse – if that's possible)
8 Football (even though I have played at Wembley 12 times – a
crime for such a bad footballer)*
7 Rugby (truly awful)
6 Motor mechanics (I don't have the finger strength required)
5 Looking after money (more about that later)
4 Staying away from the wrong kind of people
3 Sleeping
2 Crying
1 Fighting

I have never been good at fighting but for years I was happy to get stuck in regardless. That is, until over time, I gradually came to realise that fighting was not a prerequisite for either getting on in life or being a man particularly – in short, it was neither big nor clever. It was also becoming patently obvious, due to the number of pastings I continually found myself on the receiving end of, that I was in fact rubbish at it.

Fighting is just one of the many things I am not cut out to do. I have little strength, never have had, my bones are thin and brittle and I also bruise easily.

So let's face it, if you hit me I'm pretty much guaranteed to break and if I do manage to hit you back – well, don't worry about having to call the medic as I was also at the back of the queue on the day God was dishing out the manly hands.

---

* Amongst many other requests, 'celebs' get asked to play football – a lot. As well as being fun, especially for someone who never got picked for the school teams like me, it's a novel way of gauging your popularity from how big a cheer you get when the teams are announced to the crowd. In my *Big Breakfast* and *Toothbrush* days, I was more than happy with the volume of my welcomes. I was playing at Wembley once and Les Ferdinand, the ex-England international, was watching on the touchline. 'How many times you played here?' he asked. 'I think this'll be my seventh,' I replied. 'That's more than me!' he exclaimed. Not everything is always right in this world of ours.

My hands are ridiculously little for a guy of my height, stature and weight. It's almost as if The Lord was trying to tell me not to fight. I would have had no problem with this if he'd thought to make up for his 'handy' oversight in other areas of my physicality but alas no, there's little to get excited about anywhere else either, I regret to say. Little hands mean little ... knuckles and in my case they also meant smooth and round knuckles – almost completely useless for fighting with. Put them next to a half-decent man-sized set of ugly, gnarled, knobbly destroyers and it's the equivalent of putting your grandma in the ring with Mike Tyson.

But fights were going to come and fights were going to go so I had to have a plan, which I did. It was a plan that basically consisted of me getting the first punch in hard and fast after which I would whip my glasses off, close my eyes and hope for the best.

This is what had happened on the morning of the launch of the Space Shuttle *Columbia*. I had become involved in a playground altercation with another kid. Having received the aforementioned Evans first and only punch, he had to my astonishment gone down as a result – also with such apparent force it didn't look like he would be getting up any time soon! I was more shocked than he was. My plans thus far had not allowed for any such an occurrence. I had to revise my strategy and quickly. Having already opened my eyes, I decided to replace my glasses and make a run for it, which is exactly what I did.

I was safe, for now at least. However, when my adversary did come round, I was more than aware he was bound to want revenge. I was reliably informed he had been declaring as much shortly after coming to. To put it more precisely, he had vowed that come home-time he was going to kill me outside the school gates.

Suffice to say, upon hearing this I had been peeing my pants ever since.

The news of my forthcoming assassination had been eagerly telegrammed to me several times – more than I needed to hear but of course this was the usual guaranteed scenario. There was never a shortage of gleeful messengers around when there was an after-school duel to be advertised and the more likely you were to lose, the more desperate the messengers were to let you know the exact details of when and where you were going to get your head kicked in.

These messenger kids are the worst. Destined to become wasters of perfectly good oxygen as they grow older, they are the child apprentices of the kind of adults that take pleasure in the art of spreading bad news, the kind of people who need bad news to use as a currency to make themselves briefly more interesting. You know, the kind of people who take part in and watch those terrible daytime talk shows and trash each other live on national television.

My opponent meanwhile was odds-on favourite to have me over in any discernable 'proper' fight and by all accounts he was now fuming – angry as a wasp in a jar apparently. The weird kid had knocked him to the ground in full view of his contemporaries and he had lost face; not only that but that face was now a little bent and he owed me – something he would have to put right at the first available opportunity. He was in no mood to delay the process for a second longer than was required. Home-time it was to be: cometh the hour – cometh the beating. I was left feeling in no uncertain terms that when the school bell went for the final time that day I was going to get it and I was going to get it good.

I was able to think of little else. I felt sick, I wanted to go to the toilet, I wanted to cry and I wanted to die. All four of which were likely to happen before the day was over.

So, as you can probably imagine, the Space Shuttle launch was a much welcome diversion – especially seeing as we were going to be allowed to watch it on television. I even considered it might be the type of event to make the angry kid realise the bigger picture for the human race as a whole and that killing another thirteen year old in cold blood may not be in the spirit of the day.

The television room, not unlike my bottom that day, was packed and full of apprehension, so much so, that some of us were forced to sit on the floor – not that we minded, we were spellbound by what was going on, plus it meant we didn't have to do our normal lessons as they'd been put on hold until after the launch.

This was an all-round cool situation, and it was getting cooler by the minute as NASA was suffering technical problems giving rise to an ongoing delay.

'Please, let the launch be delayed for several years,' I thought to myself, long enough for the angry boy to meet the girl of his dreams, have a small family and retire to Southport. Long enough for him to realise the ultimate futility of inane hand-to-hand combat between fellow men ... and more importantly, fellow schoolboys.

But alas it was not to be. Before long the *Columbia* countdown over in Houston had restarted along with the impending 'death by fight' countdown that was currently taking place in my head.

This situation had now officially morphed into becoming another one of those moments in my life that I wished would never end, for the second it did my intended fate would surely befall me and in front of all the world to see. Like my brick wall moment with Tina, it was now that I pleaded for the planets and the solar system to pull together and show mercy upon this young and needy soul by miraculously and cosmically bringing time to a grinding halt and in so doing, save this shaking, quaking juvenile wreck of a child from pissing himself into oblivion. I swear, if *Columbia* were still waiting to take off here and now that would have been fine by me.

I decided it was time for a prayer.

'Dear God, please let time stop here for ever. Sure I know it would mean I'll never realise my potential as a human being past this point, I will never know what it feels like to take my first trip to the seaside behind the wheel of my own car, to buy my first home, to have a child, to witness another Labour government, to truly become acquainted with the ways of a woman, to stare on in wonder at the simplicity yet effectiveness of the format of *Who Wants to Be a Millionaire?* (a game show currently over fifteen years away from even being conceived), but frankly I don't care because it would also mean that I'm never going to have to face the school gates pummelling that's most definitely coming my way in what's now just a couple of hours. Please God, out of the two options I am more than happy to sacrifice all of the former for even the slightest chance of the latter. Amen.'

Time may sometimes seem like it stands still but the clouds and the clocks tell us it doesn't. Perhaps a moment is as close as we ever get. Maybe a moment is the stillness between the ticking of time, the bridge over the river, if you like, the halfway house between the now and the then.

For me this stillness is usually enough and I have learnt to enjoy such 'moments', diving into them and pushing them apart to make them last as long as possible, but back then, in the early Eighties, sat in front of that television, in that classroom, there was no such pleasure to be had, time was very much against me.

Acceptance though is often liberation. 'Let go, let go, let, go,' I said to myself and as I did so miraculously my prayers were answered.

Unconsciously, as I was sat on the floor, I began to stroke the carpet tiles – partly I suppose for some kind of self-soothing, contemplative comfort, like a wise man might stroke his chin or a dog might lick his private parts, and partly I suppose out of resignation, my resignation to the fact that, whichever way I looked at it, my goose was cooked – I was a dead man walking.

I continued to brush my right hand, palm down, across the carpet in a thoughtful arcing motion, half contemplating the wonder of what was taking place across the Atlantic, half wondering whether the mad kid was going to start killing me by punching me in the stomach or in the face first and whether I would bother trying to defend myself or just let him get it over and done with. But, as these thoughts danced around my consciousness, I found myself becoming distracted, distracted by something on the floor, something under my right hand. There was a bump in the carpet.

It felt like there was something running under the texture of the weave. I ceased my stroking and lifted my hand so I could see what it was, but there was nothing there.

'Strange,' I thought. I checked again – the carpet tile was dark brown and quite hard to see so I leant down this time to get a little closer but, nope, there was definitely nothing to report.

I resumed my self soothing, running my hand across the carpet but again I felt the bump, almost immediately this time. Again I looked to see what it was, but again nothing. Was I going mad? It wasn't beyond the realms of possibility, I was under a great deal of schoolboy stress at the time – maybe my mind had had enough of me and wanted out.

I went to stroke the carpet a third time and whatever it was, blow me it was still there; it may have been invisible but it was definitely still there. What on earth was it? And then I noticed my hand, the hand that had been doing the stroking – the three outer fingers looked like they were swollen and quite severely – not only this but they appeared to be slightly blue.

I became confused and felt the vague undertones of blind panic begin to set in. Upon further inspection, I turned my hand over and there, revealed, was the source of the mystery, a lump in my palm, the size of a golf ball.

This time, I had broken myself.

My one punch to the chin of the angry kid had been too much for my soft, little round knuckles to take, they really did hate fighting and this was the last straw, they had chosen to defend themselves instead of me and to show their disdain for such a pastime they had physically retreated into the palm of my hand.

'Ouch,' I thought as I realised it was now hurting, 'that looks awful.' 'Brilliant,' I thought next. 'This is my passport out of here. The angry kid will be fighting his own shadow at home-time if this is half as bad as it looks. My fingers are obviously broken. There must be a hospital trip in this. It might even be an ambulance job. Hurrah, thank you God, let me know how much I owe you.'

Of course I waited for *Columbia* to launch before approaching the teacher. My hand had now begun to throb and no doubt was becoming less salvageable by the minute but there was no way I wanted to miss the launch. Besides, now that I knew I was off the hook with the angry kid, my hand may have been hurting like hell but my heart was singing – to the high heavens. With *Columbia* safely on her way it was time for me to disclose the nature of my injury and get the heck out of there.

There's nothing like presenting a teacher with a genuine injury, is there?

Teachers are so ready for lesson-dodging excuses that when one is able to confront them with the real deal, one is flushed with a swell of satisfaction as the expression on their face gradually makes the journey from scepticism, all the way through to concern – stopping off somewhere in between to register a mixture of disappointment and guilt when they realise they might have to actually do something about the situation.

And so out came the trowel as I prepared to lay on the thick stuff. I took great pleasure in informing my class mistress of the obvious pain and anguish I was experiencing while offering up my increasingly ballooning right paw as evidence to such truths. I had to admit, it did look pretty dramatic. I also let her know, in no uncertain terms, that I had heroically postponed the reporting of my serious injury so as not to interrupt such a momentous event as the Space Shuttle 'take off' with such a trifling matter as my hand, which was about to 'drop off'.

Twenty minutes later I was home and free – well, I was actually in the hospital and free and boy, did it feel good. I had gone from condemned zero to resilient hero in less than half an hour. My initial sense of relief was quickly developing into a wave of unbearable ecstasy. Life felt mighty sweet, I can tell you. I was out of the woods and would soon be scampering down into the valley. I might have to go back to school the next day but there was no way the angry kid could pick a fight with me if I had a plaster on my arm. It wouldn't be worth the bad 'rep'. He would have to hold on to his anger for at least six weeks and anything could happen in that time – there could even be a war!

But, as we know, the karma police are never far away and they were about to rain on my parade, big time. One hour later I would be screaming with agony.

top
10 Things that Freak Me Out

10 Walking through crunchy snow
9 Anything that dangles
8 Trinkets
7 The lighting in department stores – it makes my eyes sting
6 The recurring dream where my head keeps falling off
5 People who don't like animals
4 My friend who doesn't 'get' music
3 My own heartbeat
2 Anyone else's heartbeat
1 Hospitals

I was screaming and begging for the surgeon to stop what he was doing, pleading with him to relent. I had been transferred to the operating theatre where I was now being worked upon. Things are never as simple as you want them to be, are they?

It transpired that as a result of my injury my fingers needed to be rebroken as they had originally been broken 'the wrong way'. I was informed of this shocking development soon after I was admitted to the accident and emergency department. I was told it would be impossible for my fingers to be set in their current state, not an uncommon occurrence apparently. Maybe not uncommon to the medical profession but it was 'news just in' to me – as was the local anaesthetic that had since been hastily administered.

The anaesthetic needed to numb the affected area had to be injected directly into the bones of my right hand. I cannot describe how painful this was and there was not one but four syringes in total! For some reason two of the syringes also had to be left in the bone during the next part of the process, which meant they were left dangling out of my skin and were currently swaying up and down like over-laden branches on an apple tree.

Everything in place, it was now the surgeon's job to do the re-breaking. This basically consisted of him taking up a black rubber hammer and smashing it down on to my hand for all he was worth.

'I'm going to hit you as hard as I can to hopefully get this done first time without having to rain subsequent needless blows down upon you. What I am trying to do can actually be achieved with just one accurate "adjustment".'

Excuse me, but since when has hitting someone with a hammer been referred to as an adjustment? This gentleman's little speech though well-meaning was doing nothing to allay my anxiety – not that he had finished yet.

'Now, young man, the anaesthetic should have taken effect but there is still a chance you might feel something.'

Feel something! He wasn't kidding, I felt every 'bloody' thing. It was as if I'd never been near a syringe in my life. Whatever had been in those things, they needed to triple the dose, at least.

After 'more than one' concerted attempt to 'adjust' my mashed-up digits, during which the attending nurses had grimaced and flinched with every whack, the action finally came to a halt: the surgeon had indeed ceased to hammer me. After wiping his brow and nodding his head decisively in a 'job well done' kind of way, he retreated to wherever it is surgeons go after benevolently bashing up the hands of little boys.

The trauma abating, my central nervous system had instructed me that it was now safe to downgrade my screaming to something less harrowing, a little less cowardly. Accordingly I did so – firstly to a respectable sobbing before fading seamlessly to a feeble whimper.

After a few minutes, and several sympathetic smiles from a couple of foxy nurses, which I happily acknowledged with the raising of a conciliatory 'Don't-worry-I'll-be-alright' Ferris Bueller-type eyebrow, milking the situation for all it was worth, I began to compose myself on the way back to regaining full heroic status. But once again all was not as I thought.

The surgeon returned.

'I'm sorry but that doesn't appear to have worked, we're going to have to go again.'

Ex-squeeze me? Baking powder?

'*What did he just say?*'

'*We're going to have to go again!*'

Surely I was hearing things, he couldn't have just said what I thought he'd said. But yes, alas, it was true.

'The local anaesthetic was not strong enough,' he went on. I could have told him that for free!

'The reason we went with the local at first is because its use does not require us to have prior written permission from a guardian as it is of little risk.'

'Or effectiveness,' I wanted to add but thought better of it.

'We will now have to give you a general anaesthetic, which means putting you under. Of course for this we will need someone to come in and sign the consent forms.'

He smiled a half smile – at least he tried. He then turned to walk away but there was something else. He came back and gestured. I drew closer, he had a secret to share with me.

'Oh by the way,' he whispered, 'I presume we are all sticking to your story on the accident report of how you fell on to your hand in the playground and not the fact that you more likely punched some other boy in a bout of fisticuffs. That's the usual way a person comes to sustain this type of injury.'

Suddenly I began to warm to this guy. Not only had he just used the phrase 'fisticuffs' – a phrase I'd never heard in real life before – but he was letting me know the score here, the way the land lay. Alright, he may have already put me through a miniature hell, and was about to 'go again' in his words, but I couldn't help feeling that he was offering to cut me a deal. The less fuss I made over the last failed 're-breaking' attempt when my mum came in, the less she needed to know about the 'more accurate' reason for the injury.

'Er ... yes, thank you,' I replied, happy to comply.

I had been well and truly rumbled by the doc and although he was poised to set about hitting me with that bloody hammer again, I had to admit – he was one of the good guys.

top
10

Things I Remember
from School Lessons

10 Tectonic plates
9 π
8 Iron filings
7 The binary scale
6 British standard lettering
5 Improper fractions
4 Expansion of brackets
3 Ripple tanks
2 French idioms
1 The angle of reflection is equal to the angle of incidence

The last three years of my education at the comprehensive school hold the most lightness for me from my school days. Having said that, I didn't learn much, not because the teachers at the comp weren't as good as those at the grammar school; it was just that the comprehensive syllabus was a year or two behind that of the grammar schools and a lot of what they were doing I'd already been taught. The result of which was a further two years of classroom boredom for me and two years of frustration for my teachers.

For ages I would be the first with my hand up to answer any questions they might ask, but after a while they realised I'd learnt it all before and began to ignore me! It was hilarious – I would be there with my hand up and they would say things like, 'Well, if nobody knows, let me explain.'

When it came to final exam time, I did somehow manage to scrabble out eight lame but just about acceptable O-level grades, as well as a couple of GCSEs, whatever they were.

Bizarrely as it turned out and very much against my better judgement (but when has that ever stopped me?), I actually decided to stay on for the sixth form. Here's a boy who couldn't wait to get out of the education system and all of a sudden he wants more. What a strange individual, but of course I had my reasons. They were mainly to do with a gap in the market I had spotted and the only way to capitalise on it was by remaining on the inside.

A Brief History of Time (aka me at secondary school).

NAME *Christopher Evans* FORM 4D

Attendance. *279* out of a possible *312* halfdays

No. of times late *1*

Clubs, Activities, Interests *Table tennis and woodwork clubs.*
Member of House Quiz team, House and school soccer teams,
cricket and basketball teams. School table tennis team.
Form representative. Front of House in 'Oliver'.

Form Tutor's Comment *Chris has settled well at Padgate and is a*
popular member of the form. He always makes a valuable
and interesting contribution to form discussions and
should prove an excellent form representative. He has
involved himself in all aspects of school activity and
is a real asset.
Date *June 1981* Signature *P. M. MacVeigh* Form Tutor

NAME *Christopher Evans* FORM 4D
TEACHING GROUP 'O' Level
SUBJECT *English Literature*
ATTAINMENT B EFFORT 2
COMMENT *Christopher's literature result was pleasing*
considering the difficulty of the paper set. He now
needs to concentrate on attaining a thorough
knowledge of the set texts and developing the ability
to write essays which contain more detailed
references to the book, with points backed up
by quotations. He contributes freely in literature
discussions but sometimes I wish he would
consider what he is going to say before he speaks,
rather often his comments turn out to be red
Signature *J. H. Hart* Subject Teacher

NAME *CHRISTOPHER EVANS*
SUBJECT *P.E.*
ATTAINMENT — EFFORT 3
TEACHING GROUP 4D MIXED ABILITY
COMMENT
Christopher must be commended on
the enthusiasm and effort he puts into
most of his school lessons and in playing
for the school soccer team. However I
am a little worried by his often
childish behaviour, particularly recently
if he does not get his own w...
Date *June 1981* Signature *D.J. C...*

PADGATE COUNTY HIGH SCHOOL

PCHS

School Report

Name *Christopher Evans* Form 4D

Date *June 1981*

For most of my years at school I had been bemused by many things, none more than the phenomenon of the school tuck shop. Both my senior schools had such a thing and both were equally hopelessly out of touch with their clientele.

The tuck shop at my comprehensive school was run by members of the PTA – good wives and loyal mothers who had a bit of spare time on their hands and wanted to do something to help the school, absolutely nothing wrong with that. The problem, however, was that they stocked what they thought the kids liked, or what they should like, not what the kids actually did like. I remember there was one item of confectionary that I had never seen in a real sweet shop. It was as if they'd had it specially commissioned by the boring biccie factory.

Where there's a problem there's an opportunity (in Chinese the word for both is the same, which explains a lot!) and by this time, via my work at Ralph's, I had good connections with the local wholesalers. I had recently also become the owner of a motorcycle, so I decided to swing into action and set up an alternative sweet emporium for my fellow students.

From day one I had it nailed. I was supplying all the latest favourites. Unlike the parents I did know what the kids wanted – after all I was still a kid myself: Refresher Chews, Wham Bars, Space Dust, the almighty Fizz Bombs, Jaw-Breakers, Sherbert Dabs, you name it, I had it ... and if I didn't I could guarantee to have it the next day. My USP was that I was also discounting my prices to beat the surrounding shops, as well as of course the good old school tuck shop which was quickly seeing business drop off. As a result I soon saw myself hauled up in front of the headmaster.

It had come to Sir's attention that I was operating a rival outlet to the official school sweet suppliers and that, as a result, their turnover was suffering, and consequently, so was the school fund – the sole beneficiary of any tuck shop profits.

He went on to explain politely to me that this was not an acceptable practice and that he would very much appreciate it if I ceased to trade forthwith.

'Damn', I thought as I hadn't considered the school fund angle. This was a reasonable point and one that had me temporarily stumped.

I bought myself some thinking time by conveying to him my sympathy as well as trying to enlighten him as to the ticking time bomb that was the death knell of the tuck shop. I explained that the whole situation was a simple case of natural market forces at work and that the school tuck shop was way out of date and now way out of its depth. What I had precipitated was bound to happen sooner or later and was in fact already happening outside the school gates in the local newsagents.

I knew I was treading on thin ice and that he was entirely justified in his initial request for me to close business but I couldn't resist chancing my arm. I'd hatched a plan. I decided to offer to cut him a deal. I would carry on trading but I would raise my prices so as not to undercut anyone anywhere. I would then donate my new additional profit to the school fund. I also ventured that this may well turn out to be more than the school fund had ever received in the past as I was moving considerably more units than the tuck shop ever had.

Now it was his turn to be stumped: on the face of it my offer, although admittedly audacious, was also entirely plausible.

He paused for a moment before realising that this was a ridiculous conversation and one that he didn't need to have. I was a pupil and he was the headmaster; this was his turf and I was trying to muscle in on it. He told me to close down immediately.

Ultimately I had no problem with this – how could I? He was completely in the right and he was a nice man.

So the funny kid with the guerrilla sweet stall packed up his belongings, bade his farewells and left town – out of business and out of the education system for ever.

part two

the
piccadilly
years

top
10 Best DJs I Have Ever Heard

10 Mike Hollis (Radio Luxembourg, the great 208)
9 Mike Read (Breakfast Show Radio 1)
8 Paul Locket (Piccadilly Radio)
7 Cuddly Dave (Piccadilly Radio)
6 Pete Baker (Piccadilly Radio)
5 Bob Harris (Radio 1 and 2)
4 Roger Scott (Radio 1 and 2)
3 Alan Freeman (Radio 1 and 2)
2 Steve Wright (Radio 1 and 2)
1 … read on

My brother was a DJ. I knew this because he came home late most nights and had hefty black record cases with Roxy Music stickers on the side. He's over ten years older than me. I was a mistake apparently – my mum was over forty when I arrived, very old for a new mother in those days. She says she travelled to the hospital to have me on the bus. I'm not sure if this is true but I've never liked buses since.

My brother David was not so much my hero but I did think he was cool – the chief responsibility of an elder brother. I wanted to be like him, I even wanted my bedroom to smell like his, which was bloody awful come to think of it – the thought of that stench now makes me want to gag. What is that smell in older boys' bedrooms? Is it the smell of 'anxiety' so to speak; and why on earth did I find it so alluring? Maybe it just smelt older and older is what all kids want to be.

My brother seemed to be very happy with his life – something that always intrigued me until one Saturday morning when I found out perhaps why he was so content. I came downstairs and there was this gorgeous girl asleep on the sofa. She really was something else, dressed head to foot in a long, black, flowing lace dress with black stockings and black shoes – in fact everything about her was long except her hair, which was cropped short in a sexy chic kind of style. Long legs, long arms, a long neck, long fingers and long fingernails painted jet black. I didn't know exactly how she'd come to be in our house but I did know she was an absolute babe.

It transpired that David had met this goddess as a result of his job as DJ at the Carlton Club, a popular nightspot in Warrington town centre situated over the top of Woolies just off the high street.

I made another mental note. Deejaying makes geeks more attractive to gorgeous women.

Both my brother and I have always looked a bit geeky although David did have a cool Fifties thing going on as a kid. Here's a pic.

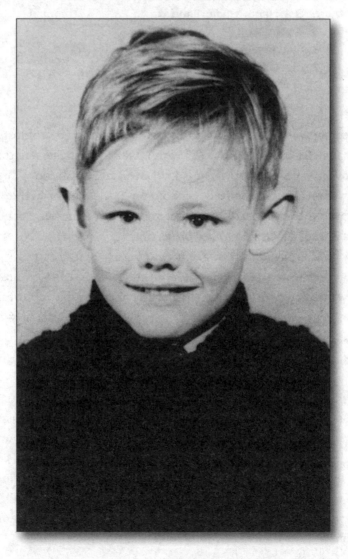

Other than him taking me to my first-ever rock concert – ELO, the Out of The Blue tour when I was thirteen, for which I will be eternally grateful, and what a 'two' nights that was* – David and I never did much together and we've never done much since. As with my sister; we all sort of live through Mum. We are a decent family but not a close family, something that isn't helped by the fact that we all live miles apart: my sister Diane is in Yorkshire, whilst David currently lives in Australia and before that New Zealand for close to the last twenty years.

That said, however, it was definitely 'our Dave', as we call him, who set me off on the road to playing records and talking in between them as a way of earning a living.

Emulating my big brother deejaying in night clubs was a cool enough goal for me to aspire to as it was, but we were about to behold a whole new world of record-spinning possibilities as the explosion of independent commercial radio was just around the corner.

---

* David organised a trip through his work for a coach load of peeps to go and see ELO. He asked me did I want to go, to which the answer was of course yes. I had never been to any kind of live event before and ELO were my favourite band apart from The Beatles. The order has since swapped and if I had to die listening to one or the other – it would be ELO … probably 'Sweet Talkin' Woman'. We set off from St Helens but it was such a cold night the coach literally froze to a halt on the M6. We had to be properly rescued from the motorway along with hundreds of other people who had suffered the same fate; it was minus ten degrees or something ridiculous. As we had no way of getting home we all slept on the floor of a local pub. I had never even been in a pub before, nor had I ever had whisky, which the landlady dished out free of charge. 'Come on you need this,' she urged me. It turned out that so many fans had failed to get to the concert that night the band put on an extra show a couple of nights later with all unused tickets still valid. The gig was truly amazing and to this date by far the best gig I have ever been to. Thank you brother. x.

top
10 First Commercial Radio Stations in the UK

10 Radio Forth (22 May 1975)
9 Radio City (21 October 1974)
8 Radio Hallam (Sheffield) (1 October 1974)
7 Swansea Sound (30 September 1974)
6 Metro (15 July 1974)
5 Piccadilly (2 April 1974)
4 BRMB (19 December 1974)
3 Clyde (31 December 1973)
2 Capital (16 October 1973)
1 LBC (London Broadcasting Company) (8 October 1973)

Where we lived commercial radio took on the form of the magnificent Piccadilly Radio, broadcast live from Piccadilly Gardens in Manchester. 'Piccadilly 261 ... on the medium wave,' sang the jingle. It was funky, it was new, it had adverts and a jazzy coloured logo, which you could send off for in carsticker form – something we all did even though most of us didn't have a car and ended up sticking them on our bedroom windows.

This was a radio station where everything was groovier than anything that had been groovy before. It was our Sixties, it was all about the music and the people who played it. There were lots more records per hour, the voices weren't as posh and plummy as on the BBC and there was more laughing. There were phone-ins where more people from around our area were able to get on the air. A girl from my class called Julia got to be on for a whole hour once, choosing her favourite records. I asked her to go out with me off the back of her appearance.

Piccadilly Radio knew exactly who it was and what it was about. It was a new voice for a new generation. It was about the North West and everyone who lived there. This deep-seated identity was its strength and one that the station would articulate whenever it could via hundreds of outside broadcasts.

I remember when I was still a snotty-nosed little kid and Piccadilly came to Warrington town centre and did a whole show from the window of Dixons electrical store one Saturday afternoon – nothing in particular happened but to me it was amazing ... it was the most exciting thing that Warrington had seen since Keith Chegwin had brought the *Swap Shop* Swaperama to the old market square. I'd never seen a rock star or been to a football match, but I had seen the DJ that I listened to on the radio in the mornings, live in the shop window on a Saturday afternoon. It was almost more than I could bear. These guys were the coolest cowboys in town and I wanted to be one of them.

From then on I was hooked.

Did I listen to the radio underneath the bedclothes at night? Yes I did, in fact one of the shows I listened to was called just that – *UTBC* – *Underneath The Bed Clothes* with Cuddly Dave.

Cuddly Dave was the late-night DJ who created a whole duvet-covered late-night world of intrigue and titillation throughout the bedrooms of the North West. He had the warmest of voices and a most alluring bedside manner. Never 'pervy', he somehow managed to attract what seemed like every single female who was listening to his show ... while they were in bed! And on a weekday!! Till two o'clock in the morning!!! They couldn't wait to talk to him. His show was huge, the girls listened because of Dave, and the boys listened because of the girls.

Dave also had a wing man that helped him out, a character called Naughty Neville. Neville would tour the areas of Greater Manchester during the show in his Love Mobile (all very Austin Powers). Dave would then encourage anyone listening to get up and out of bed and flash their bedroom lights just in case 'Uncle Nev' (this did sometimes get a bit worrying) was in your area. Watch out ladies.

The real excitement for me though was a show called *TOTT*. The acronym was a spoof on *TOTP* – *Top of the Pops*. *TOTT* stood for *Timmy On The Tranny*.

Timmy On The Tranny was an early evening show for school kids and students and was hosted by none other than Timmy Mallett! It was a nightly broadcast emanating from his fictional world of Timmy Towers.

It was Timmy, pre *Wacaday*, pre Mallett's Mallett, pre 'Blah', pre 'Itsy Bitsy Teeny Weeny Yellow Polka Dot Bikini', and all the things most people know him for now. *TOTT* was for teenagers and students and we listened in *en masse*, glued to his every word.

Timmy was 'the man' and so compelling to listen to. His show was faster than a speeding bullet. No sooner had he announced a competition than somebody was on the air trying to win the prize; if they failed to do so, the prize would be doubled or tripled or quadrupled for the next time. He used to give away towers of records:

'Tonight we are playing for 55 inches of singles and if the first caller doesn't win – 60 inches!'

Wow! With ten records making up an inch, this added up to over 500 singles!

Like Cuddly Dave and most of the DJs at the time, Timmy also had characters but lots of them and all over the place, really funny characters, like Steve Wright was doing in the afternoons on Radio 1, but Timmy's characters were far more outrageous and naughty.

Timmy talked about *Smash Hits* and squeezing spots which he called zits and girlfriends and boyfriends. He took telephone calls in lightning quick succession, three, four, sometimes even five at a time. He would send the radio car out to somebody's house which would often end up with them, along with most of their street, co-hosting the rest of the show from their kitchen, toilet or garden shed. If there was a band in town, Duran Duran or Spandau Ballet or Madness, you could be sure they would make an appearance on *TOTT*.

I was addicted to this show. The energy that was coming out of my radio every night was electric. Who on earth was this guy? What did he look like? How could he juggle so many elements and make them all sound like they made sense? He was like a mad professor in a laboratory full of wonderment and endless possibilities. I had to meet him.

The problem was, he was in Manchester, I was in Warrington.

Mum, help!

top
10
Most Significant
Cars in My Life

10 Ferrari 599 F1 (my current car, the best car I have ever driven)
9 Ferrari 250 Lusso (my wife's 30th birthday pressie)
8 Ferrari 250 California Spyder (the pride of my garage)
7 Ferrari 360 Modena (the car I proposed to my second wife Billie with. I filled it with roses and sent it round to her apartment)
6 Ford Mustang convertible (the car I drove when I lived in L.A. – I still have it)
5 Bentley Brooklands (bought it on the spot for cash, my first-ever new car! It was close to £100k and after I paid for it I had about £1500 left to my name)
4 Ferrari 246 GT Dino (my second ever Ferrari)
3 Ferrari 328 GTS (my first ever Ferrari)
2 Dad's Vauxhall Victor (his pride and joy)
1 1972 Mini reg. no. VJA 879K (the car that kick-started my dreams)

One of Mum's many financial miracles was managing to buy me the car placed at number one on my list of Top Ten Most Significant Cars.

Mum hated debt – she still does – but she was prepared to go into debt to get her youngest son on the road. She took out a £500 loan to buy me an orange Mini, actually the colour was officially listed as 'blaze' – the car had loads of extras – registration VJA 879K. It was the nuts and it was to be my passport to Elysium.

Piccadilly Radio had announced a series of summer outside broadcasts, a whole bunch of what they called Funday Sundays. These were roadshows broadcast from the top deck of an open-top double-decker bus.

I had never been to one of these outside broadcasts before but a few days after I passed my driving test there was one scheduled to take place outside Old Trafford football stadium. Not only that but Timmy was hosting. I had to go.

I set off that Sunday morning on my own. It was easily the furthest I'd ventured thus far in my new mode of transport, and as I pulled off the motorway at Salford and drove nearer to the ground I could hear the station output over the speakers in the distance cutting in and out with the wind. The traffic was getting heavier. I checked my watch – it was nearly time for the show. I decided to park my car and run the rest of the way.

I heard an almighty roar. The show had started and I was missing it. I now began to sprint, I turned a corner and there it was: to some people it may have been a tatty old orange Greater Manchester open-top bus with a rather pathetic cheap Funday Sunday banner hanging forlornly from the side of it, but to me and the rest of the crowd it was a magnificent sight to behold. For it was the chariot that bore our hero and there he was, Timmy 'King of the Tranny' Mallett – with the funny glasses.

In true radio style, Timmy was nothing like I imagined. He was small and pointy and he was young but old-looking. Nowadays he is the opposite. The truth was I hadn't really thought too much about what he would look like, but I was pretty sure what he wouldn't look like and as it turned out I couldn't have been more wrong. Not that this mattered: he was still the top dog as far as I was concerned. He could have had two heads, seven eyes and tennis rackets for arms, I would have been just as thrilled to see him.

Timmy carried out his show for the next two hours with the irresistible zest and total and utter confidence that made his nightly show so exciting. Bearing in mind that from a visual point of view there was very little going on, especially when a record was being played, not that this mattered, we were captivated by his every move. We screamed when we were asked to, we laughed in all the right places and sang along to the songs. We were more than happy to be the supporting cast of a show that was going out live on the radio.

One of the highlights of this particular afternoon was an appearance by Bruce Foxton, the ex bass player from The Jam who had formed a new band and was on to promote their latest single. I had no idea who he was at the time and thought his new song was poor to say the least, but I cheered as loud as anyone – that was the deal.

Before I could catch my breath and take it all in, the show and the fastest two hours of my life thus far was over, the crowd had begun to disperse and Timmy was clambering down the stairs of the bus in what looked a bit like an Adam Ant outfit.

All afternoon there had been kids hanging about at the back of the bus behind the barriers who were wearing Piccadilly T-shirts. It turned out these were Timmy's 'helpers', the tallest of whom was a sharp-looking guy who had been stood by Timmy's side throughout the whole show wearing impressive-looking headphones. Whoever this guy was he had Timmy's ear and now he had ours – those of us who were still hanging around to catch a closer glimpse of The Mallett Man were eager to hear what he had to say.

'Timmy is coming down and he will sign as many autographs as he can but he doesn't have much time as he has to leave soon,' said the tall kid.

I waited to see Timmy up close and hear how he talked 'in real life', which I did but after five minutes of doing so I felt a strange urge.

What I did next was another one of those instances which I can't really explain: something inside me just said it was the right thing to do. Without thinking about it, I felt compelled to run back to my car as quickly as I could. Once there I jumped in and turned on the engine. I was going to follow Timmy home.

I drove back to the bus and waited. Even the most diehard fans were calling it a day now and soon Timmy was done with the signing. After exchanging a few words with some of his helpers he wandered off over to a small car park right opposite the main entrance of Old Trafford.

What car had my hero chosen as his trusty steed?

All superstars have great cars, I thought. It comes with the territory. If I was a star, the first thing I'd do is buy a swish car.

Not so the boy Mallett. As he fumbled for his car keys I could see he was stood next to … a red Renault 5! Could this really be his? Were these really his wheels? The guy is wearing whacky glasses along with an Adam Ant top, he has dyed red hair and yet he drives a Renault 5. I was learning maybe more than I needed or wanted to know.

Though I had decided to find out the location of the real Timmy Towers I had never followed another car before, and yet here I was only two weeks after passing my test now giving it the full private dick treatment. I had no idea where I was and even less idea where I was going, but I was on an adventure and that was enough – until a few moments into my pursuit, when disaster struck.

Suddenly my little car was not happy, it started to want to steer into the kerb. I had no idea what was happening but it was obvious this car was not a car that was enjoying the thrill of the chase. Whatever the problem was it was becoming exponentially worse by the second until I was eventually forced to stop. My little baby lurched to a halt with a worrying grinding noise, and as it did so I saw Timmy tootle off into the distance, no doubt blissfully unaware his pursuer had been thwarted.

I jumped out of my Mini to investigate what on earth had happened – only to discover my first-ever puncture.

'Damn and blast and blast again.' Not only did this herald the premature end to my now unsuccessful mission, it also meant that I was faced with something I had no idea how to do – namely, the deployment of a spare wheel.

After finally locating the jack, it wasn't long before I was sweating and cursing. I have never been the world's best when it comes to manual tasks and this latest challenge was proving to be no exception. I grunted and groaned and panted my way through the process and after several false starts, like jacking the car up before attempting to loosen the wheel nuts and having to lower it and start all over again, the spare wheel was, in a fashion, now on the car.

After manoeuvring the punctured wheel back into the spare-wheel cavity, nearly removing several fingers on my right hand in the process, it was time to refocus.

Right, where was I? Oh yes I was excited and following a red Renault 5. By now the best part of an hour had passed and Timmy had long gone. 'Never mind,' I thought ('never mind' is a phrase that has featured heavily in my life – 'never mind' is the phrase of tryers not quitters and I was not about to quit again) – it wasn't yet dark, I'd never been to Manchester before. Why didn't I take a detour into the city centre and at least drive past Piccadilly Radio? Other people drive past things they're interested in – why couldn't I do the same?

Of course I had to find it first, but this was a small mountain to climb and one that shouldn't have been a problem as Piccadilly Radio took great pride in shouting out its location several hundred times a week over the airwaves. In fact you would have to be deaf not to know where it was:

'Live from Piccadilly Plaza in Manchester ... Piccadilly 261.'

This was the type of phrase, I would come to discover, that lots of stations used but often employed huge doses of poetic licence as they did so. When I moved to London my favourite by far was: 'Live from the top of the Euston Tower ... Capital 95.8.'

That sounded mightily impressive but what they really meant was that the transmitter may have been live from the top of the Euston Tower but Chris Tarrant and his buddies were in little danger of a nosebleed as they were just one flight up from the reception on the ground floor.

Piccadilly, to my good fortune, had not been quite so creative with the truth and they were indeed in Piccadilly Plaza, which itself was equally helpfully located in Piccadilly Gardens smack bang in the middle of the city centre.

If a passer-by was still in any doubt as to the exact home of 'Piccadilly magic' all they had to do was look up, for plastered in the windows of the plaza itself were seven enormous posters of Piccadilly Radio's mainline DJs. I looked up open-mouthed.

'Wow ...' I was transfixed. They were like gods, larger than life, looking down upon us mere mortals. But then—

Hang on a sec! ... *None of them looked anything like they sounded.*

Again, I hadn't before imagined so much what they would look like, all I knew is that they shouldn't look like this.

I began to feel disappointed. Here I was, early on a Sunday evening, almost on my own in the heart of a huge city that was spookily quiet, faced with the very people who kept my dreams alive every day, the same people who inspired those dreams in the first place and what was I confronted with? Seven of the cheesiest smiles I'd ever seen. These guys had the coolest voices and funniest shows on the radio but suddenly they all looked like hairdressers – except Timmy who looked more like a whacky teacher, which in many ways is what he was.

A voice is a picture in itself and maybe it should stay that way. Since working in radio I have discovered that the 'on-air turns' have a real dilemma with their self-image: they've spent so many years cultivating their on-air persona they've left their real personality behind. What most of them tend to do is end up dressing how they think their listeners see them, which is usually a lifetime away from who they really are.

So there I was, full of wonder and woe, but I really cannot overemphasise how much I could not believe that these guys thought it was all right to look like that, especially when their faces were ten feet tall and five feet wide. Not for the first time that day I realised show business might not be exactly what I thought.

My disappointment was curtailed, however, as my attention was diverted from the massive mug shots slung high above me by the violent but distant rattling of a door from somewhere down below. It sounded like someone was desperately trying to break free.

I looked to see two glass panes reflecting as they shook in the light. It was one of the glass doors that lead to the escalators inside the plaza. There was a small man on the inside almost fighting with the handle. I looked closer to see the man was wearing a strange outfit. He looked 'a bit like Adam Ant' ... no, it couldn't have been ... it was – it was Timmy and he was stuck ... hurrah! This was my chance.

'Oh my God, there he is. I have until he manages to get out of the door to decide what to do.' I said to myself.

This turned out to be longer than I needed as the more Timmy struggled with the door the less likely it seemed to want to co-operate – when he did eventually escape to freedom, he was relieved and I was ready. At least I thought I was ready.

'Hello Timmy, I'm sorry to bother you but I was at the show today. I thought you were brill, I'm a big fan and ...'

Now here's the thing. There was no 'and'. The sentence should have ended on the word 'brill', not a great word I admit, but it was nevertheless a word and an acceptable word to end on but now I had said 'and', that usually means there is more to follow. Timmy was now waiting for whatever was after the 'and'.

'... and ...'

He was still waiting and was beginning to look worried. I had to say something and I had to say it fast.

'... and ... would it be possible for me to interview you before your show one night ... er ... for hospital radio ...?'

There, that would do – it would have to and I'd said it now anyway, it was too late, the horse had bolted the gate, the cat was out of the bag, the fat lady had sung – it's all I had and I'd used it. The fact that I didn't work for hospital radio, although I had sat in on a couple of shows, didn't matter. Nor did the fact that I didn't even own a tape recorder on which to carry out said interview. On the face of it things were maybe not quite as they seemed, but Timmy need not be aware of this – and besides, he was king of make-believe.

He paused before answering, I think I recall him looking me up and down and then he said, 'Sure, why not, come before the show tomorrow, we'll do it then.'

I may or may not have said thank you, I really can't remember, my mind immediately jumping to the fact that I had less than twenty-four hours to book the afternoon off work, acquire a tape machine, think of some questions, dream up a plausible back story about my role at a fictitious hospital radio station and return to Manchester.

top

10 Items of Technology in the Evans Household, circa 1983

10 Ronco Buttoneer
9 Stylophone
8 Casio calculator
7 Two-tone trimphone
6 Music centre
5 Panasonic video recorder
4 Portable television
3 Remington Fuzzaway
2 Clairol 2000 hairdryer (my sister's pride and joy)
1 Grundig 350 Deluxe reel-to-reel tape recorder (my brother's former pride and joy)

I remembered my brother Dave had a tape recorder, it was a huge grey thing that weighed a ton – a Grundig 350 Deluxe reel-to-reel machine. It was notable also as the only thing other than my marvellous Mini that I remember Mum ever going into debt to buy.

No longer living at home, my brother had left his beloved Grundig behind. After enquiring as to its whereabouts Mum informed me that she thought it was probably at the back of the big cupboard in the second bedroom. Of course that's exactly where it was.

The next thing I needed to do was see if it worked. I clunked on the power, optimistically, and the machine hummed back into life. I even managed to get it playing – Carly Simon's 'You're So Vain' (my brother kept that one quiet!). The rest of the simple controls were easy enough to figure but crucially there didn't seem to be a microphone.

I shot off with the machine to an audio/music shop and hauled it up onto the counter with a mighty thud. The guy behind the counter looked at it somewhat bemused.

'Wow man, what-is-that?'

What I wanted to say was, 'That, my man, is my passport to a fully blown real-life conversation with my radio idol. Please can you provide me with something that might facilitate the possibility of it ever recording again – thank you!'

What I ended up saying was something far more panicky and less articulate – even though it was only lunchtime I could already feel the pressure of my first broadcasting deadline approaching fast.

The man could see my distress and kindly set about all he could do to help, eventually finding something equally as grey and antiquated as my machine that claimed to be a microphone.

'There that should do ya,' he declared almost triumphantly. 'Oh and you'll be needing a new spool of tape,' he added. 'I think that one's well shot.'

Earlier on he'd tested the mighty 350 Deluxe for me, unfortunately hearing Carly Simon in the process. I was quick to point out that this was my brother's tape machine and it was his recording of Carly Simon. He sympathised and carried on, though I'm not sure he believed me.

With my recording equipment now up and running, after the flat-tyre debacle of the day before I decided to leave the car at home and take the train into Manchester – also something I had never done before, let alone with the added burden of a small land mass in tow. The Grundig was like a dead body. What in the blazes did they put inside these things to make them work?

The beginning of my journey at the Warrington end was not so bad, the car park being quite close to the platform, but the walk from Piccadilly train station in Manchester to Piccadilly Gardens seemed like an eternity. Why these two places bore the same name yet were so far apart was beyond me.

When I finally arrived at the other Piccadilly station – the radio station as opposed to the train station – I thought my right arm was going to drop off; my right thigh was bruised with the banging of the Grundig's bloomin' great hulk and the fingers of my right hand had turned blue with the deep imprint of its wide shiny metal handle.

I was a mess but I was an early mess and that was good – three hours an early mess to be precise.

Timmy waltzed in through reception around about an hour before his show. There was no Adam Ant outfit this time but instead a multicoloured stripy tank top over a bright orange shirt; he was also wearing a big fur coat and a beret. I didn't know what it all meant but I quite liked it.

He recognised me from the night before and politely said that he'd send somebody out for me when he was ready for the interview. I waited patiently for about half an hour until the tall, sharp-looking kid from the fun bus appeared. It was quickly evident to me that this individual was someone I could perhaps learn from, he was supremely confident and I couldn't help thinking he looked like a member of Depeche Mode.

Hurriedly he led me through several corridors – something I was finding hard to cope with as the Grundig was now back banging against my leg. Between the pain and my audible wincing I remember thinking how surprisingly unglamorous the place was, looking more like an office pool than a throbbing radio station – again showbusiness was proving to be more 'business' than 'show' – when was I going to learn? Half a corridor later, we reached the office where the Great Mallett was to be found, head down, writing away – the master preparing.

The tall kid wafted out. It was now only fifteen minutes before *Timmy on The Tranny* went on the air for this Monday night, Timmy was still totally focused on what he was writing,

'Won't be a sec,' he muttered.

I went to lift my machine onto his desk in readiness so as not to waste any time.

'Shit, what-is-that?' Timmy exclaimed, looking at what looked like a small building that had just been plonked in front of him.

'It's a Grundig 350 Deluxe – it's my brother's,' I replied proudly.

'Oh … I see,' remarked Timmy, somewhat unsure of what to make of both it and me. 'Alright, you ready?' he asked.

'Yes, thank you,' I replied, my voice now quivering nervously with the prospect of my first question.

My interview with Timmy was really a thinly disguised list of questions designed to solicit advice to help me get his job one day. I have since been a victim of such 'interviews' myself – you can spot them a mile off. Whether Timmy knew what I was up to at the time I could only guess, though I suspected he probably did.

I can't remember exactly what my questions were, although I have a feeling the tape may actually still be on the machine and I think the machine is still somewhere in Mum's loft. Dare I get it out? I'm saying no – for now at least.

What I do remember vividly is the tall kid coming in again, several times in fact, always to deliver a concise piece of information or ask a quick question about the forthcoming show, speed and economy seemed to be everything between these two – there was a very no-nonsense atmosphere.

I looked at the big white clock on the office wall above the desk where we were sitting, as it ticked towards seven o'clock it counted down the time I had left with my hero. My questions would have to stop soon as *Timmy on the Tranny* was about to take to the air once again. I thought it best to wrap things up voluntarily.

'This has been Pete James interviewing Timmy Mallett for Warrington General Hospital Radio. Timmy, thank you.'

Pete James, eh – what was all that about? Pete James was the name I had decided upon using as I sat on the train that afternoon. Why? I don't know but for some reason I thought it sounded good, much better than Chris Evans. I thought it was the kind of name a DJ might have. I even practised the autograph.

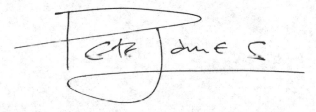

The only question I really remember asking Timmy that night is the one I asked after the 'interview' was over, just before Timmy left for the studio to go and do his show.

'Who is that boy who keeps coming in to tell you things?'

'Oh, you mean the one who looks like he should be in Depeche Mode?'

'Yes, him.'

'Oh that's Andy, he's my assistant, he's fab but he goes back to university next week – now must dash, well done, good luck – byee!'

'Bye, thanks,' I replied to Timmy as he disappeared.

I made another mental note, much quicker and bigger than I had ever done before.

'The big kid is leaving – who's gonna replace the big kid?' I thought to myself.

By this time, back in Warrington, I had left Ralph's to become assistant manager of a small group of rival newsagents so I was already an assistant of sorts, but Andy was assistant to my hero and was leaving at the end of the week.

I couldn't help feeling that Timmy had volunteered this additional information when there was absolutely no need to do so. He could have just told me that Andy was great and he was his assistant but he hadn't, he had extended to me the knowledge that Andy was leaving and soon. Why had he done this? Was it merely an unconscious and natural extension to the conversation or did he want me to know this for a specific reason? I couldn't take a chance, I had to presume it was the latter.

The walk back to the train station was a blur of excitement, all I recall is that I swapped the Grundig over to my left side so at least I would be equally bruised come the next day – the day I would write off for my first job in radio.

top
10
Things to Consider When Attempting to Make a Move in Your Career

10 Make sure you really want it in the first place

9 Really make sure you really want it in the first place

8 Think if it's going to help you get where you want to be next

7 Think where you want to be ultimately and if it will help get you there

6 Imagine if you had achieved it and how it would affect your life as a result

5 Don't consider the financial cost, as long as you can afford to carry on living it's irrelevant

4 Do consider how much of the next few years of your life it will take up and remember you can never get those years back

3 Have an exit strategy – this is so important

2 Never let your nut rule your gut – ever … the brain is not all it's cracked up to be

1 For goodness' sake, get out there and go do something about it!

The boss of Piccadilly Radio was a man called Tony Ingham. I phoned up to find out his name and immediately set about composing my note. It was brief and to the point, I explained that I had interviewed Timmy only last night, during the course of which Timmy had let slip that Andy his assistant was leaving, which to me suggested there might be some kind of vacancy coming up and although I would never presume to be able to fill Andy's role I was willing to do anything for nothing for ever – in fact I think I said I would do 'everything' for ever for nothing – if this meant I could work behind the hallowed doors of the great Piccadilly 261.

I sent the letter before lunchtime on the Tuesday and to my amazement and complete and utter joy, I received a reply from Mr Ingham on the Thursday, I went to see him on the Friday and started work on Timmy's show on the Monday. Incredible but 100 per cent true.

When I went to see Tony he told me Timmy had mentioned the fact that Andy was leaving on purpose because he thought I was quite sparky and had suspected my interview with him was more a fraudulent attempt by me to find out more about working in radio than anything else and that he would soon need a new pair of hands and why not?

Timmy had stopped short, however, of encouraging me further to see if I would do anything about it myself and now because I had, the door was open. However, the rest from here on in was up to me – and by the way I would be expected to do everything for nothing for ever!

My long working days were about to get even longer. I would start at the newsagents at the usual time, go home in the day, return in the afternoon and then, after locking up, hot foot it off to Manchester up the M62 to do 'whatever Timmy wanted'.

This started by answering the studio phones, a true baptism of fire. Answering Timmy's phones was like being a stock market trader at the moment a crash happened but for every minute of every show. He would announce a competition over the beginning of a three-minute record, give out the phone number and expect a correct, fully prepped and rehearsed caller before the end of it. If the caller turned out to be below par you'd better not have been the person to put them through.

To Timmy, the callers were everything and the calibre of kids we put on the air told the other kids who was listening to the show – i.e. only great kids were welcome; as in many things, perception was everything. The kids also had to be spread out evenly from a geographical point of view, an equal number of boys and girls was also a target, although more girls than boys was acceptable as long as it was never the other way round.

I wasn't Timmy's only helper – there were six or seven of us, some really sharp little operators, smart smart kids, good energy, lots of ideas and bags of confidence. There was Sally and Hannah and Geraldine and Paul and another Chris; they were mostly posher than me but that didn't seem to matter. They couldn't have been more welcoming, there was no air of internal competition – we were all too petrified of messing up to think about anything else.

To work on *Timmy on the Tranny* was even more exciting than listening to it. Timmy really was a genius. I still think about watching him work: he was truly insane but for all the right reasons. The pressure he put us under was nothing to the pressure he put himself under every second of every show. He knew exactly what he was doing but everything was always happening so quickly in his head he often didn't have time to tell the rest of us what it was he wanted us to do. This was a regular cause of frustration for him and blind panic for us – to be honest we were clueless most of the time.

From the second the red light went off and Timmy put on a song there was furious activity to get the next link ready. Every link meant something, every link had some colour, either a joke, a character, a caller or an interview, and every link had a beginning, middle and end – the end being the most important as, if the beginning or middle failed, a good end would always get you out of trouble.

This is just one of the lessons Timmy taught me that I have used on every programme I have ever been involved with to this day.

This golden time was proving to be a master class in broadcasting, an invaluable and unique learning experience available nowhere but right here, right now, but the heat was about to be turned up – the next stage of apprenticeship on Timmy's show was to be invited 'on the air' as a 'character'.

This was a huge deal and also a make-or-break moment. Helpers only got one or two bites at the on-air character cherry. If they were successful they would become a bit-part player in an award-winning radio show and would become famous in their own right. Listeners would write to them and want to know who they were and what they looked like; they would be asked to do more characters and be given more air time. If they were unsuccessful, however, they would be consigned to the hell of the phone rooms and sending out prizes, probably for ever.

Timmy asked me if he could see me one night after the show.

'Er, yes hi, well done tonight, I would like you to think about a character for the show, something different, something that you like, 'cos if you like it, the kids'll like it, something that you can do night in, night out. Anything – it just has to be clever and funny, that's all.' He then paused before adding, 'Oh, and have it ready for tomorrow night. Byeee' (!) and with that he was off.

See, perfect, why can't everyone in life be so straight? How much more time would we all have to ourselves if they were? Timmy didn't want a conversation, he didn't want to be your friend, but he did want like-minded people to join in his mini radio revolution.

The pressure was on and for me, pressure works: I came up with a character called Nobby N'O'Level.

Nobby had ten N'O'Levels in nothing. He would always ask Timmy a question about an educational fact to which Timmy would be gobsmacked that Nobby didn't know the answer. Nobby, as a riposte, would then triumphantly announce something that he knew, which of course was also completely wrong. Finally he would mitigate the whole episode by signing off with his catchphrase, 'Well, what I don't know ... I don't know.'

Nobby was very *Sesame Street* and Timmy was taken with him straight away – he could see that the material for the character was fact-based while also being silly enough to be entertaining and sympathetic enough for kids to like. Nobby was a tryer and you had to love him for that.

He was an instant hit and I was on the air.

What I also was, was very tired, very tired indeed, as well as fast becoming a danger to other drivers.

I had begun to stay on after Timmy's show to work in the studio. Most radio stations have two identical studios with a control room in between. After Timmy went off the air, Cuddly Dave came on from the studio opposite and Timmy's studio was free for the next three hours. I would spend the next year of my life hanging around and playing with the gear and practising various techniques and ideas until the wee small hours of the next day.

Adrenaline was my friend – it had to be – I would drive home and get in around two o'clock in the morning, still having to get up to open the newspaper shop before five. I remember having to open all the windows in the car and singing all the way home to keep awake. I could tell I was in trouble when I would suddenly stop in the middle of a Beatles chorus for no reason whatsoever – when it all went quiet I knew the next thing that would happen was that I would close my eyes and who knows what after that; I had to keep singing.

Needless to say, when I did get home I had no trouble falling asleep. It's still the most tired I've ever been. I would be panting out of breath as if I'd just sprinted for the bus, purely from the madness of the day. No complaints though, I loved every second of it but something would have to give, and soon.

I was beginning to run on empty.

top
10
Things a Boss
Should Never Do

10 Try to be popular
9 Incentivise as opposed to reward
8 Recount stories of when they were a junior employee and
   · how things used to be
7 Repeatedly state to the year how many years they have been
   in the business
6 Have their teeth whitened or their hair coloured – OK for girls
   but really not good at all for blokes
5 Return to work after a boozy 'lunch'
4 Expect anyone who gets paid less than them to care as
   much as they do
3 Get drunk at the Christmas party
2 Employ a secretary or assistant that they stand any chance
   of finding even vaguely attractive
1 Use their position to steamroller over other people,
   especially the little people

Decisions are so much easier when they are more or less made for you, even if it's down to circumstances and events beyond your control.

There was no way I could sustain the life I was leading. I was so tired. I was losing my focus at the shop in the day and it was affecting my performance on the show at night, but the show was all I cared about, the shop for me was now purely a means to an end.

The thing was, though I still wasn't getting paid 'anything' for the show (not that I minded, none of the other kids were either and that had always been our deal right from the get go), it was just that I didn't have any other source of income except my job. So for a while it looked like I was going to have to give up the one thing I loved, the one thing I thought I would never get to do and that I was now doing, the one thing that I thought I could make a life out of – the wonderful world of the wireless.

Not so, however, an archangel was about to swoop down to my rescue in the guise of the grumpy old git of a newsagent. Not Ralph from my first job but my new boss, who took grumpiness to a whole new level.

When I wasn't on the radio, or at the radio station, on the road or asleep, I would be at work listening to the radio. It was still my link to the outside world during daylight hours when I was stuck in the back of the shop for most of the day.

This shop didn't have an actual office – so while the shop girls looked after things out front, I had to do all my paperwork in the stockroom, but it wasn't really a proper stockroom even, it was more like a large cupboard, stacked to the rafters with cartons of fags and boxes of confectionery. It also had a barred-up window, which I thought was kind of appropriate.

I arrived for the evening mark-up one afternoon, breezing through the shop as usual, except this time when I went to say hi to a couple of the girls, normally so cheery and pleasant with me, on this occasion they were barely able to bring themselves to murmur a reply.

'Strange,' I thought, they were never like that, they had the air of children about them who know there is something wrong but don't want to let on in case Mum or Dad find out.

I entered my cell as usual, took off my coat and immediately noticed something wasn't right, there was something missing, I didn't know what at first and then it dawned on me ... there was silence. My radio wasn't on. I looked around, not only was it not on, it wasn't even there. I ran out to the front.

'Does anyone know where my radio is?'

'It's been confiscated.'

'What do you mean it's been confiscated?'

'He confiscated it, he said it's a disruptive influence and it had to go.'

'Confiscated. Where are we, at school?'

It transpired that the Oliver Cromwell of the retail world had come in that lunchtime and declared he'd had enough of me and my delusions of grandeur but most of all he'd had enough of my bloody radio, and what's more he preferred the funereal silence of pessimism as opposed to the soundtrack of optimism. It was his shop and that was how it was going to stay.

'What a coward,' I thought to myself, 'what a snivelling miserable snake in the grass.' I had done nothing but work my nuts off for him and he didn't even have the decency to have a conversation with me first before taking away the one little luxury that kept me going. 'Even prisoners are allowed a radio,' I thought to myself.

This was obviously why he was so bloomin' miserable all the time. He couldn't convey his feelings about anything. He had a great business, a nice car, a nice house, by all accounts, and yet he begrudged me my little radio, in the back, never loud enough to be heard out the front, never gonna disturb anyone. What a loser.

But surely there had to be more to it than this – of course there did. His rage manifested itself in the confiscation of my radio but it was obviously a metaphor for wanting me out as well. To him the radio represented me, just as I represented it – why else would a grown intelligent man stoop to such petty depths where a junior employee was concerned?

It also has to be said that he was a moaner, one of the least attractive and useful traits a human being can adopt.

When somebody moans about something, it's never about what they say it's about, it's always about something else, that's why they are moaners in the first place and if you can be bothered to dig deeper it's usually about the fact that they are personally unfulfilled in some or other aspect of their lives.

If anyone comes to me and says they want a word about something I always immediately ignore whatever it is they first talk about and then ask them, 'What's really the matter?' It always works, they either tell you straight away what it is or never come to you again for fear of having to have a real conversation about something.

So, in my opinion, if the old git wanted rid of me and didn't have the bottle to tell me so himself, I would do the job for him. I informed the girls that I had enjoyed working with them but I was now leaving and I would probably never see any of them again.

'What about the evening paper deliveries?' said one of them, in a tizz as I walked out of the door.

'No offence to you,' I replied, 'but I don't give a stuff about him or his papers any more.' I had suddenly become buoyed by a new-found sense of freedom, 'and tell him,' I added, 'that I bought that radio with my own money – technically what he did by confiscating it was theft.' And with that I was on my way.

Sadly I never saw my beloved radio again. I would give a thousand pounds for it now. But the old git had indirectly done me a huge favour, he had pushed me away from him and his doom and gloom towards a better place. Bad people always do this if you give them long enough. They can't stand positive people being around: it threatens their equilibrium of shite – they might try and infect you with their poison but once they see you're having none of it, they'll run a mile rather than run the risk of feeling happier about themselves. Ridiculous but true.

More by chance than design, I was now finally free to put all my energy into my work at the radio station, albeit having just lost my only source of income.

As a result of this drop in status I was skint within a couple of weeks, but there's always a job if you want one; anybody who says otherwise is telling porkies. It may be a rubbish job with terrible wages but there will be a job somewhere.

I had to find a job that left me free Monday to Thursday but paid enough for me to survive. I didn't care what it was or what prospects there were. As far as I was concerned my future was in radio, so all I needed was the cash for petrol to get me there and food to keep me alive.

I can't recall how it came about but the perfect solution to my dilemma was waiting for me at a rusty old lock-up garage in a small village called Vulcan, which is a tiny place a few miles outside Warrington, famous for the production of railway locomotives.

Somebody (for the life of me I can't remember who) told me about a job selling seafood out of a basket around the local pubs – shrimps, prawns and crabsticks – all that kind of stuff.

Apparently all you had to do was turn up on a Friday and Saturday night at this mysterious garage, pick up your basket, fill it with stock and then set off on your round. If you could put up with the initial banter from the lager lads then you were well on your way to earning a good few quid. It was just like being a paper boy again, but a bit smellier.

I loved it, it was great fun, the banter was banal but bearable and the pubs generally friendly and welcoming. Sure, the hours meant I couldn't go out and socialise like all my mates but I was sort of out anyway and whilst everyone else was spending their money I was saving mine and all for the greater good. I could easily make over fifty quid for a couple of nights' work. I could have the radio on as loud as I liked in the car plus I had the rest of the week free to spend back at Piccadilly.

Bingo, the miserable old git had set me free, my life had been transformed – for now at least.

Having saved up enough cash from my seafood sales plus a few other odd jobs, eventually I had enough to see me through for a while and went to work at Piccadilly full time – more than full time in fact: I was there for as many hours as they'd have me in the building. I didn't want them to be left in any doubt as to how much I was desperate to be part of what they did. All the time I was learning; it was invaluable in every sense but what I really needed was a paid position, and once again I was running out of options.

I hung on for as long as I could but there came a point when I had to face up to a reality check, I had been working there for ages now including weekends and I still hadn't earned a penny of actual wages. Of course I would have paid them to do what I was doing if I could have – I liked it so much – but that wasn't a 'real' situation and a guy's gotta live.

Regretfully I concluded that maybe the 'me working for free for ever' bit of my original deal was now no longer a sustainable situation and that at some point if I was to carry on being able to work there, money would have to change hands – preferably from their bank account into mine.

I conveyed my circumstances to the management but was told in no uncertain terms that this was not going to happen, it was not a possibility. They appreciated what I had done for them and were not ungrateful but they knew I needed the experience more than the experience needed me. I was still last in when it came to the pecking order for the next full-time paid job and things didn't look like they were going to change anytime soon; they did, however, offer me a stopgap.

The deal was, I would be paid bugger all for any work in the week, which I was still very much expected to do, but I would get paid at weekends for the Friday and Saturday night technical operating overnight shifts – the ones that nobody else wanted to do. 'Fine by me,' I thought, I did want to do those shifts – and for money, you're not kidding! As long as I could afford to eat and get there I was happy, more than happy, in fact – I was ecstatic.

I was working at a radio station and being paid for it, not much admittedly, but nevertheless I was official ... sort of.

Yeeeeeeessssssssss!

Noooooooooooooo!

As it turned out, I quickly discovered that the money on offer wasn't actually going to be enough to fulfil these two lowly criteria. On what I was receiving I could afford to either eat or drive but not both, and seeing as I wouldn't be able to drive if I was dead, I thought I'd better eat first and think about petrol second.

However it wasn't long before the writing was once again on the wall and this time I was at breaking point – I wasn't being overly dramatic or precious, I was simply skint and was forced to face up to reality. I was left with no choice – I had to leave Piccadilly Radio and I had to do it now.

Mum and Dad, Minnie and Martin, circa 1969, but where are they? Blackpool, Llandudno, Southport, Rhyl or Towyn?*

Warrington, Walking Day, circa 1974. An annual procession where we walked in between various bands and church banners. I still don't know why. So where am I? Second from front, fourth, or sixth?*

* See page 334 for answers

Wonky fringe, second button undone, ripped jumper, but hey, look at that smile – nothing's going to get this kid down.

Big sis Diane and me pretending not to argue for the sake of a nice Christmas photo.

Warrington Scouts gang show. Bottom row, second left, not happy as the kid with the pointy hat steals the show.

'OK, it may be red, but are you sure this is a Ferrari?'

Look at the babes in the front row, they're hot, man – I wonder if they're liking my tie.

'C'mon Lynne, smile. You never know where this photo might end up one day.'

Who's this badged-up dude with the side-parting taking himself ever so seriously?

Scholastic Specialists, Hartlepool.   Geo. Holdsworth & Son Ltd.

BOTELER GRAMMAR SCHOOL
WARRINGTON — 1978
Headmaster: R. J. ENGLISH, M.Sc., M.Ed.
Acting Headmaster: E. PERCIVAL, M.A., M.Ed.

'Hey, look everyone, I've turned into Velma from *Scooby-Doo*!'

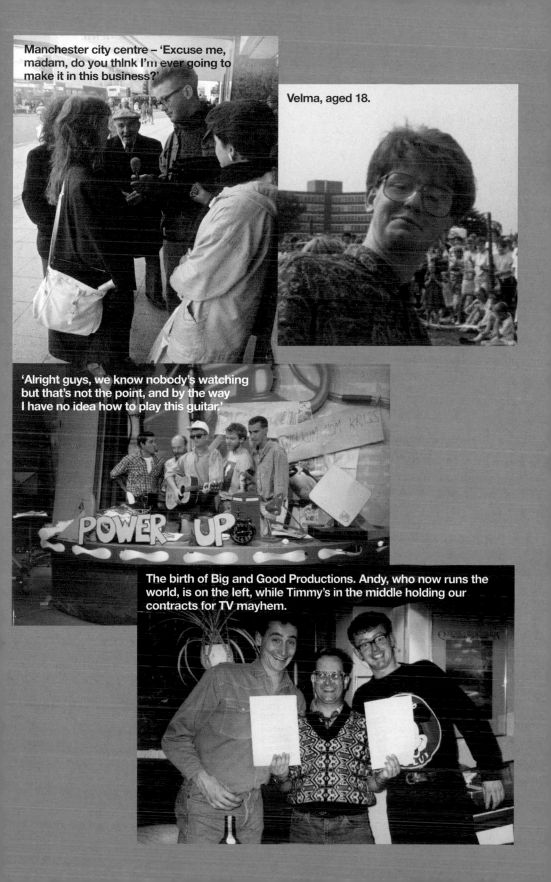

Manchester city centre – 'Excuse me, madam, do you think I'm ever going to make it in this business?'

Velma, aged 18.

'Alright guys, we know nobody's watching but that's not the point, and by the way I have no idea how to play this guitar.'

POWER UP

The birth of Big and Good Productions. Andy, who now runs the world, is on the left, while Timmy's in the middle holding our contracts for TV mayhem.

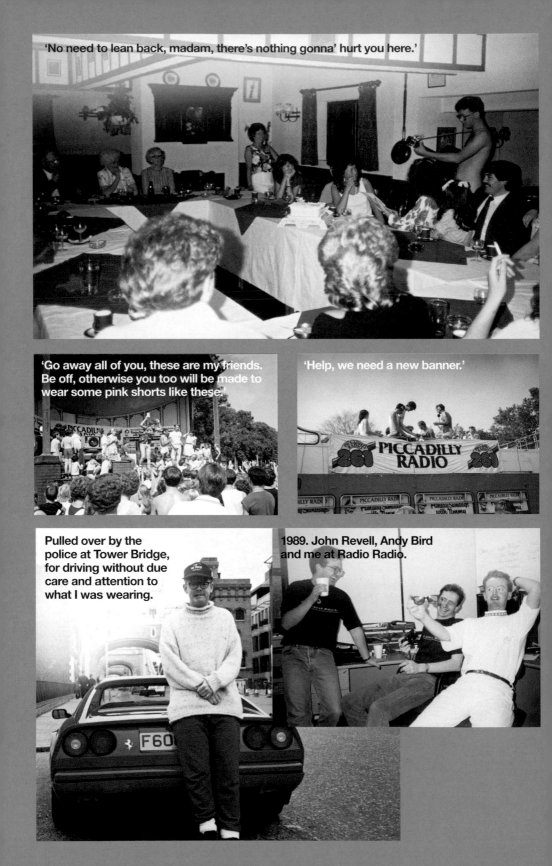

'No need to lean back, madam, there's nothing gonna' hurt you here.'

'Go away all of you, these are my friends. Be off, otherwise you too will be made to wear some pink shorts like these.'

'Help, we need a new banner.'

PICCADILLY RADIO

Pulled over by the police at Tower Bridge, for driving without due care and attention to what I was wearing.

1989. John Revell, Andy Bird and me at Radio Radio.

I used to work for a company researching audience figures for radio. One of the prerequisites for your ID card was that you had to try to look over the top of your signature.

1986 M R S The Market Research Society

Interviewer Identity Card

Radio and Television Audience Research
Room 154, The Langham,
Portland Place, London W1A 1AA.
Telephone: 01-580 1813

This Authority is Only Valid until 31st December 1986	No. 30900
Name: C. EVANS	
Number: 24066	
Signature:	

Authorisation:

Peter Menneer

Mr P. Menneer
Head of Broadcasting
Research Department

Circa 1990, me at GLR in the pink shirt, slightly camp, with one of my first fans.

The Bristol Bloom Festival, my first Radio 1 roadshow, and my first attempt to hold a two-dimensional red dot in my hand.

A special delivery for Mr Mallett as he hits No. 1 in the charts; at his house – not mine!

'Hi, everyone!' We've just got back from Queen's 'I Want to Break Free' video shoot.

ITV

'Gary, please help, I seem to have frozen in a grimace. Maybe it has something to do with the fact that TV-am have just lost their franchise.'

6.00 Always game for fun, Gary Monaghan and Chris Evans hope you'll play along as they create 'TV-MAYhem'

top 10

Things to Do When the Cards Are Stacked Against You

10 Make sure you get enough sleep

9 Eat well

8 Exercise (these three are vital and often the opposite of what you want to do)

7 Don't panic or beat yourself up

6 Take note of the new lessons you've learnt – there's always value in every experience

5 Get away – to anywhere, be it the other side of the world or the woods round the corner

4 Remember yourself as a kid and how brilliant you knew life could be

3 Think calmly, collectively and positively

2 Hatch a plan

1 Go again

I left Piccadilly with my tail between my legs, my dream in tatters, but radio was now in my blood and I vowed that one day I would make it back.

In the meantime I resolved to throw myself into the entertainment world closer to home, but I had no money and no resources with which to do so other than my precious Mini that my lovely mum had bought me. It was time to rejoin the real world.

I took a job as a forklift truck driver while I thought about things further. It was a job I both loved and hated. I loved it because I could listen to the radio all day; I hated it because the bloke in charge of me – the warehouse manager – was a complete bastard. I really wished him ill and hoped he would get killed on the way to work, I pitied his wife and children he was so horrible – unlike the big boss of the company who was one of the nicest guys you could ever wish to meet.

The business involved importing deep-fat fryers and ice-making machines from Canada. They weighed anything from a few pounds to two and a half tons and they were so tightly packed in the forty-foot freight containers they were shipped in, it was barely possible to get them out. The task of doing so involved sliding the forks of the forklift underneath the wooden packing case and then tilting the whole thing back and forth to somehow waggle it out, like you might do to loosen a brick in a wall, except this was two and a half tons of fat fryer and it was balancing precariously twenty feet above you – well, actually me in this case.

Once I got the waggle on, I had to wait for the fryer to sway away from me and then reverse quickly while the angle of the forks enabled the case to come clean out, missing the top lip of the container; as the fryer then swayed back towards you, a full backwards tilt was required to bring the waggle to a halt and allow the fryer to slide gently back fully onto the forks.

The momentum of the whole operation would often cause the back wheels of the forklift to come off the ground every time the fryer swayed away from me – over waggle and the forklift, along with the bespectacled ginger-haired driver, would be up in the air off the ground and it would be goodnight Vienna.

This never happened to me but I did get a sideways waggle on once when one of the big fryers caught the top lip as I reversed out too late. The fryer began to rock slowly from left to right but instead of beginning to settle, the rocking became more and more exaggerated; with each rock it became ever more obvious what was going to happen. The fryer had taken on a momentum of its own. I was sat in the cab of the truck, helpless and open-mouthed. I realised the fryer was going to tip at any moment and probably to the left which is precisely where the big boss's brand new beige/brown Rover Vitesse happened to be parked. I looked on in disbelief – they say things like this occur in slow motion and that's exactly how it felt.

The fryer came crashing down right on top of the boss's pride and joy which was flattened like a pancake. It looked like a joke car: all four of its wheels had splayed out like a baby deer losing its footing on the ice.

As the deafening noise subsided and the dust settled I could not believe what I was looking at. There were splintered planks everywhere from the crate; the fryer was in bits and somewhere underneath were the remnants of a now unrecognisable prestige executive motor car.

'Shit the bed,' I thought to myself, 'what do I do now?' and then I remembered that line from *The Godfather* where Robert Duvall's character informs the film producer that Senor Corleone always insists on hearing bad news as soon as possible.

I walked straight through the office pool and into Bill, the big boss's office.

He could see I was distressed.

'Well, hello young Chris, what can I do for you?' he enquired warmly in his thick treacly Scottish accent.

I had already decided the best way to break the news to him.

'Bill, imagine the worst thing I could tell you.'

He thought for a second. '... Alright,' he said smiling as if it were a game.

'OK, well, whatever that was, this is much much worse.'

He laughed nervously. 'What on earth is it? What's going on?'

There was no other way to say it so I just told him straight. 'I have just dropped a two and a half ton fat fryer on your car.'

He took a beat to take in what I had just said and then without saying a word he walked straight past me and outside to the loading bay. When he saw the car, or what was left of it, he stopped dead in his tracks, looking on at the carnage in total disbelief.

'How the fuck did you do that?' he finally said.

'It just happened,' I replied pathetically.

'Well, for fuck's sake don't let it "just happen" ever again.'

And with that he turned on his heels and went back to work. Later that day his secretary called the Insurance and the next morning they delivered a replacement vehicle – the same model of car but this time in silver. Bill's reaction amazed me and taught me several invaluable lessons:

Never keep bad news from the person that needs to know it. Tell them as soon as possible.

Never dwell on bad news – it serves no purpose save to make things worse.

Never let something that is totally sortable get the better of you. As I said, Bill's reaction amazed me, but looking back, it was entirely pragmatic: a car is just a combination of tin and rubber and it was insured – so no problem.

What I also discovered later was that Bill had vehemently disliked the beige/brown colour of his car when it had been delivered and was secretly thrilled at being able to replace it in silver.

It wasn't long after this unfortunate episode that due to a combination of bastard warehouse bloke and more recently an over-amorous female member of the office pool (who happened to be married to a professional rugby player), I decided that it was time to hang up my warehouse coat once and for all. It was back to the job section of the local paper.

top
10
Business Names I Have Been Involved in

10 Big and Good Productions (my first production company)
9 Gambon and Defreites (the private detective agency I set up with my friend Michael)
8 The Great Car Company (my first foray into the classic car market)
7 Umtv
6 Ginger Television
5 Ginger Radio
4 Ginger Productions
3 The Ginger Media Group*
2 Ginger Air (an aviation company that never got off the ground)
1 Kinkies Kissograms

I began scouring the small ads for any opportunities that might be slightly more on the entertainment side of the employment fence. In my attempt to show business my way back above the breadline I applied for a job at Bunnies Kissograms in Chester. They charged £18 a time, of which the kissogram received half. I liked the sound of that but unfortunately they didn't like the look of me; I was more Jane than Tarzan, they said.

I returned to Warrington where kissograms might as well have been spaceships – they just didn't happen. 'A gap in the market if ever I saw one,' I thought, and immediately placed my own ad in the local paper:

KINKIES KISSOGRAMS – THE SKINNIEST TARZANS IN TOWN

The kissograms that I'd witnessed were all very well but the biggest laugh was achieved when the kissogram first revealed themselves to their subject. After the initial shock it was all downhill. I decided herein lay a further opportunity and what I lacked in muscle I would make up for with humour.

---

* At its peak this company was part of an organisation worth over £1,000,000,000 pounds. How mad is that?

I devised a sequence that got funnier and funnier as it went on as opposed to fading out. My act was based around three balloons, a carving knife, a little teddy, a raw sausage, lots of cream and a blindfold on the girl; I also played the guitar and sang her a personalised song – all for six quid! It was cheap but I had to get the product out there. I had to make sure the cost was not an issue. If I was a hit then I could hike the prices all in good time.

Warrington soon woke up to the hilarity of the kissogram and before I knew it, I was up to seven or eight kissograms a night at the weekends. I soon doubled my prices as I'd planned and even brought in a couple of pals to help out with the engagements. I remember exactly where I was on the night of Live Aid when Madonna came on stage, I was pulling up in my car to Orford Park Recreation Club ready for another semi-naked performance of my own.

The kissograms were a means to an end and it wasn't long before I had saved up enough money to enter the hallowed realms of the mobile disc jockey.

I bought all the gear required for a mobile disco and secured some regular pub dates, I became resident in one pub – seven nights a week! I convinced the publican that every night would be better with music and that if he let me leave my gear there, I would do four nights for free. This meant I didn't have to haul all the gear round all week; it also meant I could sell my van and buy an MG Roadster instead. In all I was soon doing nine discos a week, seven nights in the pub and then two later on at clubs on a Friday and Saturday.

The discos were good business but another test of my resolve was just around the corner. At Christmas all the mobile DJs could charge a premium for their 'shows' and a pretty hefty one at that. You could easily make enough money for a decent holiday during the festive season.

It was two days before my first Christmas booking when, still living with my Mum, I was on the way home late one night after working at a club. I had invested in a Datsun estate car by now, my record collection was getting bigger and although my turntables, speakers and lights didn't need to move I had to take my records wherever I was appearing.

It was around three o'clock in the morning and I couldn't have been more than a mile from home when I heard my exhaust blowing – at least that's what it sounded like, it was really loud. 'Strange,' I thought, but it soon became evident what the problem was when I pulled up to park outside our house. Somehow the tailgate on my car had come open, which was why the exhaust seemed so loud. Not only that but to my utter disbelief, somewhere on the way home my entire record collection had fallen out.

I was stunned, I couldn't believe what had happened. To a DJ his record collection is everything, you have to have all the records for all ages of clientele, from the waltzes for the oldies through the Sixties and Seventies right up until the latest top twenty, as well as the novelty records for the kids. My diary was booked up all over Christmas and I had just lost every single record I owned.

top 10

**Dance Floor Fillers for
Mobile DJ C. Evans circa 1985***

10 'Let's go round again' – Detroit Spinners
9 'Love really hurts' – Billy Ocean
8 'Blame it on the boogie' – Jackson 5
7 'Eye to eye contact' – Edwin Starr
6 'Never too much' – Luther Vandross
5 'Always and forever' – Heatwave
4 'It's a love thing' – The Whispers
3 'December, 1963 (Oh, what a night)' – The Four Seasons
2 'Young hearts run free' – Candi Staton
1 'You to me are everything' – The Real Thing

The next day I woke up and still couldn't believe what had happened. Of course the night before I had driven straight back over the exact route I had come home but someone had obviously got to my records before me. All that I found was one lonely twelve-inch single of 'Relax' by Frankie Goes To Hollywood.

I was so close to throwing in the towel that morning but Mum made me a cup of tea and gave me some kind words of encouragement, enough to cause me to think about the situation a little more rationally. I could give up but what good would that do? Was this situation redeemable? What would Bill, my nice old Scottish boss, have done? One thing is for sure: he wouldn't have sat there feeling sorry for himself.

One hour later I was in Woolies buying every compilation album they sold – all the hits, Christmas or otherwise. I ended up with around twenty albums and just about enough tunes to get me through the Christmas party season – after which you could almost guarantee some of the other guys were bound to sell up and move out of the mobile DJ world, having cashed in one final time. Sure enough this year was no exception. I earned my extra cash and snapped up some other dude's record collection sometime early in the new year and before I knew it I was back on top – and with a much better variety of tunes than I had in the first place.

---

*Please note, these are in no way, shape or form, personal favourites of mine.

Being a DJ, as I had hoped and suspected, did indeed have many advantages, including that when all the other blokes were drunk and trying to chat up the girls (by the way, why do blokes wait until they are least able to do this, i.e. towards the end of the night when they can barely walk or talk?) I would be stone-cold sober. Not only that but I would have a set of wheels outside ready to go, whilst everyone else had to resort to running the gauntlet of the queue at the cab rank, a notorious hot-spot for punch-ups – second only to the queue for the late-night chippy.

It was this sobriety and availability of transport which led me to meet Alison, the mother of my daughter Jade.

By now I was the DJ at the mighty Carlton Club, the same place where my brother had DJ'd a decade or so before. Alison was a regular there and was absolutely stunning, with masses of cascading blonde hair and a dazzling smile. She also used to wear these long flowing dresses that followed her obediently around wherever she chose to float – and that's exactly what she did, she floated – magnificently. She was cool, curvy, sexy and funny, what was not to like?

Alison and I got it together one evening when a friend of hers came over and 'told' me to ask her out. To be 'told' to ask a girl out when you have also been informed that if you do then the answer is going to be yes is one of life's great joys. I promptly did as I was 'told' and Alison and I were very much inseparable thereafter.

Within not very long at all I was staying over at her house most nights – her mum was very liberal, something for which we were both hugely grateful. This 'understanding' meant we were free to do all the things young couples liked to do and we did them a lot. We did them so much in fact that one day a little baby called Jade arrived.

I was twenty-one by now and financially things were going well for me, by that I don't mean I was on the way to my first million or anything like that, but well enough for Alison and I to buy our own house. Which we did, a sturdy old three-bed terraced house with a tiny front garden, a yard at the back and a knockthrough living/dining room downstairs. But a baby was something neither of us had planned and it wasn't long before it became obvious things were not going to work out.

Alison had been nothing but supportive of me when it came to my efforts in the world of entertainment, especially when I mooted the idea of getting back into radio. I had arrived home one night and seen a guy who I used to work with at Piccadilly who was now on the telly; somehow he'd managed to bag his own slot and although not bad, he was a little bland to say the least. If he could make it, I knew I definitely had a chance, and the difference now was I also had the funds to back me up.

I discussed my feelings with Alison and she couldn't have been more encouraging and positive – this is her natural disposition. In fact it was she who pushed me to make the initial call to get back into Piccadilly. I remember specifically what she said:

'Go for it, if that's what you really want, you have to go for it.'

Alison was totally selfless when it came to my ambition but I simply wasn't around enough to be supportive of her in the far more important task of bringing up a young child – in short, I was a selfish prick. I came back to the house one day and Alison had had enough: she had gone back to her mum's with the baby.

What did I feel at the time? I'm ashamed to say relief. I saw Alison going back home as leaving me free to carry on chasing my dreams – pathetic, I know, but that's where my head was at the time. To think now what it must have been like for her to be effectively abandoned by the father of her child and, being such a young age herself, left to bring up a little girl all on her own makes me feel awful. Not surprisingly it's the one thing I wish I could go back and change.

Thank Christ, Alison is the decent person she is and has continued always to put Jade first. She could so easily have let her feelings towards me dictate her decisions but she instead has remained steadfastly loyal to Jade and her well-being, and has done all she can not to let her own feelings get in the way of any chance Jade and I may have of getting to know each other. Jade has always come first with Alison, regardless of whatever else may be going on, testament to what a truly fantastic mum she has been and is one of the many reasons Jade loves her to death.

Inevitably, from the point Alison moved back to her mum's we grew further and further apart. With our relationship effectively over I decided to move to Manchester, but before I did so, Alison insisted we meet to talk about the future as far as Jade was concerned.

We arranged to meet one evening to discuss what we would do as a long-term strategy considering we had a child together. We met in a pub called the Britannia in Warrington. I'll never forget that night. Alison laid it on the table, plain and straight. That's her style. She said if I couldn't be relied upon to be around on a regular basis it would be best if I stayed out of the picture altogether.

Alison had had enough of me not being there when I said I would be and stated in no uncertain terms that she was more than capable of bringing up her daughter on her own. If I wasn't prepared to help her, she would much prefer to get on with things by herself rather than having Mr Unreliable hovering around, wondering whether or not he was going to turn up. Understandably her support for me and my career was no longer what it once had been – her priorities had changed and Jade came first, now and forever.

Alison and I both agreed that if one day when Jade was older and wanted to find out who her real father was, then that would be up to her. In the meantime Alison wanted to be free to find someone else to be with in life and if that person came along, then she also wanted Jade to have the chance of having a proper full-time dad. So we decided, for the next few years at least, that it would be best for me to disappear from the scene altogether.

I talked to a friend who had grown up without her real dad being around about my situation. She told me that she loved her stepdad, i.e. the guy her mum had got together with when her real father had left, and furthermore she neither cared nor wondered who her real father was, nor did she have any inclination to track him down.

So that is what we did. We parted company and went our separate ways. There was no screaming or shouting, just a flat sadness. As I drove back to Manchester that night and away from my responsibilities I felt a nagging sensation deep in my gut. I'd convinced myself it was the right thing to do and in many ways it was, but at the same time I knew of course it was entirely wrong. I supported Alison and Jade financially from day one but so what? Jade was my daughter and I had decided to leave rather than look after her. Something that I now realise was unforgivable.

Having said all that, I'm pretty sure this arrangement would have worked out fine if it weren't for one thing – the fact that I would one day become famous and with that would come a whole load of unexpected consequences, including the inevitable intrusion into innocent people's private lives, which Jade and her mum would have to deal with. Neither Alison nor I thought for one second that this would ever really happen – at least not to the extent it did – not that night in the Britannia pub in Warrington over two halves of lager and a bag of salt and vinegar crisps.

top
10
Memories of the great Piccadilly
Radio exponential learning curve

10 Take calls
 9 Send out prizes
 8 Prep callers for on air
 7 Log records
 6 Perform characters
 5 Edit tape with razor blade and chinagraph*
 4 Operate portable tape recorder†
 3 Operate the radio car
 2 Operate the studio
 1 Present a show

Now that I had moved to Manchester, the radio station completely consumed my every waking hour. I had more or less picked up from where I left off, going in during the day when the place was entirely different from how it was at night and weekends.

The sales, promotions and admin teams rushed around all day whilst the whacky commercial production guys with the loud shirts and funny voices (honestly) could be found in full flow, hidden away in their studios, lost in the throes of creation. The newsroom buzzed with an impressive roster of journalists – many more than you would find at a similar station today. News was very important to independent local radio in those days and many of the stations were home to proper old hacks with the legendary drinking habits to match.

As the days, weeks and months went by, I got to know more and more people and was asked to do more and more odd jobs, working on other shows, more studio management and lots more work in the radio car.

I loved the radio car. It was a Ford Cortina estate with the Piccadilly logo plastered across the bonnet. On its roof was mounted a bulky

---

* A chinagraph is the pencil/crayon we used to mark the edit point on the tape with. I used to love editing. As you removed a length of tape you would put it round your neck in case it was the wrong bit before making sure by listening back.

† These were mini reel-to-reel tape recorders called Uhers – they had to be charged up like car batteries and were a constant source of worry and woe.

retractable thirty-foot aerial – a proper bit of kit which always caused a fuss wherever it pitched up.

The radio car was a real workhorse, taking the radio station to the listeners and putting the listeners on the radio station. One of my jobs was to drive it to wherever it needed to go and set it up ready for action. Having located the site this basically involved pressing a button, waiting for the mast to elevate and then pointing it in the general direction of Manchester city centre. A highly hit-and-miss 'fine-tuning' operation would then commence which usually involved a quite pissed off and condescending studio engineer back at the base shouting at me via a short-wave radio in a patronising manner for the next ten minutes.

Before ISDN lines became de rigueur, the radio car was one of the few ways of gaining semi studio-quality sound at sports fixtures and the like. I remember all too well freezing my nuts off in the car park of St Helen's Rugby League Club, while Stuart Pike – now a top voice on Five Live, was attached to the other end of my cable commentating on how 'The Saints' were faring out on the pitch.

Sport was a massive part of Piccadilly's output and football especially, with Man U. and Man City leading an impressive cluster of local clubs regularly involved in the thick end of the old First Division.

One of the most exciting shows you could be asked to work on was a show called *Sport on Saturday*. *Sport on Saturday* was a non-stop four-hour maelstrom, packed full of action from beginning to end.

There was so much going on during this broadcast that the presenters only had time to focus on what they were saying, leaving them no time for operating any of the equipment. This meant the control desk had to be operated separately, usually by a technical operator, a rather grand name for someone who just about knew how some of what was laid out in front of them might work – at least that's how I always felt.

Working on *Sport on Saturday* was a learning curve like few others and again I couldn't get enough. The operator would sit behind the main control console where the DJ would normally sit while two sports presenters would sit opposite over the desk at the guest mics. The presenters would then spend most of the afternoon with their heads buried in makeshift notes and rip and reads (ie. hurriedly prepared scripts), just trying to hold themselves and everything else together. They would have the output of the station in one ear and the producer in the other, updating them with scores and any additional information they might need to know or that might be useful. It was a highly impressive scene to witness.

The console, the guardianship of which was down to the likes of me, was not unlike a mixing desk you might witness at a gig, consisting of faders, sound meters, gains of one type or another and a whole host of illuminated buttons with little letters on them which either did or didn't do what they were supposed to. When it came to *Sport on Saturday* the faders, normally linked up to records, CDs and cart machines during other shows, were connected to ten or more outside sources which were permanently dialled up throughout the afternoon. They were our live links to all the reporters at the local grounds.

The big guns, however, were behind us in the shape of four enormous clunking great ten-inch reel-to-reel tape machines, slowly turning like huge wheels in some sinister Victorian workhouse. They were mighty indeed and they commanded respect.

Each one of the four machines would have a direct input from full commentary of one of our featured games. Now here's the fun bit – when there was a goal, the operator would have to instantaneously swing around on his chair and thrust a scrap of paper in the take-up reel approximately where the goal took place. It was then down to the pressure of the ensuing tape to hold the scrap of paper in place. Consequently, as a result and if we were lucky, we would have some idea of where the goal might be when it came to full time.

It was then the operator's job to spool back on all four machines and splice the goals together for the final highlights package – very hairy, highly precarious, unbelievably messy but surprisingly productive.

At the end of a sports show, as you might imagine, there was always a real sense of relief, quickly followed by a sense of overwhelming achievement; celebratory beers in the bar afterwards were often the order of the day.

I don't believe there's anything better than live sport on the radio. Sports commentators are by far the most gifted of broadcasters – they are the people I have the most respect for in my industry. They make what they do sound so easy and it makes me shudder with dread at the thought of ever having to do it myself. The excitement they manage to convey is infectious and the accuracy with which they choose their words as the action changes from one thing to the other lightning fast is jaw-dropping – and whilst all this is going on they still find time to be articulate, humorous and even poetic – I hate them. Of course I'm joking.

I was recently told that a good commentator actually has to state the action before the crowd reacts to that action, otherwise it will sound like he's behind, so he almost has to guess what's going to happen next! If he gets it wrong he risks sounding like a dufus; if he gets it right, however, the oohs and ahs serve only to enhance his commentary, making the whole thing sound like a carefully prepared film score designed to highlight the scene in all the right places – now that's quality.

Like most places of work, at the radio station there were good jobs and bad jobs. Driving the desk for big shows and operating the radio car were up there with the best; whereas tape reclamation and record logging were most definitely down there with the worst.

Tape reclamation involved taking all the old tape that had been discarded during editing from out of the tape bin and sticking it all back together again for reuse. Whereas tape cost a fortune – me, a razor blade and a roll of sticky tape were a relative bargain.

As dull as tape reclamation was, it was nowhere near as dull as the music logging. The logging of records was a legal requirement, so that the various royalties could be paid to the various people concerned in the making of the records in the first place. Every song that was ever played on the radio had to be logged by hand.

The easiest way to do this was to take all the records off the DJ during or after the show and log them then and there, but often it would be late at night and there were more interesting things going on, so I would more likely leave my logging until later – big mistake, huge.

What was already a mind-numbingly tedious process now became a prolonged pain in the ass marathon of detective work, all my own fault of course. I would have to listen back to the shows, identify the records, locate them in the record library and then take down all the details to pay the contributors – the label, the record number, the artist, the name of the song, the writer/s, the publisher and for how long the record was played.

The humdrum of this process was compounded by the fact the record industry had thus far not agreed on a uniform place to write all these details, so they would be in different places for every disc; sometimes all the details would be on the sleeve, sometimes they would all be on the record label, sometimes a mixture of both ... soul-destroying. It often took longer to log the records for a show than the show itself, especially if you did it the way I did.

By this time, by the way, Timmy had moved on: he had flitted to London and to the zany world of early morning television and his kiddie-filled creation called *The Wide Awake Club* and *Wacaday* – the programmes that were to make him rich and famous.

Timmy had a theory that there would always be kids and they would always want entertaining, whereas in his opinion adults would use you and lose you, leaving you for dead. It was a theory I didn't quite understand then and one that I still don't quite understand now, but for Timmy it was a logic that worked and one that proved to be mightily lucrative for him.

He quickly became the most successful children's television presenter of his day, taking children's television to a whole different level. He set new benchmarks with his energy and creativity, making most of the other kids' shows look interminably dull by comparison. Piccadilly's loss was very much *TV-am*'s gain: *Wacaday* was a smash, literally taking over breakfast television during the summer months and at weekends. Timmy was everywhere – for such a little guy he couldn't have been any bigger; rock stars used to be ordered to appear on the show by their kids! And Timmy even went on to top the charts himself after being chosen by Andrew Lloyd Webber to front his remake of 'Itsy Bitsy Teeny Weeny'.

Both Timmy and his show were a ratings winner – of that there is no doubt. I just wish everyone could have seen or at least heard him doing the things we witnessed him doing on the radio. *Timmy on The Tranny* will always be number one for me.

top
10
Things that Will Happen to You and that You Will Have to Accept

10 Your mum will one day stop finding you cute
9 A friend will betray you
8 You will start to exhale a sigh of relief whenever you have a 'sit down'
7 You will one day be older than the current James Bond
6 You will one day be older than the current Prime Minister
5 Your body will start to fall apart
4 You will listen to the same songs and find new music 'strange'
3 Naughty afternoons with the curtains drawn will be replaced by repeats of *Columbo* and a cup of tea
2 Girls will always cry – it's what they do
1 Your mentor will one day leave you to fend for yourself and you will never learn as much from anyone ever again

Change is the only one true constant and is always going to happen no matter what we try to do to stop it. In the end only the fool stands in its way, the wise man accepting things for what they are and moving on. Any other strategy is an abject waste of energy, time and emotion, and so it was when Timmy left to seek his fame and fortune in London. But as always there was a flip side to the situation.

The fact that Timmy was no longer around at Piccadilly meant that we had to change too. I, like the rest of the Timmy-helpers, may have lost our guru, but there were still many more lessons to be learnt and we were now forced to stand on our own two feet in Radioland.

The time had come for us to develop our own characters and find our own voices. It was all very well hiding behind a character on someone else's show but what would we say and how would we say it if we were ever given our own shows? It wasn't long before we all began working with other on-air talent – none of them anywhere near as dynamic as our old boss but all different and unique in their own special radio ways.

Independent radio was still a very free medium at the time, trusting and encouraging its producers and presenters to do whatever they thought might be worth listening to – all good to watch and learn from, and not always how to do it but often very much how not to do it.

The existence of such a variety of individuals all pulling in the same direction, albeit admittedly with different ropes, is unfortunately very much a thing of the past, independent radio having long gone the way of tightly formatted predictable output designed to appease the advertisers. I blame the Americans.

A short rant

The argument for tightly formatted output came from America; this is how things had always been there and as more and more radio stations popped up over here and bigger radio groups were formed, the more this model began to be adopted. A big mistake in my book – and after all this is my book.

The model is based on the fact that a radio station needs to guarantee a definitive audience so its commercial clients know who's listening and thus advertising can be sold to the highest bidder. The more stations the group's owners can get to sound the same, the more potential customers they can deliver to specific advertisers, but a side effect of this is the sacrifice of anything surprising, new or different, which is the very reason why commercial radio was so popular in the first place.

The vast majority of commercial radio is so bland nowadays. I find that very sad, the irony being that many of the colourful characters who now run it came from the original crazy days of the 'let's give it a go and see what happens' era. Not only this but when it comes to Britain, the American model is fundamentally flawed in the first place because of one thing – the existence here of the BBC.

In America there is nothing that comes anywhere close to being like the BBC and what nobody realised was that in an ever-increasing cutthroat world of commercialism, where costs and standards would inevitably have to be compromised in order to keep making money out of a thinner and thinner slice of the pie, the BBC would be able to continue producing high-quality product that would keep sounding better and better compared to its dumbed-down rivals. This, in turn, would cause the more discerning and ultimately desirable audiences, the likes of which the advertisers would kill for, to leave commercial radio once and for all – which is exactly what's happened. As a result commercial radio has never been in worse shape than it is today.

I don't think it's beyond the realms of possibility to take an overall philosophy for a radio station and sell it to advertisers, as opposed to a minute-by-minute breakdown of exactly what will be said and played at every second of the day, albeit guaranteeing a product but at the same time removing any room for creativity or personality. And the mad thing is, this is the only way their next big hit is going to be discovered – the next new voice or idea that could catapult their station ahead of the rest needs the space and freedom to be found out.

The two caveats to this are Classic FM and TalkSport, who both know and respect their audiences inside out, so much so that their audiences in turn trust them enough for there to be some freedom within the schedules. TalkSport especially I find an excellent listen, and Classic FM is a previous winner of the prestigious Sony Award for Radio Station of the Year.

Listening figures for radio are up yet commercial radio is in decline – this speaks volumes. It's not because of the dominance of the BBC but simply because somewhere along the line commercial radio lost its balls and became boring.

The sales guys started calling the shots over the production guys and the tail started to wag the dog. Today the sales floors remain intact whereas the vast majority of production floors have disappeared altogether. What on earth do they think they are going to sell?

Entertainment must come before advertising. It can never be the other way round – content is king. In the long term, the audience will realise what's going on and vote with their dials, anyone who presumes otherwise will be out of business, probably for good and quite rightly so. Surely, the better the entertainment, the more money you can make around that entertainment, but there has to be entertainment there to start with.

The beginning of this suicide by over-advertising was the 'promotion-based feature', a phrase just the mention of which was enough to make a producer's blood run cold.

'We're gonna have another winning weekend,' came the cry from the sales floor. This was where a whole weekend's output would be hung around the promotion of a certain product. Basically it was a straight money deal, usually excused by an hourly competition.

'All this weekend we're giving you the chance to win blah blah blah ...' I know, I've been there, for my sins I have uttered such phrases.

Features like these do not have entertainment at their heart, they are purely designed to make as much money as possible. Eventually the audience come to realise this and see them for what they really are, an endless stream of unimaginative ideas. They then begin to resent this hijacking of what was once colourful and entertaining airtime, ultimately losing interest altogether and switching off.

This programming 'con' is the difference between an amusement arcade and a bouncy castle: the amusement arcade may well be full of flashing lights and loud noises but they are merely there to hide the fact that nothing else remotely amusing is going on other than some poor soul gradually being squeezed of their hard-earned cash.

The bouncy castle, on the other hand, may cost 50p to have a go on in the first place, but after that is almost guaranteed joy, smiles and laughter all the way, with the exception of the odd twisted ankle and sprained wrist.

I can only presume Rupert Murdoch was brought up with a big bouncy castle in his garden at home when he was a kid as Sky television seemed to embrace this philosophy from the beginning. People would rather pay extra for programmes they want to see than have to put up with lame excuses for entertainment that they don't want to see even if it's for free, even if they might win a flat-screen television in the bargain, especially when it's obvious these programmes are just thinly veiled revenue streams driven by avarice and laziness.

It's bizarre that this was the exact type of dross we were warned to expect from Sky by the same terrestrial broadcasters who are now mostly responsible for churning it out.

One more thing – while we're on the subject of sales guys completely messing this industry up for everyone else – the broadcasters and the public and anyone else in between, what drives me really crazy is ...

If a (TV or radio) station's audience starts to deteriorate, and as it does so begins to attract a lower demographic, instead of stopping, regrouping and attempting to recapture its lost, more desirable and now disenfranchised audience, what do the sales guys do? Bring in a whole set of equally lowly advertisers to appeal to the dregs, drug addicts and no-hopers that are still tuning in and probably only because they can't be bothered to get their fat arses off the sofa to stretch for the remote control.

Rest assured, as long as the sales team hit their targets and get their bonuses they don't give a hoot what's going out on the air. They are the 'bankers' of the television industry. They don't care how long ad breaks are becoming and what's offered up as so-called entertainment in between them as long as X + Y = £.

I swear, if the sales guys could justify 59 minutes of adverts per hour and just the one minute of actual content, maybe even less, they would go home with their heads held high as long as their pockets were bulging, guiltless of the fact it was they and their like that slaughtered the goose that used to lay that oh so very golden entertainment egg.

If the BBC does ever get bullied off the air, God help us all.

End of the short rant (please forgive me)

Back at the ranch at Piccadilly, my weekend overnight shifts were soon to be supplemented with weekday overnight shifts – more official hours meant more official pay, whoopee! My feet were now firmly under the Piccadilly Radio table and I was willing to play footsy with anyone who would have me. There wasn't a show I hadn't worked on, there wasn't a 'jock' I hadn't worked with.

I started to be given warm-up jobs for the various road shows and it wasn't long before I was appearing on the breakfast show as the tea boy, again as a character rather than a real person. This time I was called White and Two Sugars.

One of the ruses with 'Whitey', as he was known, was how he always wanted the DJ's job but was so unbelievably inarticulate and narrow-minded that he didn't have a hope in hell. This wasn't going to stop him, of course – he was in show business and he was going to milk it for all it was worth. Not only did he want the DJ's job but he also wanted his life. This would make up the basic premise for each on-air exchange.

A lot of the DJs had sponsored cars, supplied by local companies, emblazoned with their names on the side. I thought it might be fun to see if Whitey could jump on the sponsored car bandwagon and bag a set of wheels. He was on the air, after all, so why couldn't he have a car like the top guys?

The sponsored car thing was a huge big deal for some of the DJs, the make, model and type of sponsored car they had saying a lot about their perceived popularity and coolness – in their minds at least. A couple of the presenters were leaders of the sponsored car pack, always managing to secure the latest snazziest models and quietly having a secret duel to try and outdo each other every September when it was new reg time.

This all came to an embarrassing head one year when one of the guys suddenly couldn't get a deal – for a car of any kind. The story goes that this was such a crushing blow for him, he went out and bought a brand new car out of his own pocket and then had his name sign painted on the vehicle along with an imaginary sponsor. This was made all the more ludicrous by the fact that, previously, he had always claimed what a bind it was to have to endure the rigours of a sponsored car with such overt livery attached to it.

Based on the DJ-sponsored car philosophy, I had decided that if White and Two Sugars was to get a car, it would probably be a Skoda or something similar. Skodas had for a while been the butt of a lot of jokes and as a result the company were doing everything they could to change their profile, a battle they were gradually beginning to win – there was even a rumour of a sporty version.

I was told I was free to make some enquiries as long as it was all good 'business' on the air. Not for a second did any of us think anything would ever come of it, but as the daily on-air reports of my sponsored car-seeking mission progressed, gaining more and more programme time, local garages realised that if one of them was to give the tea boy some wheels, there was a good chance they would receive some decent publicity, maybe even more than the other car sponsors, with their 'reluctant' DJs having to pretend a free motor car was a cross they were forced to bear.

So lo and behold, the day came when Whitey was offered his own diamond white Skoda – there was a sports version of this latest model and this was it. I couldn't believe my luck, none of us could, they were offering me a brand new car and it was mine for twelve months – if I wanted it, which of course I did. When it arrived I thought it was beautiful – Reg no. E363 WNE ... I'll never forget it and of course, *Name ... on ... the ... side ...!!!* The brightly coloured caption read:

'WHITE AND TWO SUGARS BLENDS PERFECTLY WITH SKODA.'

And if you don't believe me:

Everyone thought it was hilarious – I thought it was amazing.

Along with the radio from the newsagent's, it's the one thing I would buy back from my past – in a heartbeat.

top
10
Genuine Names of 80s Nightclubs in the North West of England

10 Cinderella Rockafella
9 The Dance Factory
8 Legends
7 Peppermint Palace
6 Rotters
5 Placemate 7s
4 Mr Smiths
3 Thursdays
2 Fridays
1 Saturdays*

The main Piccadilly DJs went by the collective name of The Magnificent Seven and often went on the road as a group, touring the local nightclubs, performing party nights and appearing in the same order as they did on the air. For no more than approximately half an hour's spot each they could earn hundreds, sometimes even thousands, of pounds – I had been right, DJs really did have the easiest life – ever.

Sometimes in return for a few quid or a drink I would tag along and play the records in for them as they messed around with the crowd. It was great fun and all more experience.

Then there were the continuing live roadshows. During these, I would work as the warm-up guy, another sweet, sweet job. I would wind up what was already a very excited and lively crowd for the big, first on-air cheer of the day; after that I just had to keep them interested and vocal for the rest of the show, nothing that a few free T-shirts and the odd CD couldn't sort out.

As with everything in life, though, the more you do, the more you should become good at things, but at the same time the more chances there are for something to go wrong. The two most renowned mushroom experts in the world were a married couple, they met through their passion for mushrooms and they both died of mushroom poisoning, what more do we need to know?

---

* Seven different dance floors, seven different DJs including the one and only 'ooh Gary Davies'.

I was due a mess up soon and I was going to get one – in fact I was in line for two.

The radio station was appearing at a local summer festival along with what was now a full roadshow rig. Things had moved on from the funbus days and this piece of kit was state of the art for its day. Until, that is, I was let loose on it.

The Piccadilly Radio stage was to have an ongoing programme of events throughout the afternoon, including the live show. This was a much longer stint than usual and was to last in all for around six hours, as a result of which we were given a supply of props to do 'stuff' with. This 'stuff' could be anything as long as it engaged enough people to make it look like Piccadilly Radio had something going on.

The 'props' were made up mostly of promotional freebies we'd been sent over the last few months, including several boxes of disposable barbecues that were new on to the market. I took one look at these intriguing new inventions and immediately thought we could have some fun with them – we'd also been supplied with trays and trays of raw chicken legs ready to be roasted and enough of them to feed a small army. 'I know,' I thought, 'I will hold an hourly cooking competition, free food, the new throwaway barbecue and, most important of all, fire! The kids'll love that,' and they did, all afternoon. I felt like Robo-redcoat. I was getting bigger crowds than any of the other attractions, even well after the live show was over.

At one point I had such a good crowd that I decided even if I took a break they would probably stick around. So I lit the latest row of barbies and announced that I would be back soon and looking for some new contestants.

The crowd cheered and gave me a round of applause as I went backstage and climbed aboard the support bus for a quick drink and a change of shirt.

It could only have been five or six minutes when the crowd started to chant for my return. This was fantastic, I felt like a rock star. None of the named DJs were still around and yet here was the crowd shouting for the warm-up kid.

Although secretly I was gagging to run out there and soak up the applause, I decided to play it cool and wait for a while. Cool has never been my thing – I should have known better. After a few more moments, the cheering became literally manic, I could have sworn I even heard the odd scream.

I simply couldn't resist any longer. I had to get back out there, so that's what I did: I ran out back on stage for the first encore of my show business life.

'What's the matter with you lot – are you crazy? Can't a guy have a quick break and a drink, for heaven's sake?' is what I was about to say, but I couldn't even see the crowd for huge plumes of black smoke which were now filling the stage. The six barbecues had all burnt through their bottoms and set light to the floor. The only reason anyone was screaming or shouting was for the idiot with red hair and glasses to get back out there and do something about this before the whole truck was razed to the ground.

When I went into work the next day, it was not a pleasant experience.

'Did you hear about Nobby? [People still called me by my original character name – and on this day with good reason.] He only set the OB truck on fire.'

This particular 'day in the field' continued to be the source of much merriment between my colleagues for the remainder of my days in Manchester.

The management, in their wisdom, also decided I was to be charged for the damage I had caused. A little unfair I thought – not that it bothered me that much as I had so little money anyway another bill I couldn't afford wasn't going to make any difference.

top
10
Stars Recognised
by a Single Name

10 Jesus
 9 Moses
 8 Cher
 7 Bono
 6 Prince
 5 Noddy
 4 Morrissey
 3 Madonna
 2 Sweeney
 1 Umberto

Having created a near disaster outside of the radio station, it was time for me to retreat back to the comparatively safe confines of the studio – or at least that's what I hoped. But it was not to be, a much bigger and altogether more career threatening gaff was heading my way.

Mike Sweeney, a salt-of-the-earth, gravelly voiced Mancunian, was presenting his Sunday-morning show that he co-hosted with a big gay man, camp as a row of tents, who went by the name of Umberto. Both are still around, both still very good at what they do. The duo were an odd pairing but one that worked like a dream. I wish I could still listen to them now. Someone should put them back together, they were brilliant.

Sweeney (I'm not being impolite – that's how he used to refer to himself) like most DJs had an unending need to talk, whereas Umberto just sat back and picked his moments, a skill even more impressive when you consider the fact that Sweeney controlled the microphones.

The show was a huge hit, the fact that it was Sunday morning served as a perfect platform for Umberto's obsession with the tabloid newspapers and celebrity gossip along with Mike's passion for sport and music.

The key to their success was that neither of them was remotely interested in what the other one had to say – about anything. It was this beautiful irony that made them a total mismatch but a compelling formula. It was hilarious to listen to. Sweeney was such a 'bloke' and here he was being forced to get on with one of the most overtly gay men in the world – priceless. Of course in real life they loved each other, I think.

I was answering the phones for them one Sunday morning after completing a Saturday overnight shift. I loved working on their show so always volunteered to stick around for phone duty. After my night shift this particular morning, Sweeney had started on another one of his sports conversations to which Umberto had pretended to fall asleep, it was already funny. Sweeny then looks through the glass to me for some support.

'See, our Chris in there likes his sport. I bet he saw the fight last night 'cos he would have been up. He was workin' 'ere all night ...'

Sweeney was referring to a world title fight that had taken place in the States in the early hours of the same morning which I had indeed managed to catch on the telly.

'Come in 'ere kidder and let's talk about the fight like real men ...' All the time Umberto audibly snoring at the mic.

'Wow,' this was now my favourite show and Sweeney really wanted me to go on the air and for the first time ever as me, not as a character, something I'd never done before. I was filled with a mixture of nerves and excitement.

Sweeney announced that he would play a record and then he and the kid on the phones would talk big man's sport – boxing. Umberto humphed his disapproval.

I had three minutes to set myself with something to say, beginning-middle-end – never forget. I also had the same three minutes to find a cassette to record what was about to happen – I had to get this down on tape.

There was a facility in our control room called a snoop. This was a recording device that when set to 'on' via a large red switch would record but only when the microphone was live. The snoop was mostly used for monitoring purposes by the management because it meant they could just hear the links without the music. It was also used from time to time by some of the DJs to listen back to their shows or for preparing on-air demo-tapes, if they were after other work.

The snoop would automatically record the next link that I was to be involved in – if, that is, I could find a cassette in time. Cassettes were much harder to come by than the big spools of tape we usually used, as there was little call for them except from the newsroom where the journalists might take out a portable cassette recorder to cover a story.

So to the newsroom it was. I rushed in to find it deserted as it was the weekend skeleton shift and the one journalist that was on duty had nipped out for a break. Seeing as I had no idea where they kept their cassettes and it was nearly time for the link I decided to cut my losses and instead just focus on what I was about to say, after all I could always listen to it later on the log. But then just as I was about to dash back to the studio, the fickle hand of fate once again tapped me on the shoulder.

'You will mess up my son, *you will mess up*.'

As I brushed past the locker section, I noticed one of the locker doors was open, it was the locker of my best mate Gatesy – another tech op. As long as I'd known him he'd never kept his locker locked – there was never anything important in there as he was never given anything important to do but as I looked, sure enough, sat on top of a load of his old rubbish, like a shining light, was one brand new, glistening, boxed C-90 TDK cassette.

'Perfect, Gatesy, you are a saint, I love you, always have, always will.'

Gatesy, real name Michael Gates, had been my best friend for the last year or so, I had lived with him and his mum and dad at their house in Bolton, we ran a stall together in Bury market to make extra cash and we even placed an advert in *The Lady* magazine to try and get some work as private investigators. As well as being a very gentle man and very funny, he is also the most intelligent human being I have ever met – an Oxford graduate who plays classical piano for fun – and sometimes completely naked, regardless of who may be looking on. He is an old-style true intellectual eccentric and how he became a technical operator at a local radio station instead of a top professor somewhere none of us could ever figure out, not that any of us cared – we all loved him.

To this day I have never heard anyone say a bad word against Michael. He's an all-round good egg. He once went to the airport to drop some friends off in a minibus they'd hired when, during the time it took him to say goodbye and see them off, a group of old people got onto his bus by mistake – they thought he was there to pick them up and that this was their bus.

'So, what did you do?' I asked him.

'Well, I just took them to where they wanted to go,' he replied, without the slightest shred of irony. Truly gorgeous.

Anything that was mine was his and vice versa, so I knew there was no way he would mind me using this cassette. Into the snoop it went and seconds later I was on the air, desperately trying to remember the beginning, middle and end of what I'd prepared to say.

When it came to my bit 'it was all so fast', as they say, but Sweeney seemed to think it was funny enough. Umberto had kept up his snoring, we had ignored him, he had ignored us and somewhere along the line the listeners had found out some more about the big fight.

I was so chuffed I wanted to listen back to the sequence straight away but I was busy with the phones. As a result the cassette stayed in the snoop and the big red switch remained set to record, during which many, many more links came and went easily enough to fill up the whole side.

After the show was over Sweeney and Umberto would go their separate ways, although I often fantasised that they were actually secret lovers who met up again in the car park and went off together to their Trafford Park penthouse full of soft furnishings and other frou-frou. After they had left this particular morning my attention turned back to the snoop. I'm sure what I had said hadn't made much sense but it was all part of the learning curve. I would retrieve the cassette, listen back while driving home, make my notes and put them in the memory bank for next time.

Little did I know I was oh so close to there never being a next time.

The snoop machine was over the other side of the control room behind the switchboard. I walked over to it, clicked off the switch which released the tape and out it popped. Now literally, at this second, who walks into the control room but none other than me old mate Gatesy. I was riven with excitement at my latest radio appearance. Michael on the other hand was full of the fuzziness of his habitual Sunday lunchtime hangover.

'Gatesy, how are you, ol' lad? Did you hear me with Sweeney and Umberto this morning? They asked me on the show to talk about the fight last night.'

'No, I didn't actually – to be honest I only got up half an hour ago.' He was a little vacant but no more than I'd come to expect. He often stayed out until all hours, usually securing the company of an unbelievably attractive woman in the process, always a source of wonder to the rest of us.

'Er, I don't suppose you have seen a cassette, have you?' he asked, now appearing distracted, almost worried.

As he said this, I was holding the cassette in my hand, but he obviously hadn't noticed ...

'Er, well there's this one that I found in your locker.'

'What do you mean, the one that you found in my locker?' As he said this, it was almost as if he began to crumple in front of me. He suddenly turned grey and he sounded like he cared. He never cared about anything.

'I was looking for a cassette for a snoop and I was in a rush and this one was in your locker, on the top of your things. I didn't think you'd mind.'

Michael's face now contorted into an expression I didn't think was possible for a human being. His mouth went all wavy like a cartoon character's* and beads of sweat started to form on his forehead. I thought he was about to faint. What the hell was wrong with him?

'Yes but you haven't used it yet, have you?' He was now beginning to shake.

'Yes I have, I have used it, I used it to tape my link on Sweeney's show.'

I don't know how to spell the next phrase he uttered but it was something between a gulp, a squeal, a whimper and a scream, I think there may have been a yelp in there too.

'I used it to tape me talking about the big fight last night.'

'Oh my God, my God ... my God, my God my God my God. How long was the link?'

---

*

'I dunno, about four minutes maybe five.'

'So that was it – just that?'

'Well no, because it ran till the end, I left it in, so it's used up a whole side.'

Gatesy now began to weep, I promise you, he was actually crying real tears.

'Which side has it used?'

'Er, the whole of side A.' I offered with a pathetic inflection of optimism.

At this point Gatesy fell on to his knees and started to sob, like a young child who's just been told their pet hamster has died – died in a really bad and horrible way, maybe squished – something like that. He cried and snorted and blubbed. There was snot everywhere but at no point was he angry. As I said he didn't do angry, this was the mark of the man.

Eventually after what seemed like for ever but was probably no more than a minute he just about managed to utter the words.

'We're both going to get killed.'

When Gatesy was finally able to conjure back the powers of speech, he explained to me what the problem was.

It turned out the cassette in question was not brand new at all, its label may have been blank but the cassette most definitely was not. It was in fact full of an exclusive recording of Bob Geldof in his first big interview since Live Aid. He was the hottest thing in the world at the time and this was an interview conducted with him at the venue of his next big charity concert entitled Rock Around the Dock. Somehow Piccadilly had bagged the exclusive and now everyone wanted to buy it off them.

Though the cassette wasn't worth more than a couple of pounds itself, the rights to the interview on it had been syndicated to the commercial radio network for a considerable sum, over £40,000. It was to be Gatesy's job that afternoon to dub off the master, the now redundant little cassette we were both staring at.

It didn't take a genius to realise the gravity of what I'd done.

Michael was right – we were both going to die.

I told him I would take the blame and tell the boss it was all my fault, which of course it was entirely. Michael said that he was grateful but he was sure we would both be fired on the spot regardless. He was already considering his options and he advised me to do the same. The thing was

I didn't have any options – this was it for me, radio was my world and as I'd only just survived setting fire to the OB truck, I now feared the worst.

The man in charge of our fate was a chap called John Clayton, senior producer and deputy programme controller. I went to see him on the Monday, first thing in the morning. For a good few moments at least he was too angry to speak to me – unlike Michael, John did do anger and he did it very well.

Eventually John gave me the benefit of what he was thinking.

'If I'd have been able to get hold of you yesterday afternoon you would both be dead by now. Last night, I would still definitely have killed you Nobby, but probably not Michael. As it stands if you ever do anything like that again, I *will* kill you but I am calmer now and ... we all make mistakes, so I'm going to let it pass ... *But* ... please please do not take any tapes from anywhere ever again unless you know exactly why you're doing it and exactly what's on them. Now piss off and carry on doing whatever it is you do for us.'

God bless you, John Clayton.

As for Michael he decided radio was no longer for him. Shortly afterwards he spent his savings on a language course before moving to Finland of all places. He still lives there to this day in between travelling the world in his profession as a language and culture expert advising global brands on cross-culture communication. He is also happily married with four children. I'm not sure if he still plays the piano naked, although I suspect he probably does.

top 10

Records I remember from My Piccadilly Radio Days

10 'Money's Too Tight to Mention' – Simply Red
 9 'Girls on Film' – Duran Duran
 8 'Too Shy' – Kajagoogoo
 7 'If You Let Me Stay' – Terence Trent D'Arby
 6 'The First Picture of You' – The Lotus Eaters
 5 'Oblivious' – Aztec Camera
 4 'Chocolate Girl' – Deacon Blue
 3 'Living in a Box' – Living in a Box
 2 'You are my World' – The Communards
 1 'Don't Try to Stop It' – Roman Holiday

As Michael moved to Finland I slowly moved more and more onto the air.

The usual passage of apprenticeship followed with a try-out in the middle of the night on the graveyard shift: 2–6 a.m. This is a show I had witnessed being performed hundreds of times before, sometimes well, sometimes really not that well.

These nightly marathons were useful hours, however, for a young disc jockey trying to find his voice; it was the longest show on the network, making it easy to rack up lots of flying hours relatively quickly and as any pilot will tell you, it's all about building up those hours. In many ways operating a radio console is very similar to learning to fly, with certain things having to become automatic before you can concentrate on the next thing – like entertaining people for example, which let's face it is pretty essential if you are going to try and make a living out of this.

To start with, just playing all the records and jingles in the right order and managing to say, 'that was' and 'this is' along with the odd time check proved to be enough of a challenge – any chance of saying something funny or colourful on top was a rare bonus, for the first few weeks at least. Some people have been on the radio for years and still haven't managed this last bit – harsh but true.

Another challenge for the presenters of *Nightbeat*, as it was called, was the lack of availability of well-known songs to play. Due to budget restrictions this was limited to six records per show! And if you used all six in the first half hour, as I did, this meant you then had three-and-a-half hours to fill with little more than pan pipes and lift music hardly recognisable and barely worth the vinyl it was printed on.

Once again a problem became an opportunity as they so often do. I was free to create – and creating was what I did best. Ideas were needed and lots of them, the great thing was that anything that I came up with would probably sound more entertaining than playing these godawful records, so there was plenty of room to experiment.

I tried out tons of ideas during my duty on the graveyard shift, mostly phone-in ideas – competitions, agony uncle, blind dates, challenging bored listeners to get out of bed and drive somewhere and all meet up, races to the studio, night-time picnics.

One of my favourite slots and one of the most successful things I ever did was a thing called moon bathing, where I encouraged the night owls not to be outdone by their daylight-loving counterparts and get out there to acquire a moon tan – people sent me pictures of themselves in their deckchairs wearing Speedos out in the garden in the wee small hours, it was hilarious. It's amazing what people will join in with if it's all done in the right spirit.

I even had a suicide slot where I would play the most depressing record from the lift music selection at the same time every night. It was a track called 'Deck of Cards' by Wink Martindale – a bad bad bad song, miserable enough to plunge even the happiest of souls into darkness. For this I would ask people to ring in and tell me why they were particularly happy that night and then invite them to stay on the air and listen to this song … After it was over I would ask them at which point during its playing had they first contemplated death – the answer was usually somewhere within the first thirty seconds.

No idea was too flimsy for *Nightbeat*, no show a better place to learn. I used almost every idea I came up with. I had to, there was so much time to fill.

Make your mistakes in private is another great lesson I have learnt, or at least when there are fewer people around. This was most of the time on *Nightbeat*, but I didn't care as I was on the air and I was learning with every show. No two shows on the radio are ever the same, there's always something to test you or some new avenue down which to wander.

With the passage of time, again came more regular stints. Soon whole swathes of *Nightbeat* were mine and mine alone – it may have been a job few of the other DJs wanted but I would have happily presented the show every night if they'd asked me to. I was living the dream. I even started to receive a few letters. Listeners would ask could they come to the studio and sit in on the show. They would bring me presents and midnight picnics. There was one amazing lady who had fostered over sixty children, all of whom had kept in contact with her, but that wasn't all: somewhere in her life she had struck up a friendship with Dirk Bogarde! She'd met him at a book signing and had become something of a confidante, both of them corresponding with each other on a regular basis. She brought in all these amazing handwritten letters and showed me one in particular where he referred to her as his Salford Rose. This was one of the first times I realised that it's often the most unlikely people who have the most amazing stories.

Another time I received a call early on in the show, sometime just before three-ish. It was a local nightclub who said they had a celebrity in who was most upset as something terrible had happened to him and he wanted to come on the radio and talk about it.

'What – at three o'clock in the morning?' I replied.

'He says it's a big story and if you want it's yours.'

This was my first brush with the madness of celebrities. For some bizarre reason, celebrities feel the need to tell the whole world everything about themselves (by writing an autobiography, for example!) whilst often complaining about their lack of privacy. An annoying trait brought on by self-obsession and megalomania, two conditions with which I would become all too familiar with myself before my time on this mortal coil was done.

As far as the phone call from the local nightclub was concerned I'd never had a big story before – in fact I'd never had a story at all and this by all accounts might even be a scoop.

'Sure, tell him to come over,' I said. I had another four hours to fill, and all content was welcome, planned or otherwise.

Straight away I started to tell the story on the air of what had happened. The story about the story is often infinitely more interesting than the story itself. I explained that the celebrity, a hugely popular household name, was currently on his way over to the studios and although I had no idea what he was going to say, I suspected it may well be worth sticking around for, at least I hoped it would.

The celebrity turned out to be Bernie Winters – he of Mike and Bernie Winters fame – the likeable television double act consisting of two Jewish brothers, who had now gone their separate ways but for years had graced our screens. Mike was skinny and handsome, Bernie the more roly-poly, smiley kind of character.

When Bernie arrived he was in a right old state – in floods of tears, his eyes red raw. It was obvious he'd been crying for some time and he still was, although I was yet to find out why. Before we went live I asked him for some idea of what was the matter but he was insistent that he would only talk about it on the air.

'Fair enough,' I thought, 'in for a penny and all that.'

I asked him was he ready, to which he replied he was. He became more composed but was still audibly upset. The red light went on. I began to speak.

'Ladies and gentlemen, I am now joined by one of Britain's favourite entertainers, Bernie Winters, who has something he'd like to share with us. Good evening, Bernie ...'

Bernie said hello and very graciously thanked me for giving him the opportunity to speak on the radio. He then went on to inform the listeners of the death earlier that day of his beloved doggie Schnorbitz, his famous St Bernard canine sidekick.

I was gobsmacked – we all were. What a bizarre story to have as your first scoop and what an even more bizarre way of coming across it. Schnorbitz was a dog deeply loved by television viewers all over the country – of that there was no doubt – and evidently adored by Mr Winters himself, but if you'd have asked me to predict what he was going to say when he walked in that night there's no way I would have guessed it was to announce to the world the death of his furry friend.

Along with the post of regular overnight presenter came sporadic depping jobs on more prominent shows, shows with proper formats, content and even songs people recognised!

Depping on the radio is called swing jocking. It sounded pretty swish to me and it was. Eventually it involved me leaving my beloved *Nightbeat* altogether and moving on to the weekend early breakfast shows – plus I was now first replacement for anyone on holiday in the weekday part of the schedule.

If I was happy before, I was *flying* now, but there was yet more good news to come. I was also offered my first full-time contract. If I accepted – which of course I did, like a flash – I would no longer have to worry where my next buck was coming from. I was now officially on the payroll and for the princely sum of £10,000 per annum. I was rich.

With more shows came the need for more ideas and more writing. I have always written my radio shows, almost everything of what I intend to say. I may not end up saying much of it, sometimes none of it at all, but it's always there if I need it. I am first a producer and then a presenter – always have been, always will be, always beginning, middle and end, preparation, preparation, preparation. Chefs have a great phrase for it – the more you do off the board, the less you have to do on the board. The less pressure, the more freedom.

The Dalai Lama even applies this theory to death. He says, if you throw a dinner party and you leave everything until the last minute then you are more likely to have a really stressful time and wish you'd never bothered. He goes on to say that death is very much the same – the more you prepare for it, the less chance of it being stressful and therefore more peaceful and although none of us particularly wants to die in the first place, it is a surefire thing that it's going to happen and generally accepted that a peaceful death would probably be the nicest way to go. If the Dalai Lama ever tires of Buddhism, he should take up producing.

It's always amazed me the number of people who fall on to the air on television and radio who haven't given a second thought as to what they might want to say. What on earth do they think is going to come out of their mouths that could be remotely worth listening to?

I hear this kind of thing all the time when I listen to the radio and it drives me insane, I don't want to hear some halfwit scrabbling around for ideas on the air, I don't want to have to put up with constant streams of ums and ers whilst they are wondering what to say next, having been too lazy to have considered it beforehand. Don't have the meeting on the air – have it before the show or don't bother turning up.

Also the really crazy aspect of this approach is that you just end up sounding like an idiot. Five minutes' preparation for a three-hour radio show is never going to work – do the maths!

The same can be said of awards shows: when people haven't prepared a speech, they just come across so badly. I know – I have been that fool. Those brilliantly off-the-cuff speeches that people love so much and that often steal the show – I don't think so. They have been thought about and rehearsed for hours beforehand. Only a dimwit tries to wing it when there's a scriptwriter available. Not that there's anything wrong with departing from a script once it's written, but there has to be some sense of where we're coming from and where we're going to just so we all feel comfortable. Magical mystery tours are fine as long as the driver knows the route.

I once witnessed a guy win three awards in the same night. He'd spent his whole life waiting for this night but it was obvious he hadn't given an ounce of thought as to what he might say if he won. The end result was not pretty. He ended up swearing overtly the first time, slagging off his current employer the second time and then slurring most of his words the third time, as he was now so drunk. It's no surprise he hasn't even been nominated for an award since.

It takes a lifetime of hard work and endeavour to build up a reputation but only one ill-judged moment to bring it crashing down – another lesson I would come to learn through first-hand experience.

top
10 Things Never to Joke about on the Air

10 Friends
9 Family
8 Money
7 Religion
6 Drugs
5 Illness
4 Exes
3 The elderly
2 Dogs
1 Cats

American Beauty – **a perfect film in my opinion,** and while we're at it the best mid-life riposte to my favourite film of all time, *The Graduate* – opens with a scene where Lester Burnham, the main character, played sublimely by Kevin Spacey, wakes up on what is to be the last day of his life. He has no idea it's the last day of his life – why should he? He's still relatively young, he's fitter than he's been for years and having recently split up from his godawful wife, for the first time in as long as he can remember he has a renewed libido and everything to live for.

But then – *pow!*

Along comes his next-door neighbour, supposedly homophobic but really latently homosexual ('a lot of them are, dear'), who suspects Lester of having an affair with his son, which he isn't but this, coupled with the fact that the neighbour also secretly lusts after Lester himself and is having to suppress this, along with the rest of his emotions to protect his legacy as a war hero, drives him – via a heady cocktail of anger, bitterness, jealousy and sadness – to blow poor old Lester away.

D'oh, don't you just hate that? Right at the moment when you think you've got life where you want it, along comes the bogeyman.

This was my Lester Burnham day.

It was 1988 and I could not have been happier. I was writing some material for the current drivetime show that I was filling in on. The drivetime show on any radio station is a big deal, the mirror to the breakfast show and often a stomping ground for future breakfast DJs.

With each different show would come a different daily routine. For drivetime I would: get up in the morning and listen to the guy on breakfast; dip in to hear what he was up to; take a quick look at the telly and then nip out for the papers and start to have a good old mooch as to what was going on in the world.

Anything was potential material but I would have to stay away from any subjects that had already been talked about on the other shows in the day – the safest way of doing this was by focusing my attention on the early evening papers and mainly, because of its importance locally, the all-encompassing *Manchester Evening News*.

No one tells you 'this is the day you're going to die', furthermore no one tells you that you're going to read a story about a little old lady ordering a birthday cake for her cat in the morning, talk about it on the radio in the afternoon and a few hours later be out of work.

This is what happened to me. The cat in question was nineteen, which in human years, so the story claimed, was 133 apparently. I went on the air and said that this was clearly a dodgy conversion rate of cat years to people years as no human to my knowledge had ever come anywhere close to reaching such a grand old age.

I urged the cat world to revisit this generally accepted but highly inaccurate formula for converting cat 'years' to human 'years' and to please come up with a more realistic one. I then went on to say that this was probably why other nutty cat owners ended up leaving hundreds of thousands of pounds to their cats when they died because they obviously had no concept of numbers and what they meant.

I then for some stupid reason added another line which was so bad and unfunny it still makes me cringe today. I said:

'However there is a good side to cats – that's the left-hand side, cooked medium rare with a garlic sauce.'

After this last line the switchboard lit up like a Christmas tree, but for all the wrong reasons.

Never ever mess with the emotions of owners and their pets – another one for the memory bank – especially cat owners. They are to be given the widest of all berths. Jeremy Clarkson can say what he likes about lorry drivers, prime ministers and old people's homes, but I swear if he ever took on the cat lovers of this sceptred isle he would be toast before he had time to say, 'Vroom vroom, feel the torque on that, Mrs.'

The show finished at six o'clock and by five past I was out of the door and out of work – silly, silly boy.

I was now an ex DJ. I was in total shock, what on earth had I done? What a complete and utter idiot. That night I went to bed and I had the opposite experience of what it feels like to wake up after a nightmare – you know, when you experience the relief of thinking something terrible has happened and then realise that it hasn't. Well, I woke up and it still had.

It was the third week in the month so I had close to no money in the bank, being now used to spending more or less what I earned every month. I had technically broken my contract so had no chance of being paid. Not only that but the next day the garage rang up to ask for their car back so I had to say goodbye to my beloved sponsored Skoda. Within twenty-four hours I was both broke and car-less and had just flunked the job I had hankered after since being a small boy.

top
10 Christmas Presents

10 Apple and orange
 9 Bar of Cadbury's Dairy Milk
 8 7" single, notably Chuck Berry's 'My Ding-a-ling'
 7 Selection box
 6 Atari game console
 5 Model railway layout
 4 Scalextric
 3 Chrysler Silverado 4x4 pick-up (a real one I bought for
    myself)
 2 Bike – the one I was really ungrateful for
 1 A flashing red light at work one Christmas Day afternoon

Piccadilly was the third biggest independent radio station in the country at the time and having been on air there, I hoped this would stand me in good stead to get another job relatively quickly. Even though it was likely to be at a smaller station at least I'd still be doing what I loved. My optimism, however, proved to be without foundation as after writing to every commercial radio station in the entire UK network and receiving some particularly scathing, not to mention hurtful replies, I was made abundantly aware of the fact that not a single one of them wanted to employ me.

I was living with my new girlfriend by now in her house in Didsbury. At twenty-six years old she was four years my senior and how important those four years can be when you're a young man of twenty-two.

Sara was a newsreader on Piccadilly – that's how we'd met. She'd had a fair few cocktails at the Christmas party the year before and decided she wanted to take me home. When the music stopped and the lights came on she asked me to go and get her coat for her and then asked me to wait outside with her whilst she hailed a cab – when the cab arrived she practically bundled me into to it.

'You're coming home with me,' she declared. I wasn't going to argue with that – Sara was an absolute babe and if her beer goggles were telling her to take the young ginger kid back for the night, that was more than fine by me.

The next day when Sara woke up (I hadn't slept a wink all night – I was too 'excited' about the whole episode) she apologised and said she was sorry but that she might have been using me for a Christmas quickie. She then promptly leant over me to grab a cigarette from her packet which was resting on the bedside table. I remember her lighting it and then staring out of the window as she exhaled the smoke, like a satisfied assassin rewarding themselves after the perfect kill – she was the ice queen.

I said I had no problem whatsoever with what had happened – on the contrary I had had a marvellous time – she was absolutely gorgeous and I never thought I stood a chance with her anyway. If I was a one-off it was fine by me, I could live with just the memory of such an exhilarating night. She offered me a drink but I had to go – I was covering the Christmas shifts at the radio station and seeing as I was already late and had no idea where I was, I thought I'd better get my skates on.

Two days later it was Christmas Day, and while the rest of the country was tucking into their turkey I was alone with a cup of tea in the main studio, having been charged with making sure the pre-recorded programmes that made up Piccadilly's festive schedule went out smoothly. As this task consisted of little more than watching two great hulking tape spools go round and round and round, my mind was free to wander, inevitably back to the unexpected but highly enjoyable episode with Sara a couple of nights earlier. I was still thinking about this when I noticed out of the corner of my eye the red phone light in the studio had started flashing – it was the ex-directory studio hotline. Only a few people had this number. When it rang, it was usually one of the bosses having a moan about something. I checked the output before answering the call; the taped show seemed to be going out fine – as far as I could see there was nothing wrong.

'Hello studio,' I said, secure in the knowledge that whoever it was they were not calling to have a beef with me.

'Hello, is that Chris?' The voice was deep and wonderful and female.

'Er ... yes it is.'

'Hello, it's Sara. Happy Christmas.'

I couldn't believe my ears.

'Er, Happy Christmas to you. How's your mum?' I didn't know what else to say.

'She's well thanks ... Now about the other night.'

And with that she proceeded to inform me that, as she had quite rightly said, she had indeed been using me the night of the staff party but she was now calling to ask me if I would be willing to be used a bit more. I said I would love to – 'a bit more' turned out to be the next five years.

Sara was an intriguing blend of sexy and sensible. She looked like Purdy from *The Avengers* and had the voice and pedigree to match – she was, as they say, a real catch. She was also very generous when it came to educating me further on the subject of what women really want in all aspects of a passionate and stimulating relationship. By the end of our time together, my eyes had been well and truly opened and it was all very much down to her – she was, in many ways, my Mrs Robinson.

She was also financially independent. After my departure from Piccadilly as a result of the cat joke she assured me that, although I may have had the weight of the world on my shoulders, the fact that I was penniless should not add to that weight. She said money was not an issue – I should forget about that and just focus solely on getting another job in radio, no matter how long it took.

I couldn't have asked for any more support but this didn't stop me from despairing as to how exactly I was ever going to break back into the one thing I knew I wanted to do for the rest of my life. I think I can honestly say this period was the only time I have ever been genuinely depressed. I had no idea what to do next.

I had tried everything I could think of including ironically travelling down to London one day to hang out outside Radio 1 waiting to talk to Steve Wright. He had read out the tale of my cat joke and what had happened to me as a result as part of his 'showbiz news' the week before, enough reason I felt to suggest he might have some empathy for my situation and be able to give me some useful advice. Unfortunately on the day in question he rushed out of the building with such haste into a waiting cab that I lost my nerve, and not wanting to hold him up I just asked for his autograph instead. Even now when I recall this story it still makes me laugh out loud.

Day after day the situation became more desperate and my mood ever darker. The phone never rang, the postman never came and the weeks soon began to drag. I still couldn't believe how dramatically my life had changed in the space of just a few weeks.

I could feel myself giving up. I began to contemplate another life, a normal job – what kind of job I had no idea but sat at home day in day out in a terraced house in Didsbury, show business and the magic of the microphone seemed a million miles away.

We all need some luck, we really do, and anyone who says otherwise is talking tripe. The harder you work, the luckier you get – maybe. But if you analyse that phrase it's a little bit silly – you could also say, for example, the more you're born the luckier you get, or the longer you're awake the luckier you get. I think it's much more a case of the more decent you are with people, the more decent they're likely to be with you and the more they may consider you in their future plans. Folks love to work with other folks who are good at what they do but who are also good to have around and are as little of a headache as possible. Having been a boss I have come to realise how rare these individuals are and how important it is to try and cling on to them when they pop up – and so it was with me.

Remember the tall kid from the first time I saw Timmy on the fun bus outside Old Trafford football ground? Well, guess what he ended up doing – he ended up running the whole of the Ted Turner network in America before moving on to work with Mickey Mouse and his chums at the Disney corporation. (Told you he'd do well.) Several years before, however, it was also he who eventually made that old-fashioned big green phone of Sara's finally ring.

I'll never forget that phone, I began to hate it. During my more unstable moments I even questioned whether the damn thing was still working, to the extent that sometimes I would phone Sara at work and ask her to call me back just to check. There was no doubt about it, I was going slightly mad.

The call from Andy would prove to be the single most important telephone call I would ever receive. Without it I have no doubt my career as I now know it would probably not exist.

Andy – or Big Bird as we called him, because he was big and his name was Bird – was always at the cutting edge of whatever was going on. He loved working in radio and now television but had no desire whatsoever to appear in front of the microphone or camera – in fact, he couldn't think of anything worse. Consequently this freed him up to concentrate wholly on production. He really was an amazing energy to have in a studio. Another virtuous talent of his – and he has many – has always been getting astonishingly well paid for whatever it is he's doing.

Big Bird had long since moved to London and was currently involved in setting up a new radio station called Radio Radio, a satellite radio station owned spookily enough by Richard Branson, a man with whom my path was destined to cross much more intimately several years later. Radio Radio, his latest business venture, was unique in as much as it would only broadcast at night. This was originally its selling point, but would ultimately lead to its demise, with the available audience being so small and unable to yield any worthwhile market for advertisers. For now though it was all guns blazing as they were gearing up for a huge launch, having signed up some serious talent for their on-air team including the legendary Johnny Walker, Whispering Bob Harris and Tommy Vance, to name just three.

Big Bird had been appointed as a senior producer and was looking for an assistant; he briefly explained what was going on and asked me if I fancied giving it a go. He said he was aware of the fact that it might not be what I was looking for, as it was a job in production as opposed to presenting, but it was a job nevertheless and meant I would be back in radio and working with some of the industry's most illustrious names. He also took pains to point out that the pay was almost non-existent, but I could stay with him for free as long as I was willing to sleep on the floor of his living room as he only had a one-bedroom flat.

I thought about his offer for all of … a second before informing Andy that I could be there within 24 hours. I then called Sara, who gave me her blessing, even though me moving to London without her was a much more drastic step than either of us had envisaged. Still, we both knew it was something I had to do.

After an emotional farewell on the platform of Manchester's Piccadilly train station, I sat down in the carriage, my vision still blurred from the tears. Both Sara and I secretly knew that this moment could spell more than just a change in employment. I watched as she waved me off, wearing one of those desperate half-smiles – the only kind you can manage when you're trying to hold it together on the outside whilst being torn apart on the inside. She loved me enough to let me go. What more could I ask for?

part three

fame, shame and automobiles

top 10

Things No One Tells You about London

10 It's bloody huge
 9 It's much greener than you think
 8 It really is very expensive
 7 The underground is so windy
 6 People walk faster
 5 Big Ben looks smaller
 4 There's a distinct lack of 'chatting'
 3 You never see old people
 2 Hardly anyone is from London
 1 It's much warmer than up North

After being brought up in Warrington I thought Manchester was big, but nothing prepared me for the sheer scale and size of London – it was massive and so different to anything I had experienced before. London also has an innate toughness about it and a rulebook all of its own – it is the definitive rat race and one that I could not wait to join.

By contrast, Big Bird's flat was the smallest flat I'd ever seen in my life, albeit the most expensive. It was a one-bedroom rabbit hutch in a place called Holloway and had cost him close to £80,000. I couldn't believe it, you could buy a substantial detached house in Manchester for the same price. This was crazy but Big Bird didn't seem to mind and nor did any of his neighbours. This kind of price was the going rate and they were keen to get going.

My bed was a sleeping bag on top of a lilo in the living room – the airbed had a slow puncture so every night before I went to sleep I had to blow it up, knowing that when I woke up in the morning I would be flat on the floor but, hey, Andy was letting me stay there for nothing and I couldn't have been more grateful.

Andy was turning out to be a total brick – as solid as they come. The first morning he woke me up with a huge mug of coffee and a bowl of cereal, he explained how the day was going to work and that I needed to be ready to go in about ten minutes. Dazed and confused but as excited as you like I couldn't wait to discover what was in store for me in the big city.

I remember us taking the underground and how totally metropolitan everyone was. I also remember how incredibly hot I had become by the time we got off at Tottenham Court Road. Blimey, I was roasting – London was so much warmer than Manchester. I made my first London note: 'No coat tomorrow.'

The offices for Radio Radio were in Rathbone Place just off Oxford Street. They were still in the process of being kitted out with desks and computers along with the odd bits of radio gear – tape machines, etc. I can recall many things about that first day but one memory stands out above all – the first person I saw after we'd walked up the stairs.

She was a woman called Carol. We saw her when we walked through the main office door but we had been able to hear her a good minute or so before, from several floors below. This woman was loud – I mean really loud. This woman was the living embodiment of London.

'Who's that?' I whispered to Big Bird.

'Oh that's Carol McTraff,' said Big Bird laughing. 'We call her McTraff because she deals with the traffic but her real name is Carol McGiffin, she's hilarious.'

Other than Andy, Carol was the first 'new' person I encountered in London. Little did I know she would also be the first person I would marry.

Although I was now back in the radio game, thoughts of me ever being in front of the microphone again were immediately erased from my mind as this was London, where almost everyone who was on the air was already famous and more often than not a born and bred Southerner. I was from the regions, I had a regional accent and no one had ever heard of me. 'Brilliant', I thought, 'not the greatest package to bring to the table'. I quickly accepted that if I was to make anything of myself here, it would have to be in production. I decided to use what I'd learnt from being on the air to make me the best off the air. I now had a new mission statement – to become the greatest radio producer in the world.

It was time to start learning again and as long as I like what I'm learning about there is no more voracious a student. From that first morning I knuckled down to anything I was asked to do, from assembling tape machines to running out for the lunch and even booking guests, something I'd never done before.

On only my third day, I even took on the role of a roving reporter and was dispatched to a magic shop with a microphone and tape recorder to Charing Cross underpass near the Embankment. One of the senior producers had received a tip-off that Michael Jackson, who was flying into Heathrow that morning, was going to go straight from the plane to a magic shop there. It was well known that Jackson was a big fan of magic as well as a prolific shopper – so it didn't seem an unreasonable possibility.

When I arrived at the location, there was already a guy there from the *Sun*'s Bizarre column who had heard a similar whisper. His presence buoyed me somewhat. I could almost feel another scoop coming on, they'd been few and far between since my middle of the night confession with Bernie Winters (whatever did happen to Bernie Winters?).*

After enquiring from the owner of the shop as to whether or not he was expecting a famous visitor any time soon and receiving a shifty 'no comment' we both thought it was worth sticking around. As it turned out we stuck around all day. We even stayed on until a couple of hours after the man had shut up shop and gone home, convinced it was all a ruse to put us off the scent and that the man would sneak back to open up again the second we disappeared.

Well, maybe he did but not on our watch. At around nine o'clock we decided to call it a day – and besides, the hack from the *Sun* received a phone call assuring him that Jacko had been firmly ensconced in the Dorchester since just after midday and by the looks of it wasn't going anywhere soon.

So there I was, having spent a whole day out in the field with nothing to show for it except a new acquaintance with a tabloid journalist, one pair

---

* After a much publicised and acrimonious split with his brother Mike, Bernie hosted several television shows including *Make me Laugh* which kick-started the career of comedian Brian Conley. He also hosted the long-running ITV quiz show *Whose Baby?* in the mid '80s, which he took over from Leslie Crowther. It was during this period that he teamed up with his St Bernard dog, the aforementioned Schnorbitz, whom he both owned and trained himself. Several years before Schnorbitz's passing – the episode Bernie was so insistent on announcing on my radio show – the dog had almost come to grief when he famously fell into the swimming pool at the home of the actor Terry Scott, only to be rescued by none other than Barbara Windsor. In 1991, on 4 May, *Star Wars* Day – May the 4th Be With You – Bernie went to rejoin Schnorbitz in that great kennel in the sky. Happily, before he did so, Bernie also made peace with his brother Mike, though they never worked together again.

of aching legs and a tape recorder that hadn't even been turned on. I thought I was in for a rollicking but nobody seemed to mind. In fact when I got back to the office everyone had gone to the pub. Not only that but there was a note left on my desk inviting me to go and join them. Two minutes later I was there.

'Drink, Chris?' someone asked.

'I don't really.' It was true – a pint and I would be no use to anyone. 'Alright, just a half though, please.'

'A half please, barman.' This was not a phrase I would be hearing for much longer.

Working in London, I soon discovered, was as much about what you did in the evening as what you did in the day. From the very beginning I found myself going out almost every night. And if Big Bird didn't know how to get into somewhere, Carol did – she was the original girl about town; she was also not averse to turning up for work slightly the worse for wear, not that she was alone – this was the London media way, everyone seemed to play as hard as they worked.

Within that first week I visited places such as the Limelight Club, a trendy hangout at the time favoured by the likes of Ben Elton and Harry Enfield – I know this because I found myself stood next to them at the bar. I couldn't believe it, they were both heroes of mine and here I was rubbing shoulders with the guys. Ben even nodded to me as if to say, 'How you doing?' I was made up. The same night we moved on to another hangout called Zanzibar where I witnessed the London 'set' in full swing. It was a normal Wednesday but these guys were partying like it was New Year's Eve.

There was this one character over in the corner who seemed to be knocking back one drink after another and surrounded by people in constant hysterics.

'That's Rowland Rivron,' Andy informed me. 'He might be coming to work for us – you'd better come and meet him.'

Moments later Mr Rivron was inviting us to join him in his favourite tipple, a rather large vodka and tonic, I can honestly say it was the strongest drink I'd ever tasted. Rowland was also the lucky man who happened to be dating Wendy James, the sizzling hot lead singer of the band Transvision Vamp. A couple of hours later I found myself sharing a cab with them on the way to a club somewhere in Harlesden. I was sat in the front seat whilst they were busy in the back, pausing only when Wendy leant over to pass me a cassette of The Clash, 'Get the driver to put this on, would you?' she said, not waiting for a reply. I was more than happy to oblige. This was all very rock 'n' roll and The Clash were the perfect soundtrack.

The opportunity to find a reason not to go straight home after work was never very far away. During only my second week Prince was due to play in town at Wembley Arena.

'Do you want to go?' asked Carol.

This was nuts.

On the night of the concert the record company not only provided us with tickets but also sent a car for us. When we arrived it was beers all round, again all courtesy of the record company; half an hour later there we were watching The Great Purple One live on stage – but of course there was always another party.

This particular night it was back at Camden Palace, a very famous London club which now goes by the name of KoKo. Prince had hired out the whole place for his after-show bash. Prince's 'after shows' are notoriously legendary as he usually plays at them and often for longer than he does at his concerts. Tonight was no exception: he played Wembley for around two hours, whereas he played the after show for closer to three! This was all too much for me. I needed to calm down. Two weeks into my time in London and I was losing my focus – literally. I had never drunk so much in my life

Somewhere in amongst all this revelry Radio Radio had launched on to the airwaves, whilst in the process also adding yet more famous names to its on-air roster. Jonathan Ross had agreed to host two one-hour slots a week – this was in 1989 by the way! Jonathan was the new kid on the block on television, he was the king of late-night cool on Channel Four and quite rightly too – he was very very good and very very different to anything I had seen before. His show, *The Last Resort*, was by far my favourite on TV. Apparently Radio Radio had to offer him thousands of pounds per show to come and work for us back then – little did I imagine ten years later I would be paying him, albeit nowhere near as much, to come and work for me.

Steve Davis was another well-known name on our schedule – yes, that's right, Steve Davis, the snooker player. We signed him up to host a specialist soul music show. Steve is a massive soul fan – so much so, he bought up all the rights to his favourite record label.

The best part of working with Steve was going to the pub over the road afterwards for a pint of lager and a game of pool. He was still at the top of his game at the time and was more than happy to take anyone on. I only played against him once. I don't think it's up there with his most memorable confrontations, but I'll never forget it. I did manage to pot two balls, but accidentally and straight from the break, after which Steve came on and cleared up. I wouldn't have wished it any other way.

A lot of my working hours now shifted to night time when we were broadcasting. This was no bad thing – at least my liver and I didn't think so, we were both glad of the break. I was now embracing my new role in production and was loving every second. I was also about to discover the art of 'talent management'.

top
10 Legends I Have Worked With

10 Dudley Moore (*The Big Breakfast*)
 9 Jools Holland (*Don't Forget Your Toothbrush*)
 8 Michael Caine (*TFI Friday*)
 7 Paul McCartney (*TFI Friday*)
 6 The Stones (made a documentary movie with them in the States)
 5 Cher (I once spent twelve hours in bed with her shooting some skits)
 4 Helen Mirren (another sketch for *TFI*)
 3 Peter O'Toole (*TFI Friday*)
 2 U2 (several times, two notably – more about those later)
 1 The Dude (Radio Radio)

Sara had now moved down to London and we'd rented ourselves a flat just off the Camden Road. We couldn't have been happier, we were back together and still very much in love.

Originally from Buckinghamshire, Sara already knew loads of people in London, including her best friend who lived just down the road from us in a mansion block in Swiss Cottage. She was thrilled to be back within spitting distance of her old pal and had no problem when it came to finding a job in news, securing a position even before she arrived; not only was she highly intelligent but she had a beautiful announcing voice as well. On top of this she spoke no fewer than five languages – three of them fluently! Alas, though, London and our new lives would ultimately prove to be too much for our relationship and within a year Sara and I would go our separate ways. I would continue to dive head first into my career while Sara went to live in France via a brief spell in Norwich of all places.

For the time being, however, life both at work and at home continued to be exciting and stimulating, although it was quickly becoming evident that, as a business concern, Radio Radio was about as much use as a glove puppet without a hand up its bottom. It was becoming ever more apparent that nobody either knew or cared about satellite radio – and probably never would. It was also clear that we were mostly broadcasting to ourselves, a fact that didn't sit well with some of the more well-known presenters – one in particular as I was about to find out.

In those first few weeks I had impressed my new bosses enough to be given a contract and was now on twice what I had been for presenting in Manchester for producing in London. With my new title of junior producer and more money came more responsibility: I would now be solely responsible for the production of several of our shows.

I have highlighted the word 'production' because this can mean many different things depending on the situation. With some shows there's little or nothing to produce, the DJ knows exactly what he's doing and anyone trying to help will only end up getting in his way. The most useful thing for a producer to do in this case is to keep as low a profile as possible.

This was one such show.

The DJ concerned was more than capable to say the least when it came to being on the radio. He was and still is an extremely well-respected name in broadcasting – a legend in fact – but at Radio Radio he knew no one was listening and even though, like everyone else, he was being paid a small fortune to work there, he was not happy – this is not what he did, he was not on the radio to broadcast to no one regardless of the size of the cheque. He was also a realist. He hated bullshit and everything and everyone that went with it.

So I'm sat behind the glass in the control room one night and it's like one o'clock in the morning. Now the week before I had met a man called Tim Blackmore, a very highly respected producer and another legend in the radio world. Tim was the person who taught me the mark of a good producer was to understand the person they were working with and then provide them with whatever they needed to perform at their best. If all that amounted to was giving them space and grabbing them a cup of coffee every now and again – then so be it. My guy was one of these guys: apart from a polite hello when he arrived and a genial goodbye when he left, plus the aforementioned odd coffee in between, there was nothing else he either wanted or needed from me.

I didn't mind, I was just happy to watch him work. He was a maestro, an economy of words being at the heart of his style. Not that he was lazy, it was just that he could achieve more with less – the finest of arts. But then there's less and then there's even more than less before less becomes so little it's nothing – and this is what was about to happen.

The Dude (not his real name, but one I have chosen to use for the purposes of this story) puts on an album track and then tells me he's going to the loo – 'nothing strange there', I thought, and as the album track was by no means short, everything looked like it was going to be OK. When the track reached halfway, after three or four minutes, we were still OK and although I wasn't yet concerned, I was beginning to become a little intrigued as to where my guy was.

Three minutes later and I'm very concerned. If anything went wrong on this show that I could have stopped but didn't, I guessed that I was gonna get fired – and me getting fired was not an option.

Now bearing in mind my guy and his 'style' I am still reluctant to do anything about the situation because he is the man and he knows this game inside out and one second before the song ends – you just know he's gonna slide back into the studio, slip back down into his chair before opening the microphone and no doubt giving us all another few choice words of infinite wisdom. If I was to do anything to stop that happening – getting in his way, ruining his karma or doing anything else that might put him off – I would be guilty of upsetting his cool, a crime for which he had been known to go absolutely ballistic.

I was frightened, I have to admit. I was frightened of the situation and I was frightened of The Dude. I was so confused as to what to do, I didn't do anything at all and as the track faded out, the transmission monitor fell silent. I had failed to avert the 'dead air' situation that was now occurring. There was now nothing on the radio and, as I'm sure you're aware, this is not generally what the radio is for. The shit was about to hit the fan, the vast majority of it I suspected heading right my way. The Dude was still nowhere to be seen. After several seconds, during which I was frozen with the prospect of my impending doom – the next track started – at which point I began to feel physically sick ...

Alright, so now the ship had begun to sink, we had approached the iceberg and I, as captain, had failed to take any evasive action whatsoever. Anything that happened from now on would be all my fault. I had to do something and quickly – suddenly all my feelings of hesitation and uncertainty abated – replaced instantly by pure fear, the fear of imminent unemployment and a one-way ticket back to nowhere.

I flung open the control room door and sprinted off down the corridor towards the toilets where I hurtled through the door, panting with anxiety. I scanned the urinals – they were all vacant. 'Of course they are, you dick,' I heard a voice in my head shouting – 'no one has an eight-minute piss!' I rounded the corner past the sinks to check out the cubicles, skidding on the tiles as I did so.

All the cubicle doors were either open or ajar, all that is except one … Upon further inspection I could see the red mark on the lock signifying that this cubicle was indeed engaged and seeing as there was only me and The Dude in the whole of the building, I felt safe to assume it was probably The Dude that was inside.

I stopped and stared at the door. Suddenly there was an eerie calm as I noticed cigarette smoke rising gently from inside.

'Shit, fuck, fuck, shit, what do I do now, what in Christ's name do I say? This is ridiculous.' My thoughts were running wild, the music from the next track of the album taunting me as it piped through the crappy old speaker mounted in the ceiling.

I stood there stock still, staring at the door, wanting to cry but at the same time wondering what the hell to do next. Indecision becoming a new habit that I was quickly going to have to break, it was doing me no good at all. Thankfully I didn't have to procrastinate too long. The Dude was about to speak.

'Hey kid … is that you?' he drawled.

'Er … yes, yes it is,' I replied (who the fuck else did he think it was?).

'I know why you're here,' he went on. 'You're here to get me off this john and back into that studio. Well, let me tell you, I ain't goin'. There's nobody listening out there and that's not what I do, so I'm gonna stay in here for a while until I feel like coming out again.'

I had to tell him the score – this was a monumentally important moment to me.

'But you can't,' I said, 'you just can't – you've got to get back in there.' There was a pause before another drawl emanated from inside the cubicle.

'Give me one good reason why I should come out, kid, and I promise you, as sure as eggs is eggs, if you can I will, but here's the thing – there ain't none. You know that and I know that, this whole station is a crock of bull.'

Of course he had a point and if I'd been him I might well have thought the same thing. He didn't need to do this for a second but I definitely needed him to do this and I needed him to do it pretty fucking quickly. When all else fails, how about the plain old truth? This is all I had left to bargain with.

'Dude, if you don't get back in that studio and say something, I will lose my job and I really need this job – I need it like you have no idea.'

Again there was a pause, maybe five or ten seconds and then:

'Ahhh – shoot, come on kid, don't lay that one on me, now you're making me feel bad.'

'I don't mean to make you feel bad, Dude, honest I don't but it's the truth. If you don't come out they'll sack one of us and it isn't going to be you, it's going to be me and then I'll be fucked.' I wasn't exaggerating, I was deadly serious.

Again I awaited a response.

'Shit kid ... I didn't ever think you were gonna say something like that ... do you really think they'd do such a thing?'

'In a heartbeat,' I replied

'Man ...' he sighed.

I could have said something else at this point but there was nothing left to say. All I could do now was hope The Dude would take pity on me. I anxiously awaited his verdict with regards to my fate. After a few seconds I could hear the sound of various activities taking place behind the door. The chink of a belt buckle, the zipping up of a fly, along with the random grunts and groans that usually accompany such a process, culminating in an explosion of water flushing down the pan.

Seconds later the lock snapped open and out strutted The Dude. He was still in no mood to be hurried but I couldn't help feeling things were looking up, perhaps as a result of my little speech. I had been straight with him, a trait I knew he would appreciate and though he was a complex man, he was by no means a bad man. His beef was with the bosses and the terminal plight of the radio station, not with me, a junior member of staff and my fight for survival.

Without looking at me he went over to the sinks to splash his hands and face with water. After checking himself in the mirror he turned in my direction. He had a little speech of his own.

'Alright kid,' said The Dude resolutely, 'you got me. Go back to the studio, I'll be there in a minute.'

'Before the end of the track?' I chirped excitedly.

'Sure, before the end of the track – now go and chill – and hey, none of this never happened unless somebody says it did and even if they do, it still didn't happen – the lock on the john got stuck, you came to get me and somewhere in between we figured it out.'

At that moment I could have kissed him. Before the end of the second track, the Dude was back in front of his microphone in time for the next link.

As it turned out, no one noticed the gap in between the tracks or even the fact that both songs were from the same album.

The Dude was right. There really was no one listening.

top
10
Books that Have Inspired Me and at Times Kept Me Sane

10 Marcus Aurelius – *Meditations*
9 Deepak Chopra – *The Path to Love*
8 The Dalai Lama – *The Art of Happiness*
7 Bertrand Russell – *The Conquest of Happiness*
6 Alain de Botton – *Essays on Love*
5 Charles Dickens – *A Christmas Carol*
4 Ernest Hemingway – *The Old Man and The Sea*
3 Lao Tsu – *The Way*
2 Bernie Brillstein – *Where Did I Go Right?*
1 Sam Goldwyn – *The Goldwyn Touch*

Inevitably Radio Radio tanked as we all suspected it would and with it the hopes and dreams of satellite radio for ever, but hey, this was London so we had a party anyway. This city really was a strange place.

After Radio Radio disbanded, all the staff went their separate ways whereas I just went the one way – back to the flat Sara and I had rented in Camden. Only three months into our new lives in London and once again Sara found herself in the company of a boyfriend who didn't have a job, but as always she continued to be brilliant, beautiful and totally behind me 100 per cent. She helped me prepare some new CVs, I sent them off and rekindled my old pastime of staring at our phone, willing it to ring. I had learnt a lot in the last couple of months, had mixed with some of the greats of my profession, but once again I was out of work and felt things going cold. I wanted more of the same and I was willing to do practically anything to help make that happen.

Some time during that night in the toilets back at Radio Radio I had obviously made an impression on The Dude and little did I know he was now out there working his magic very much on my behalf.

The old BBC Radio London had recently closed down and was to be relaunched shortly as a new, more cosmopolitan, forward-thinking station. It would also receive a new name – GLR, Greater London Radio. The Dude was to be part of the debut line up and the new boss who was looking for fresh people with a fresh new vibe had asked him if he knew of anyone who might fit the bill. Along with a couple of other names The Dude had very kindly mentioned me, as a result of which I was contacted and asked to come in for an interview.

Wow, this really was something – I now had a shot at working for the BBC.

To get into the BBC was no mean feat, especially as a producer. It usually involved some kind of university education or at least a stint at broadcast school. To circumvent this type of route was almost unheard of but if the BBC were happy to see me, I was more than happy to see them.

When I said I was asked in for an interview, I ought to clarify that the BBC don't have interviews so much, they have a process called 'boarding'. It's one of the typical BBC phrases that still exists to this day, like holidays are always referred to as 'leave', a surefire way of spotting a BBC employee and the use of which for some reason still makes me giggle.

To be 'boarded', a potential candidate must face an actual 'board' of people who will cross-examine them with a combination of different questions. It's a very good idea that works well and with the make-up of the board often being a huge source of intrigue itself.

'Have you heard who's on the board yet?' the whispers soon start to circulate.

The members of the board are usually cast from various departments from across the BBC and even the top jobs and internal moves are still determined in this traditional way, from the Director General all the way down to researchers and broadcast assistants. I was currently at the 'all the way down' level but this was a job with the most respected broadcaster in the world and I was preparing to give it my best shot.

My board was to take place at the radio station which was located in Marylebone High Street, a very swanky part of town, posh shops with the clientele to match, with lots of actors and other showbiz types residing in the area, many of them in the pretty mews houses which lay hidden off the main drag.

On the day of my appointment I had decided to walk there to help clear my head, the route from my house meant I could take in Regent's Park along the way, the perfect place for a quiet think and for me to contemplate what kind of questions they might ask me. The park, with its mighty trees and acres of green grass, helped calm me down and gain some perspective. I'm always exasperated at how few people make use of these amazing spaces and their beautiful surroundings.

As I arrived at reception, my peaceful preparation had worked – I was relaxed and focused, a good place to be. I was, however, minus one essential item.

'Don't you have a tie?' said the guy who was due to go in before me. His name was John Revell, who happened to be the second person I had met after Carol on my first day at work at Radio Radio. John had previously worked as an in-store DJ at Virgin Megastore before moving on to the doomed satellite broadcaster. We had hit it off immediately that first morning whilst struggling to assemble a Revox tape machine. Neither of us had the first idea what we were doing and it resulted in one of those situations where you can barely talk for laughing.

'No, why, do you think I need one?' I replied, suddenly feeling on edge.

'This is the BBC, they like all that, you gotta show you know the appropriate thing to do – the etiquette – and right now wearing a tie is probably pretty much up there at the top of the list.'

'Shit, fuck – fuck, shit!' He was right, I thought I had looked perfectly acceptable in jeans, a shirt and jacket but I had to put a tie on – it wasn't worth the risk. I wasn't going to not get this job because I wasn't wearing a tie. I had the rest of my life not to wear a tie.

'You can borrow my tie if you like,' he offered kindly.

'But don't you need it?'

'Yes, but they always take five minutes to discuss things after seeing someone, so you can have it after I've been in.'

'Gee thanks man.' What a star.

In he went and twenty minutes or so later he was out again. John said he thought it had gone well and that the guys in there seemed decent enough; he said it wasn't as tough as he thought it was going to be and he advised me just to be myself and let them know how much I loved radio and wanted the job. He then duly took his tie off and handed it over.

'There you go,' he said. 'Break a leg.'

The board was made up of three people – the new boss and two other suits, except they weren't suits, they were smart casual – quite cool for execs, all with a different line in questioning, serious but not solemn. My boarding got under way. The questions, few of which I had expected, came thick and fast. I'm sure I was way off the mark with most of my answers but I kept the bullshit down to a minimum whilst cranking up the enthusiasm to maximum. Towards the end of the session, their mood had lightened and I began to sense a feeling that they might even like me. Could I really be in with a chance of working for the BBC?

I finished with a flurry of how and where I had come from, experiencing the relative freedom and creativity of commercial radio which I suggested could be useful if married with the professionalism and resources of the BBC – it was just what the corporation needed. In my mind the Beeb presented broadcasters and producers with endless opportunities but was lacking in ideas whereas commercial radio was basically the opposite. This final argument, though a little audacious, brought a smile to their faces – always a good time to shut up – I decided to leave it there.

Matthew Bannister, the boss, thanked me for my time, congratulated me on my energy and positivity and informed me that they'd 'let me know'. As I rose from my chair and turned to the door I wanted to punch the air – I may not get the job but I couldn't have done any better and that's all a person can ever ask of themselves – but then ...

... just as I was about to press down the handle on the door to 'escape' along with remembering to breathe, which I had momentarily forgotten how to do, Matthew called me back.

'Er, just one more thing ...'

'Shit – fuck, what was it? What was he going to ask me now? Please don't let it be a sneaky last-minute question designed to trip me up,' I thought to myself. I turned and smiled through gritted teeth, attempting to appear nonchalant but filled with a terrible sense of foreboding.

'Sure, what is it?' I squeaked unconvincingly.

'Err ... is that the same tie the last guy had on?'

Ha ha, very bloody funny, the three of them were in stitches.

'No,' I replied with a huge sigh of relief and a relieved smile. 'Who on earth would be so stupid as to turn up for a BBC board without a tie?'

Two days later I got the job, as did John. The tie was a winner – and so were we.

top 10 Jobs at a Radio Station – in My Very Biased Opinion

10 Work Experience
9 Broadcast Assistant
8 Assistant Producer
7 Producer
6 Executive Producer
5 Head of Department
4 Assistant Controller
3 Controller
2 Network Controller
1 DJ

Greater London Radio was to become a very special place for me and one without which I would not have achieved much of what you most likely already know about.

GLR's ethos was that it should be a much bolder station than its predecessor Radio London had ever dared to be, based on the fact that the local BBC station for London was in many ways a one-off. London is, after all, one of the most famous cities in the world – people come to live and work here from all over and the new GLR wasn't going to be embarrassed to acknowledge this. It was decided it would capitalise and seize upon all the opportunities such a rich and fertile environment had to offer and would stop pretending to be like all the other local BBC radio stations.

Big ideas call for big names, so once again I witnessed a small army of well-known personalities drafted in to fill the schedules – many of whom had been more used to telly, some having never done any radio before. This is where I came in.

I was charged with the task of producing a young lady by the name of Emma Freud, who was slated to host the mid-morning weekday slot. Emma was a much-respected television broadcaster and one of the sharpest cookies in town. She came from one of the most famous dynasties of modern times, her great-grandfather being Sigmund Freud –

the father of psychoanalysis – and her own father the eccentric, intellectual and much-loved though now sadly departed Sir Clement. As a result of such breeding, there was nothing Emma wouldn't tackle; her confidence knew no bounds – or at least that's how it seemed, although underneath she was actually quite a fragile little soul. She took to radio, however, like a duck to water. Failure was not in her vocabulary – she was totally brilliant.

Emma typed all her own scripts for every single show; she prepared her research notes more thoroughly than anyone I had ever worked with. Not only that but she insisted on learning how to self-operate the studio, something a lot of 'celebs' shy away from. She was never late and was never once antsy or starry, no need for talent management here – Emma was the real deal, a consummate professional, the best of the best, a joy, what more can I say? I loved working with her.

As Emma's show grew in stature and popularity, I was now labelled as the kid who taught London TV types how to do radio and as a result was given my next charge – a shy, retiring young man by the name of Danny Baker.

Danny was an old television colleague of Emma's from LWT's *The Six O'Clock Show*. It was a show I'd never seen as it came off air before I arrived in London but by all accounts it was a very big noise for several years, a fact Danny was very keen not to let pass me by. *The Six O'Clock Show* was a Friday teatime show designed to start the weekend off with a bang. This was another prophetic coincidence as Danny and I would one day work together on a similar show at a similar time and on a Friday night. You know the one.

I will never forget the first time I met Danny. He came for a cup of coffee after Emma's show one day – Jesus Christ (and I don't often take the Lord's name in vain) – he just talked and talked and talked and he's been talking ever since.

Danny really is a one in a gazillion – the most energetic man I know as well as one of the cleverest. No one can hold a torch to Danny when he is on form. He is alight twenty-four seven and is now one of my best friends. That first day, however, I wasn't sure if I ever wanted to see him again, let alone work with him in a confined space twice a week for the next year.

Danny had been asked to host the new weekend breakfast show, a real shot in the arm for the listeners as the lady who'd been doing it for the previous hundred years was a more 'traditional' broadcaster, shall we say. Her audience didn't have a clue what was about to hit them. Nor did I for that matter.

Danny's opening link on his first show, his first-ever link on the radio, was at six a.m. on a Saturday morning and consisted of the following sequence of events. He opened the fader connected to the microphone and when the red light came on he immediately started to bang on the console of his desk with his fist, like a warmonger whipping up the mob:

'GOOD MORNING LONDON', he bellowed. 'THIS IS RAW MEAT RADIO, THERE'S A NEW SHERIFF IN TOWN AND FROM NOW ON THIS IS HOW IT'S GONNA BE – HEAR YEE, HEAR YEE.'

With his other hand he then proceeded to ring a handbell for all it was worth before next producing a huge old-fashioned bell horn and honking it profusely.

What the hell was this madman doing? The banging on the desk was making everything distort so much no one listening at home would have been able to understand the first word of his radio revolution. And what was all the shouting? Was he trying to broadcast the first ever radio show that didn't need a transmitter, let alone a microphone? Whatever it was, though the method needed a little fine tuning, the intention was clear, to me at least, if maybe not to anyone else as I was probably the only one who could hear what he was saying.

Danny was going to do it his way – period. The listeners were either going to love it or hate it. Fortunately for everyone, once we'd fitted a new microphone and they could hear him – they loved it: Danny was a hit, a humungus, unstoppable, unpredictable, hairy, raw-meat-radio hit.

Like the majority of the best, Danny was a leave-alone guy: once he'd grasped the basics of what he needed to know, which took him no more than a couple of shows, there was little he needed from me. I just spent the next few months benefiting from the first-hand experience of witnessing another mad genius at work but I got the added bonus of the pictures as well as the sound – exhausting but great fun.

I wouldn't want to be in Danny's head for a second but I want him in my life for ever.

* * *

For the first time in a long time after Danny had settled in and probably the first time in my career, I felt myself cruising – a very dangerous place to be. I was a BBC staff member, I was on a very good wage – but I was treading water. Both the station and the shows I was involved in were doing well, all I had to do was keep my eye on them, but as you get better at something, inevitably you learn less and less. This is precisely what was happening to me. I concluded that if I wanted to keep moving forward I needed to take the next step, wherever that was and whatever that might be.

top
10 Pivotal Moments in My Career

10 Going to watch Timmy at Old Trafford
9 The phone call from Andy
8 The Dude
7 *The Big Breakfast*
6 *Don't Forget Your Toothbrush*
5 *TFI Friday*
4 Making a load of money
3 Losing a load of money
2 Fame
1 Matthew Bannister

When you're hot in the London media scene, everyone tends to know about it. Fortunately for me it wasn't long before the word was out that there was a sparky young producer over at GLR who might be ready for a move. This just happened to coincide with the need to fill a vacancy over at the mighty Radio 1.

I was twenty-five years of age and about to be offered a producing post on a national BBC network. It was a job which I would accept without hesitation after completing the obligatory boarding process, of course. A year or two before, I couldn't even imagine being allowed to look round Radio 1, let alone actually get a job there. All I had to do now was tell Matthew, who was still my boss at GLR, that I would be leaving.

I owed Matthew plenty and this was a sad occasion for both of us. After discussing my circumstances, Matthew said he understood my position and couldn't blame me for wanting to advance my career. What an all-round top man. He helps make you what you are and then he sends you off with a hug and a pat on the back. We shook hands but then as I went to walk out of his office, history was about to repeat itself.

'Er, Chris ... just one more thing.'

I thought he was having a laugh by reminding me of the first day I met him when he called me back to ask about my tie.

'Sure, what is it?' This time I was a little less squeaky but equally surprised.

'Is there *anything* I could say that might change your mind?'

He wasn't joking and I was touched by the sincerity of his question but nevertheless the writing was on the wall, I had to take the offer from Radio 1 if I wanted to progress my career.

'Honestly, Matthew, I am flattered that you even ask but really there isn't. Radio 1 versus GLR. It's a no contest.'

'Alright ... what about ... if I gave you your own show?'

'*What?*' What did he just say? Did he say, 'What about if he gave me *my own show!*'

I didn't do the on-air thing any more. I was a producer now. My presenting days were over – done and dusted, dead and buried, not only that but this was London, the home of 'all killers, no fillers' when it came to hiring talent. What on earth was he talking about?

'How about you produce Danny on Breakfast at the weekends,' he continued enthusiastically. 'And then you stay on and do a Saturday afternoon show yourself?'

He both looked and sounded like he meant it.

'But me – why?' As far as I knew, he wasn't even aware what I sounded like on the radio.

'Because I think you might be good, you're funny.'

Christ on a bike, Matthew was offering to put me back on the air and not just anywhere – on the BBC and in London – regional accent and all.

Radio 1 would have to wait – for both of us!

top
10
**Things that Make a Successful Radio Show
(the type of shows I do, that is)**

10 Know your audience

9 Play on your strengths

8 Avoid your weaknesses

7 Reflect the day

6 Reflect the world

5 Empower the listeners

4 Never forget music is your friend (The Beatles are always on hand if you need them)

3 Be yourself but just a bigger version

2 Put yourself down before anyone else has the chance to

1 Content, content, content

I now had a new show to create and this time my own. I couldn't wait to get going.

Whenever I'm faced with the prospect of a new show, all I do is consider each hour as a clockface, an hour of time to fill and the better the things you fill it with, the more effortlessly and entertainingly it will pass by. The content should also, when it comes to light entertainment, leave the listener or viewer in a better, more relaxed, or more thoughtful frame of mind.

Break it down, break it down, break it down. That's what I do, that's the key.

To plan an hour of radio I actually draw a clock. I use a CD to draw around – it's the perfect size. I then fill in all the things that *must* happen at the corresponding times, shade in those areas and then see how much room there is for anything else to happen. That's the *me* bit.

I still use this method today. Over the page is a drivetime clock from my Radio 2 *Drivetime Show*.

For this, my first London radio show, it was very important for me to trade off the back of what I knew the listeners were guaranteed to like, i.e. quality records and information and then nip in and out with a bit of my stuff. I would do this gradually for the first few weeks, then as my confidence and relationship with the listeners grew, I could start to exchange more of the solid gold musical bricks for those speech-based ones of my own.

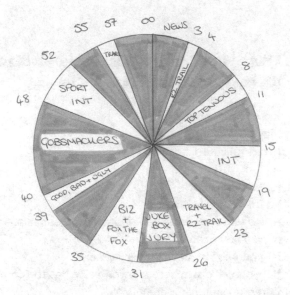

After the news, which was usually around three minutes, to open each hour I decided to play two records back to back instead of just the one, that's another eight minutes. My first link would be a menu telling you what's coming up on the rest of the show followed by another record – another five minutes. Then I'd do my first feature, a phone call or an interview followed by a fourth record – another nine or ten minutes.

If you do the maths here, it's already close to half past the hour. Suddenly, being on the radio is not such a formidable prospect!

I wanted this show to be informal, that's how I would make it different. I was nowhere near as slick as some of the polished pros around me – so I decided to make a virtue of a far more conversational, relaxed and open style. I was also conscious of the fact that this was a local London show and I was an out and out Northerner; somewhere along the line I would have to come up with an idea that would get me round this issue.

The show went on the air under the title *Round at Chris's*. It was a title I thought would help. I wanted to convey the idea that this was my home and anyone was welcome. I genuinely encouraged people who knew me and who might be listening to drop by – which thankfully they did.

Covering the London angle was a little trickier but it was the weekend and our listeners were more doers than talkers; they loved to get out there, in amongst it, and seeing as it was Saturday afternoon – how about a what's on guide?

Not the most groundbreaking idea, I admit, but it was simple, useful and effective – after all we were in one of the most exciting cities in the world, there was always loads going on, how about we just let people know when and where. If some kind of what's on guide could be delivered in an upbeat and entertaining way, I thought it was more than justified being part of the programme. Shows always need pegs to hang their coats on and the more pegs the better – the imparting of information is a great way to do this.

The what's on guide would primarily be based around things I knew little or nothing about, so I concluded it was probably best to get someone else to present this segment. Who was the most London person I knew? How about the crazy lady with the cockney voice as loud as a foghorn? Carol the traffic girl from Radio Radio – my future wife! She *was* London, remember.

Carol, having never actually been on the radio before, jumped at the chance of having a go. I have to admit she was a little clunky to start off with but weren't we all? She found her radio voice soon enough though and in no time at all was hailed as our very own *Time Out* Totty.

Carol was all over the social scene and knew exactly what was going down, from designer sales to the latest new comedy clubs. When she arrived at the studio, she was always totally prepared and impeccably dressed – although sometimes still a little hungover from another late night out. Not that this was a problem – on the contrary it added to her character as she regaled the audience with her tales of the previous evening's merriment. This only served to enhance the weekend feel we were trying to achieve. Well done, Carol, and the listeners loved her. She was very good and she was very funny and for some bizarre reason the majority of our listeners also thought she was black, something to this day I've never quite understood.

Carol's what's on guide popped up in each of the three hours around the quarter to mark, with a telephone guest at each of the half hours, along with a couple of competitions and the odd set piece. Bingo – we were home and dry.

Round at Chris's was a show by the people for the people and it was only a matter of weeks before members of the public started turning up asking if they could be in the audience. The thing was, we didn't have an audience, it just sounded like we did but the more the merrier, we invited them in and more and more they continued to come. It wasn't much longer after that we were also inviting those listeners who did come in out to party with us for the rest of the day. Very quickly this is what the show became known for – a party on the radio that spilled over into real life when the show ended. A blueprint of things to come!

Going for a drink with the audience afterwards became a regular occurrence and something we would talk about the following week on the air. The more we talked about it the more it happened and the more fun everyone was having. As I look back on things, the lines of show business and the real world were pretty much blurred from the start. We were happy to show up and more than happy to do our bit, but the thought of going home never entered our minds. We were having a blast.

Carol and I would often be the last two left standing, usually ending up in a bar near her flat. She was the most fun, full of stories and tales of adventures, often including outrageous behaviour. If she'd have been a man I'd hate to think of the number of fights she'd have got into but because she was a girl she could get away with murder.

She also had another attractive quality which I was becoming ever more aware of – she had the greatest legs I'd ever seen. And they were so long. The longer we stayed out the longer they seemed to get. Sara and I had long since split and somewhere in amongst the broadcasting, the booze and the bun fights, the thought of Carol's legs consumed me and one day I found myself asking her if I could take a closer inspection. It was a weekday afternoon, the sun was shining and she was wearing the cheekiest of white pleated short skirts.

As in life – when it came to passion and romance with Carol, there was no holding back. She was all woman and there was no volume control. A fact to which her neighbours would no doubt testify.

The Saturday show started to get talked about for all the right reasons by all the right people. It was so uncool it became cool. We were taking London by the scruff of the neck, this was our time and it wasn't long before the show was moved to the more prestigious Saturday morning slot.

Matthew, the boss, happy that his hunch about the quirky, ginger-haired kid from up North had paid off, decided maybe I had yet more juice in the tank and offered me an additional regular evening slot. He said he'd like a show for school kids and students that ran weekday evenings, Monday through to Thursday. As this was the exact same timeslot as Timmy had been doing in Manchester and a show I had been brought up with, I couldn't wait to get started as I already knew the format inside out.

I called this latest show *The Greenhouse* and filled the studio with plants every night. I needn't have bothered of course – this was radio, after all, but I thought it added to the on-air effect plus any guests who came to visit us would hopefully be struck by the memorable sight of a studio packed full of foliage and flora – something a little different to remember us by.

The Greenhouse was not a big ratings winner – it was never going to be – but those who did listen enjoyed it immensely: they recognised it had a heart and a purpose and was tapping into what kids needed at that time of the night. Once again we were succeeding – know your place, know who's out there, give them what they want and sneak in a bit of what you think they might want and hope for the best. They'll soon tell you if they don't like it.

By this time I was living in a three-storey mews house in Belsize Park on the north side of Regent's Park. It was as funky as you like with a big sliding window out from the living room on to the street and a spiral staircase from the kitchen on the ground floor all the way up to the bedrooms. I was renting and although it wasn't cheap, I didn't need my money for anything else. There was also a new car on the scene, a 1972 MK III Triumph Spitfire – I was living the dream.

top
10 Seminal Items of Technology that Had the World Aghast

10 Eight-track car stereo system
9 LED/LCD digital watch
8 Betamax video machine
7 Spectrum ZX81 personal computer
6 Atari home entertainment centre
5 The Sony Walkman
4 Sega Megadrive
3 Fax machine – £3,000 when they first came out and a salesman came to your house and treated you like God
2 Telephone answering machine. You could only rent them at first – £1,500 a year from BT!
1 The Squarial

As remote as I thought my chances of getting on the radio in London had been, even more remote was any idea of me appearing on television. But these were heady times for the media in general – hundreds of new broadcasting platforms were being discovered every day, new and novel ways to reach an audience and with them new opportunities to make money. Where satellite radio had failed, satellite television had now taken its place and was looking for both content and people who could provide it.

With every new technological revolution there is usually a race between two or three formats to gain supremacy. This kind of war is usually highly brutal and bloody with everyone ploughing in hundreds of millions of pounds in an attempt to kill off the competition, all of them knowing that when it comes down to it the winner takes all. It's a game of very high stakes and big balls, not for the faint-hearted.

The two main protagonists involved in this new stream of television were Sky with their big grey dishes and BSB with their funny-looking squarials – both companies keen to get their particular receiver screwed to our walls. The key to this was buying up the rights to various programmes, movies and events that would then tempt any potential viewers to choose their package over their rivals. As part of this process

> All of which, I think, leaves us with Danny Baker and Chris Evans. Baker (GLR, 10am, Sundays) has the unpremeditated banter of an inspired South London street-trader, while Evans (GLR, 10am, Saturdays) has the same free-association skills (albeit in a weird curdled Scouse) but combines it with such superb set-pieces that the only thing which stops me coming right out and declaring him to be London's best DJ is that he's in his early twenties and already (thanks to a breakfast show on BSkyB) earning £1,000 a week.
>
> Since he's already making his pile, he's not getting a haemorrhoid from this arsehole.

BSB decided to go one step further and create a channel for younger viewers based on the success of MTV. This new channel would be called the Power Station and was owned by a guy called Nik Powell.

Nik had made a name for himself by being one of the three men who had started the Virgin brand, the other two being a chap called Simon Draper and of course Richard Branson. After leaving the Virgin group Nik had then joined forces with the ex Beatle George Harrison and Stephen Woolley to form a venture called HandMade Films with which he had several hit movies. All things considered he was quite a guy. He also happened to be married to the 60s pop star Sandy Shaw.

Nik had heard me on the radio and thought I would be perfect to host his daily breakfast television show. It was to be two hours long and very much a radio show on the telly, with videos taking the place of records and me popping up in between to provide some sort of additional colour. He asked me in for a screen test, took one look at it, realised I had absolutely no idea what I was doing and offered me the job straight away – along with a very handy signing-on fee plus a salary of £25k a year.

£25k – wowzer, this would double my annual income and sure it meant I had to work on the telly for two hours in the morning and on the radio for two hours every night, plus a few hours' pre-production on top, but I didn't care. I had boundless energy pumping through my veins and each new opportunity simply fired me up even more.

Two hours a day of television, having never done any before, was of course a baptism of fire, but what a way to learn. Fortunately, once again, there were very few people around to witness my mistakes – and there were plenty to witness. Although when I say my mistakes, I should say, our mistakes because guess who was producing me? Big Bird – Andy was back on the scene, once again at the forefront of a new operation.

We had just the most fun making *Power Up*, which was the name of our show. We had a fully kitted-out television studio and gallery to play with every day. This is where I would learn all the camera tricks, digital video effects and other television trivia that would give me a head start when it came to working on *The Big Breakfast, Don't Forget Your Toothbrush* and *TFI*.

Characters were instrumental in filling the show's content as well as getting most of the crew on camera – as there was no one else to play them. There was almost one character per link: Mystic Mick and his Magic Brick would bring us news of the future. The Man in the Kagool would mysteriously wander in and out of the back of shot, the one-string guitar guy would shuffle on and play a song every now and again and our in-house pet squirrel Martin would be berated to leave the phone alone before being unceremoniously whipped off screen via an invisible length of fishing line.

All total nonsense, all very *Wayne's World* – almost exactly the same in fact, based on the premise that anything that made us laugh might make the viewers laugh. Again I found myself in the middle of an ideas-eating monster – we just had to keep those ideas coming.

The viewing figures for BSB meanwhile were dismal to say the least but the breakfast show was just about managing to register some kind of blip on the research. Nik decided to protect his biggest asset and invited me to lunch at a pub on Parsons Green in Fulham. It was called the White Horse and Nik wanted to meet me there to offer me a new deal.

'Look Chris, we really love what you and the team are doing and we want to make sure you're happy.'

'Nik, I couldn't be happier.'

'Yes but you've probably heard about the figures and some of the other shows that are moving to a straight music video format as a result.'

'Yes I have but that's all fine, we are rocking.'

'Well, that's precisely it, you are rocking and we want you to know that we are 100 per cent behind what you're doing.'

'Great, that's good, thanks.'

'And that's why we want to double what we pay you.'

Yes he really did say that. 'We want to double what we pay you.' What was it with these London people?

I didn't know what to say so I said this: 'Nik that's really nice of you but it's not about the money for me, it's about taking the programme forward and seeing what we can do next.'

It wasn't exactly what I meant but it was sort of what I meant. Of course I cared about the money but only because I'd never had any. I was far more passionate about what we were going to do on the show every day, and Nik was slightly taken aback. I didn't mean to be ungrateful but here was a guy who had just doubled this kid's wages and the kid barely seemed to bat an eye.

Whatever emotions I had suppressed whilst sat opposite Nik in the pub that afternoon screamed out of me as I drove home later in the day. Woohoo! In the last eighteen months my salary had gone from £15,000 a year to the princely sum of almost £70,000. What a laugh. It was time to buy a new car and how about a place to live?

top
10 Pads

10 Terraced house in Warrington

9 Studio house in Belsize Park

8 Old rectory in Kent

7 2-bed flat in Belsize Park

6 Terraced house in Notting Hill

5 Villa in Portugal

4 Country estate in Surrey

3 Farmhouse in Surrey

2 Semi-detached house in Chelsea – I never went there, sold it to George Michael who never went there either, he then sold it to Puff Daddy, who I also think has never been there

1 Lionel Ritchie's old house in L.A. – by far and away the coolest house I have ever owned

I went to see and fell in love with something called a studio house. It consisted of one big room with stripped wooden floors, a vaulted ceiling and a gallery bedroom. Within that room was everything except the toilet. From the bath you could watch television and from the bed you could see the bath. There was a small but perfectly formed galley kitchen, a real fire and French windows leading out onto a tiny garden. It was my fab London pad and I loved it – it was also the breathtaking sum of £105,000. The second part of the package, my new car, was a blue 1960s Jag, with chrome wire wheels – it was to die for. Life was sweet, sweeter than sugar and honey pie, but my main focus was still on the work – that's where my future lay. Although my fledgling television days were about to come to an end.

In the race for satellite television dominance it was becoming quickly evident that Sky was going to be the bride whereas BSB was going to be the bridesmaid. BSB's days were numbered and it was only a matter of time before it would close down and admit defeat. To add insult to injury Sky would take BSB over and even adopt part of its name.

As British Sky Broadcasting was born, my salary having recently been doubled was now double nothing. The Power Station, being part of BSB, had to switch off and power down. Just before midnight on the final day of transmission we all huddled together in front of the monitor in reception to have a few farewell drinks and witness the playing out of the last video. It was The Doors' 'The End'. There wasn't a dry eye in the house.

Thanks to Nik and Don Atyeo, our laid-back but brilliant Australian programme boss, not to mention all the crew who I worked with day in and day out, it was here that I had gained an invaluable education in the art of producing a low-budget, two-hour, daily television show. I still have several large boxes of videotapes to prove it, which I cherish as much as anything else I own.

You can't buy experience like the hours I racked up on the Power Station let alone hope to get paid for doing so. And it was these same hours that would put me in pole position to host a show which intended to wake Britain up like it had never been woken up before. *The Big Breakfast* would be along in less than a year, but there would be more television shows, not to mention a marriage, in between.

The radio show back at GLR meantime was still flying and offers of additional work started to come my way. I remember one particular such offer, a voiceover for a McDonald's television advertising campaign. It was for several thousand pounds. I had no idea such vast sums could be earned for such little work. It was a 30-second ad that would take less than an hour of my time – but not so fast.

'You're not going to do it, are you?' said a guy I worked with.

'Why not?' I replied.

'Well, it's for McDonald's and you know what they stand for. Your shows are cool and McDonald's definitely isn't cool, at least not to your audience.'

Hmmm, this thought had never crossed my mind, I'd never had to consider such a dilemma before, maybe he had a point. The money would have come in handy as I still had a hefty mortgage on my house to pay but what he'd said had made me apprehensive. So much so, I decided to pass.

Imagine my surprise a few weeks later when the ad finally aired with the voice of none other than the guy who told me not to do it … and he was a bloody vegetarian.

The guy in question was Andy Davies. Andy used to sell ad space in the back of a computer magazine whilst listening to Emma Freud's weekday morning show, the show I was brought in to produce. He called up one day and asked if he could come in and sit in to see the show go out as he was a big fan, hated what he did for a living and would love to have a chance to help out if we ever needed a spare pair of hands. Good for him – that's exactly what I had done several years before at Piccadilly Radio.

When I began my evening show I called Andy to see if he was still interested as we were short of people to man the phones. From there, again like me, he started to work on other shows and it wasn't long before he was able to leave his telesales job and come and work at GLR full time.

When we set up the Saturday morning show Andy was very much the third member of the team – along with Carol and myself – going by the on-air name of 'Handy the Producer'. We were the perfect radio threesome, although Carol and I were about to break away and form a splinter group of our own.

We had been on and off as a couple for a while now and although for the majority of the time we got on like a house on fire, there were several cogs to our relationship that kept on getting jammed. It was as if we were both reluctant to admit we wanted to be with each other on a permanent basis, especially having enjoyed such a wild time together for the last few months or so. Could two people still have as much fun as we were having if they were more of an item? Or would this change the dynamic too much? We had to either shape up or ship out. I think there is a point in most relationships when this happens and Carol and I had reached ours.

One day the subject turned again to the future and whether we were wasting our time or not when out of nowhere I suggested, 'Why don't we just get married.'

'Don't be stupid,' she said. 'You and me married? That's insane!' She was laughing her now famous laugh hysterically.

To say that Carol was not the marrying type would be putting it mildly. She was fiercely independent and to my knowledge hadn't been involved in any serious kind of relationship for a good few years, certainly not since I'd known her. But I genuinely thought it could work; maybe this was what we both needed. A reason to commit and there's no bigger reason than marriage.

I think it must have been the gravity of the proposition that eventually cajoled Carol into saying 'yes'. And we were both slightly mad, why not be slightly mad together?

Once we had made the decision to go through with it, we wasted no time in booking a slot at Camden registry office. Although we only told a couple of people about the actual wedding, we organised a party the same night where we announced our nuptials to the world in the form of fifty or sixty open-mouthed guests who didn't know whether to believe us or not. Carol and I thought it was hilarious. We set up home together and changed the title of our radio show. *Round at Chris's* had now become *Round at Chris's and his Mrs.*

top
10
Things to Take to a Meeting if You Think You are Going to get Shafted

10 A clear head
 9 Perspective
 8 A plan
 7 Self-control
 6 More people than the other guys
 5 A smile
 4 A bottom line
 3 A walk-away figure
 2 A lack of ego
 1 A lawyer

The broadcaster TV-am was to be the final bridge in my journey to Channel 4. Andy and I had pitched a show to them based on what we had done at the Power Station for a Saturday morning slot. We had called the show *TV Mayhem* and it was to be my second bona fide television experience as well as being my first experience of independent production, something that would one day make me a multi-millionaire. Andy was well ahead of the game and knew the value of owning your own content. Carol for her part, an experienced television production manager, came on board to look after the pennies, something she was uncannily gifted at.

The show itself was fab, unlike TV-am's fortunes, which after a cracking ten-year period of popularity and profit were suddenly anything but. During the first few weeks of our run, TV-am lost its contract to GMTV in a franchise bidding war and although the network handover date was several months away, it was decided maximum revenue was now paramount and all costs at the station were to be slashed immediately. Big and Good Productions (named after 'Big Bird' and 'Good Evans') were last in so it was a safe bet we would more than likely be first out.

'What do we do now?' I asked Andy.

'We take the money and scarper,' he replied.

'What money?' I said, 'we don't have any money, they're cancelling our show.'

'Yes, they are but we have a contract for forty shows. They might not want to air them but they're still going to have to pay for them.'

I had no idea what he was talking about. Surely we couldn't get paid for shows we weren't going to have to make?

TV-am called us in for a 'friendly' meeting where they had intended to thank Andy, Carol and me for all our efforts with the new show, apologise for what must have been a big disappointment and give us a pat on the head. Andy was having none of that, however – that's why he hired a lawyer to come with us to the meeting.

The expression on the exec's face when we walked in was a picture, he had no idea what had hit him. Within fifteen minutes, TV-am had settled with Big and Good Productions and to the tune of several hundred thousand pounds.

Shit the bed again ... this media world was getting goofier with every deal.

For the next few months, as the GLR show rocked happily along in the background, other than having more fun with my new wife, I basically filled my whole day working, keeping fit and then going for a beer. I was now going to the gym five days a week and spending any spare time I had at home where I would constantly be writing new ideas, trying to come up with anything that might work on the television or radio.

I had decided to let business take care of itself. It was a ploy that had seemed to work thus far. I would do the creative work and let other people take care of the money. Besides it was becoming ever plainer to me that very few people in the media actually did anything discernible at all other than feed off the ideas guys in one way or another. It was ideas that made this business tick and as far as I could see anyone who came up with them was bound to be on to a winner sooner or later. Over at Channel 4 there was a group of such people about to do exactly that.

Breakfast television, which had been a disaster to start off with, was now big news – there was money in them there hills and Channel 4's Michael Grade had decided it was about time they got their hands on some of it. Invites were put out to tender for their own early morning slot.

The pitching process for this much-coveted contract consisted of several rounds, culminating with two companies going head to head and actually making programmes to be broadcast in real time, although not to the general public but rather directly back to the bosses at Channel 4.

The first I heard about all of this was when I was asked to go and see a company called Mentorn – one of the biggest independent television production companies at the time, responsible for producing such hits as *Challenge Anneka*. They had sailed through the initial bidding stages and were now, from a shortlist of ten, hotly tipped to get down to the final two. Mentorn now wanted me to be part of their bid as they thought I would strengthen their appeal – it was well-known that Channel 4 were looking for something different and had suggested new talent might be the key. Although flattered, I was surprised by their interest as I still hadn't really achieved anything on television, but the radio show was gaining more and more notoriety and it was obvious that people in high places were beginning to tune in.

Mentorn wanted to be able to say that I would be the presenter of their show and no-one else's. They were willing to buy me off the market in an exclusive deal to be part of the package to take into the final pitches and for this privilege they were willing to pay me £10,000.

Out of all my experience with the media and money thus far, this was the craziest I'd encountered to date. Ten thousand pounds for doing nothing except agreeing to have my name on a piece of paper. Television really was a strange world full of even stranger people but if they wanted to keep sending cash my way, that was fine by me. This was my third significant payment from a television company which, added together, now totalled more than I had earned in the rest of my working life.

But this is the most unpredictable of businesses and to everybody's surprise, along with Mentorn's disbelief, they were kicked out at the penultimate stage. No one was more shocked than the boss of the company, Tom Gutteridge, a relative giant in TV. They had been a shoo-in to get to the final and although I felt some sympathy for them I could hardly say I was devastated, having been involved very little with their bid either emotionally or creatively.

The ten thousand pounds, however, meant I could buy the next car in what was now becoming an impressive list of vehicles I had owned – a 1956 MGA Roadster in old English white with red leather interior. Thank you, Mentorn.

Back at GLR I continued with my trusty radio show, not really any the wiser and not really knowing what was going on with the whole Channel 4 breakfast thing. Not that this would remain the case for long as I was about to receive a phone call from a man called Charlie Parsons offering me a job that would change my life beyond all recognition.

Charlie was a very respected programme maker, specialising in new styles of television. He had worked on *Network 7*, a diverse rolling alternative news show for Channel 4 on Sunday mornings where all the reporters were young, had trendy haircuts and wore black. He was also the creator of *Club X* and the infamous *The Word*, which he produced through his company Planet 24. Both programmes, though often annoying, were without doubt signature shows of their time and now Charlie wanted me to be involved in his bid for the Channel 4 breakfast show, a bid which unlike Tom's and Mentorn's had made it through to the final two.

Channel 4 approached Charlie because they knew he would come up with something different and he hadn't disappointed them. He had his finger well and truly on the pulse; he knew how important it was to employ younger brains to come up with ideas for younger audiences. This was one of, if not the, key ingredients of his success. His development department was an exciting albeit exhausting place to be.

Charlie invited me for a cup of coffee. Immediately I liked him, as soon as we met I could see he was different (hyper is another word you could use here) and so enthusiastic – about everything, even the word hello.

'Alright, tell me about your idea – shoot,' I said. I could see he was gagging to get on with it.

'Well, it's not my idea exactly, it's an idea dreamt up by an old friend of yours,' he replied with an intriguing glint in his eye. 'Actually, it was Duncan Grey.'

My evening show at GLR, just like Timmy's at Piccadilly, was staffed mostly by helpers – college students looking for some experience in broadcasting, some boys, some girls, the boys usually spotty, the girls usually absolutely beautiful for some strange reason. One of those boys was a young man called Duncan Grey, a very intense individual whose overriding expression was a permanent troubled frown. Duncan had found himself at odds with his recent Oxford University career and had decided instead to drop out in order to chase a life in the media. Everyone who knew him thought he was crazy as here was a boy with a big brain, a born academic if ever there was one, but Duncan had other plans. He was fascinated by entertainment, obsessed with it almost, entertainment was where his big brain longed to be.

When I was first introduced to him at the radio station, I was at my desk one afternoon preparing that night's show. I remember him barely being able to say hello: he was so nervous.

'Who is this kid?' I thought to myself.

'This is Duncan, can he have a week on your show?' one of the bosses asked.

'Sure,' I said, 'why not?'

If I'd have had to bet, I would have said he wouldn't last a day, let alone a week, not only on the show but in life – I don't think I'd ever seen anyone look so unsure of why they existed.

As it turned out, I couldn't have been more wrong: he stuck around for almost a year and turned out to be an invaluable member of the production team. Now Duncan had gone on to work for Charlie … interesting. What had the bespectacled brainbox managed to come up with that had Charlie in such a froth – literally?

Duncan is a theorist, almost forensic when it comes to thinking about and preparing ideas; he had decided that kids were the key to a new audience. Whatever Planet 24 did, they had to make sure it was an out and out alternative to what was on the other two channels, basically shows for grown-ups – both pretty dull and bland as far as the younger viewers were concerned.

Duncan's idea was simple, all the best are. He had suggested that the Planet 24 pitch should be based around a mirror image of what was happening in most houses at that time of the day. Indeed the show would come from a house, a real house with real rooms and even a real family, a different one every week. But the house would be like a cartoon house, with bright colours reigning supreme, a house all the kids watching would want to live in – a throwback to the type of hangouts The Monkees and The Banana Splits had on their TV shows.

At the helm of the proceedings would be a regular presentation double act, a younger couple with their own television family. This would include the crew, a computer whizz kid, various 'experts' and two alien puppets from planet Zog by the names of Zig and Zag. There would also be regular appearances from Charlie's business partner Bob Geldof as well as his gorgeous wife – the ice-cool Paula Yates, who would interview/seduce the latest stars every day whilst they reclined in her boudoir.

Already it sounded like fun and the more he told me about it the more he became animated and the more the show came alive. By the end of his spiel I was completely sold while Charlie was completely exhausted. I told him he could count me in. Charlie thanked me for my time and rushed off to deliver the news back to his team – but hang on a minute, there was something missing. He hadn't offered me any money. Isn't that what all TV people did?

Not Charlie, he knew he didn't need to. For Charlie the idea was the thing, personnel could always be hired. If I didn't want do it he would get someone else who did. Ideas were where the real value was. Ideas had to be dreamt up. People were everywhere, but ideas were priceless – ideas were everything.

top
10 Memories of
The Big Breakfast

10 The dead body in the river
9   Don't phone it's just for fun – my first run-in link and catchphrase
8   My pre-show bath – 6.46–6.50 every day without fail
7   'More Tea, Vicar' } Two tunes that still hijack
6   'One Lump or Two?' } my headspace from time to time
5   Ben the Boffin – we had a big bro'–little bro' bond going on
4   Zig and Zag – simply the best
3   Paula – telling the shark experts to eff off
2   Gaby – the Hutch to my Starsky, the Bodie to my Doyle
1   The first ever show – when I got stuck in the loo as the
    handle came off in my hand two minutes before we were due
    to go on air*

The Big Breakfast ended up winning the franchise by a mile. It was bold and brash and most importantly a direct alternative to anything else on offer at that time of the morning. It was like Saturday morning kids' telly but every day, which caused it to evolve more quickly. Again it was a deluge of ideas, which only served to make it more compelling – no one knew what was going to happen next because *we* didn't know what was going to happen next. It was never going to last for ever – this we did know – but it would certainly cause a huge fuss whilst it was around.

On the first day of broadcast *The Big Breakfast* more than quadrupled the Channel 4 audience from 100,000 to almost half a million; by the end of the first few weeks this had risen to 750,000 and within a year we were over a million. After that the next target was to beat the once indomitable *GMTV*.

Both the show and everyone on it were hailed as an overnight success, and that's exactly how it felt even though, especially as far as I was

---

* Last-minute nerves got the better of me and when you gotta go, you gotta go. The toilets, like everything else, were brand new and when I went to turn the handle on the door, it came clean off in my hand but the door remained locked. I was shouting for someone to help but everyone was already on set. I had no choice but to smash the door down. Thank God it was made of cheap plywood, otherwise I wouldn't have stood a chance.

concerned, it wasn't the case. But whenever things come good it suddenly feels like it's all been so much easier than it actually has. Success has a knack of taking away the pain of hard work and I had never experienced or even imagined success on the scale of *The Big Breakfast*.

Gaby Roslin was my co-host, but it was oh so nearly somebody else who just happened to drop out at the last minute. Thank heaven they did as

TO: BB Team.
From: Michael Grade, C4

CHANNEL FOUR TELEVISION 60 CHARLOTTE STREET, LONDON W1P 2AX
TELEPHONE 071-631 4444 DIRECT LINE 071-927 8700
TELEX 892355 FAX 071-255 1616

MICHAEL GRADE CHIEF EXECUTIVE

FAX
Charlie PARSONS
The Big Breakfast   9.92

Dear Charlie (et al),

My warmest congratulations to all at Old Ford Lock for the spectacular success of the Big Breakfast. I am now an avid viewer, the ratings have held up for a terrific start. It is everything we all hoped for. I couldn't be more pleased with the start. I'm sending down a case of adrenalin and plasma!
Yours, a fan

[signature]

CC   Liz, John W
     + Andrea

Gaby turned out to be the perfect partner. She was just a tad older than me and from the more traditional school of television presenting; she was also a drama student. I'm sure she won't mind me saying that I added the humour while she steered the ship. We were a good team together, covering each other's backs whenever things started to go wrong, unlike some presenters who use such situations to score points against each other. A fruitless exercise that serves no purpose whatsoever, especially to the viewers who just want you to get on with things.

Every single day on *The Big Breakfast* was an unforgettable pleasure. Sure, we shouted and screamed at each other behind the scenes – me in particular – but we all just wanted to get things right and sometimes this involves 'difference of opinions'.

There are hundreds of stories about *The Big Breakfast* that I'd love to share with you, enough to fill a whole book on their own, but the pages are against us so let me just pick the one – here goes.

top
10 Female Pop Stars

10 Suzi Quatro
9 Annie Lennox (Eurythmics days)
8 Kate Bush
7 Chrissie Hynde
6 Jay Aston – Bucks Fizz
5 Debbie Harry
4 Boy George (it was a good couple of weeks before I realised he was a bloke)
3 Sharleen Spiteri
2 Kylie
1 Kim Wilde

One of the worst things about doing a regular show is when your partner in crime decides to take a holiday. When Gaby was off it was nothing short of a nightmare. Here you have someone who knows both you and the show inside out and they disappear for a fortnight to be replaced by someone who has no idea about either. Add to these facts that sometimes the bosses would draft in a 'name' who had never presented television at all before and we are talking daily disaster. We had some terrible experiences as a result of this – maybe that's why God decided to send me the guest hostess from heaven to even things out a little. Good old God.

Ladies and gentlemen, allow me to introduce Kim Wilde into the proceedings – Kim Bloody Wilde, I tell you. What an awesome female.

Kim was to be a guest presenter for a week and this was one of the rare weeks none of the boys on the crew minded Gaby having off. We still loved 'The Great Roz', of course we did, but this was Kim Wilde we're talking about here. Kim was in the 'never presented on telly at all before' bracket but did any of us care? Not for a second, we were all in love with her and had been for years. When she arrived it was as if Cleopatra had just entered the gates of Rome.

She was glamorous and giggly and so so so much sexier than even any of us had dared to imagine. Kim was a big fan of the show and threw herself into the spirit of things right from the off; doing anything that was asked of her, which just happened to include one Wednesday morning having to crawl into a one-man tent with me during an ad break.

Every show, just before the eight o'clock news, we re-ran the main title sequence to start the next hour, after which Gaby and I would burst on the screen to declare the day and date and why it might be significant. We called it 'Today's the day'. It was a neat idea that took no time at all whilst also giving the viewer added value and often involved a product new to the market – hence the presence of a brand new, revolutionary one-man tent.

The producer, bless his cotton socks, thought it would be a good idea for Kim and me to be in the tent when the shot came to us but with the flap zipped up. On his cue we would rip open the zip, reveal our happy, smiling faces and bid the world good morning. Having already been in the tent for about a minute waiting for the ad break to finish and for the titles to start, we were beginning to find the situation somewhat comical. Like two kids hiding in a wardrobe hoping not to be found we began to snigger and feel naughty all at the same time. We were also so close our noses were almost touching. From nowhere a voice told me it was just one of those moments that you have to grab in life, so with the title music having started in our earpieces, I whispered to Kim, 'We could do anything now and no one would know.'

'What do you mean?' she asked quizzically, becoming intrigued.

'Well, anything, as long as we weren't still doing it when the zip opens.'

The title music was about halfway through and the production assistant had started counting down to our cue.

'What like?' she enquired, raising an eyebrow as if to encourage me to do whatever it was I had in mind.

At which point I simply went to kiss her.

I didn't care – I just had to do it, after all what's life for if not for kissing Kim Wilde in a one-man tent seconds before welcoming the world to a new day live on television? After no more than what was initially a nibble really on that famous full top lip of hers, Kim kissed me back. I took this as a green light to go for it – what followed next was the most memorable, fantasy-filled, nigh-on miraculous five-second snog any red-blooded male could ever experience.

Paula's boudoir at *The Big Breakfast*, 1993. Uncle Chris, my niece Rhianne, and Aunty Paula and Aunty Gaby.

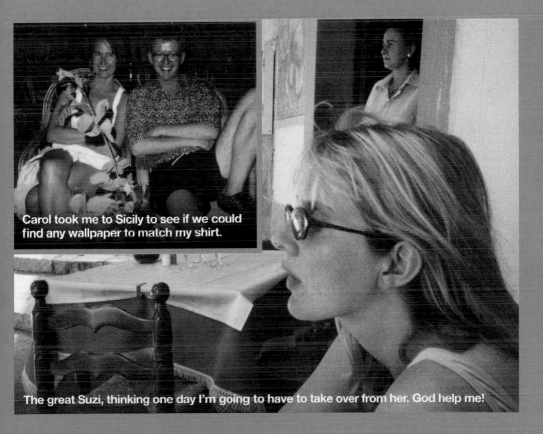

Carol took me to Sicily to see if we could find any wallpaper to match my shirt.

The great Suzi, thinking one day I'm going to have to take over from her. God help me!

My first attempt at impersonating Padraig Harrington, while sitting next to Paul McCartney.

Danny, US shock-jock Howard Stern and me. We should have all gone to Specsavers.

A serious case of white man overbite, after winning two gongs at the Comedy Awards.

The *TFI Friday* football team and our shy and retiring midfielder. I think his name was Paul something.

My writing partner Will and I escape the Vinny Jones-lookalike doorman.

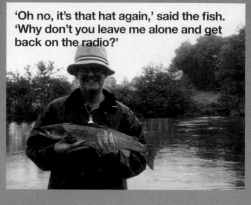

'Oh no, it's that hat again,' said the fish. 'Why don't you leave me alone and get back on the radio?'

'Hello? Is that the police? Please can you rescue me, I seem to have been kidnapped by a ginger bloke for the last five years of my life. I just want to go home.'

'Hey, ladies, do you think I look a bit like Michael Caine?'

The beginning of one of our weekly Naked Parades on *TFI*. I would like to take this opportunity to thank the art director for the unnecessary size of the black rectangle.

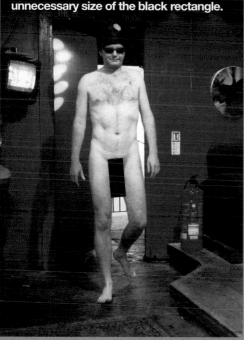

Jimmy Five Bellies, with Danny and me, wondering whether it's safe to let Gazza out of the van.

Happy 80th, Mum. Look at your kids all growed up.

My two *Big Breakfast* bathroom buddies, Lord Zig and Sir Zag of the Planet Zug.

Big sis and little bro. My daughter Jade and Noah, the newest addition to the growing Evans clan.

Jools Holland and me, both aged 13.

The late Allan 'Fluff' Freeman. Finally he doesn't have to put up with idiots like me anymore.

Danny Baker meets Concorde. But all he's given to eat is this pillow.

Ginger Air would have been a far better name.

comic genius

Hairy chest, hairy chin – either way it was a win-win.

'Hey Richard, let's pretend I'm Jenson Button and you're Ross Brawn. What do you reckon Holly?'

As the countdown ended and the director gave us our cue, the zipped-up door of the tent now filling the screen remained fastened for just that little bit longer than it should have done. And now you know why.

'Cue!' the director said again, 'what's going on in there?'

The next Monday Gaby was back on the show.

'How was Kim last week?' she asked.

'She was incredible,' I replied.

Gaby looked a little put out.

'Oh no, not at presenting, Gabs, you know there's no one comes close to you as far as that's concerned – I'm talking about as a woman.'

'What do you mean as a woman?'

'She's my new girlfriend – I kissed her in a tent on the show last week and now we're going out.'

Gaby half smiled at what she thought was a joke but it was true – Kim and I had since got it together and were now an item as by now my marriage to Carol was unfortunately no more.

Out of all the questionable things I have ever done, and there have been many, marrying Carol is way up there. Impulse can be a good thing – in fact, impulse can be a great thing, but I have concluded that perhaps it is an emotion best employed in situations that may not be that important. Impulse is different to having a gut feeling. A gut feeling is more considered. It's the feeling after the thought, whereas there is little thought to impulse and especially to the consequences of it. My marriage to Carol was based on impulse and the hope that it might work as opposed to any concrete reasons as to why it actually would.

When I think back now, it's like it never happened. It's hard to believe we were ever husband and wife.

Carol is the star in any room, in any situation. She was born with an extraordinary self-confidence and a take on life that's unique compared with any other I have ever come across. I still don't understand what makes her tick but whatever it is, it makes for a highly entertaining human being. She is also as hard as nails and not to be messed with.

After I had made a few quid in the first flushes of *The Big Breakfast* we bought a modest but pretty house on the edge of Hampstead Heath. It was a magnificent location in which to live but, as always in life, when the heart's not happy it doesn't matter what the address says and if it takes someone having to leave before the situation can improve then that's what has to happen.

I know for sure I was really not very happy at all and I suspect Carol was not feeling dissimilar. We were both being nicer to everyone else than we were to each other – a surefire sign of a couple in turmoil. We were starting to bicker at home and when we weren't bickering we were becoming more and more distant. Slowly and silently we were making each other miserable and as neither of us are the miserable type, this was not a sustainable situation.

Looking back, I can see how my success was more likely the determining factor in our break-up. Carol has a lot to bring to the table and now here she was married to a guy who was the talk of the town. Shrinking and violet are not two words one would naturally associate with my first wife, and quite rightly so.

Princess Diana once famously said of Prince Charlie's affair with Camilla Parker Bowles, 'There were three of us in this marriage, so it was a little bit crowded.' Well, when it came to Carol and me, there was no longer even enough room for two!

And you know – sometimes that's just the way it is. There's nothing wrong with it, it's not a crime, it's just a fact. Carol and I both wanted to be the lead singer of the band – therefore the band was destined to split.

I remember the afternoon it happened. It was a Tuesday and I was upstairs in bed. My days were divided into two because of my early morning start. I would be up and out with the lark and so I would always have a couple of hours' sleep in the afternoon to stop me feeling like I was on drugs come the evening – anyone who has done regular earlies will know exactly what I'm talking about.

I was lying, eyes wide open, thinking the same thing I had been thinking for weeks.

'I am so unhappy, we are so unhappy, why are we together, what are we going to do about this?'

I am not an individual that is at ease with confrontation – I am a man after all. And this was also Carol we were talking about here – not the easiest person to bring round to any point of view other than her own on even the most trivial of subjects, let alone her marriage. But I had to do something, I was dying inside.

I got up out of bed and went downstairs to the kitchen.

'Alright?' she said.

'Not really, no,' I replied.

'Why, what's the matter?'

'I don't think we should be together any more.'

There, I'd said it, with those few words it was out in the open.

One hour later, I was in my car driving away from a woman who had once been my best friend, a woman with whom I'd shared so much joy and laughter and yet we had now come to a point where we could barely recognise a single thing we had in common.

How does something like that happen to two people? All very sad.

top
10
Things to Consider When
You Split Up with Someone

10 Try not to leave on a row
9 Try to resist going back
8 Don't bleat about it to friends
7 Don't jump into bed with someone at the next available
opportunity
6 Don't worry about who gets what – it's all just stuff
5 Try to remember the good bits
4 Don't beat yourself up about it
3 Don't listen to lawyers – they will mess with your head
2 Always remember you liked each other at the beginning
1 Sort out somewhere to sleep that first night

Directly after my split with Carol I was the first person to actually stay in *The Big Breakfast* house for real. I slept in Ben the Boffin's room. Ben was our computer games expert, a slot he presented from his make-believe bedroom; make-believe for him maybe but reality then for me – for a few nights at least.

They really were a bizarre few days – the press, having heard of my marriage break-up, were looking for me all over the place when I was at the house/work the whole time. 'How's he getting in and out of the show without us being able to tail him?' they wondered. Well, I wasn't, I was in temporary residence at numbers 1 and 2 Lock Keepers Cottages, the home of the mighty *BB*.

The bosses at Planet 24 didn't mind me staying there, not for a second, but they were genuinely concerned about my circumstances and wanted me to be happy and so took it upon themselves to find me a new, more permanent address. This was to be a two-part process, the first part of which would involve me moving in with Zig and Zag, the show's two massively popular space alien puppets.

Zig and Zag were, in real life, two former art students by the names of Mick and Keiron. They were based in Dublin and despite the huge popularity of their creations, they felt there was no need for them to move across to London, preferring instead to fly over once a fortnight to pre-record their segments. Zig and Zag were a smash, by far the most popular things on the show and if this was what it took to keep Mick and Keiron happy then we would all have to make it work.

The Zig and Zag pre-records took place every other weekend and to be honest were a complete pain in the neck, but it was more than worth it as the guys were so good. That said, it was an organisational nightmare.

First of all you're dealing with a crew who have been working all week on the main show and who are now being asked to come in one weekend out of every two. Next you have to write eight scripts, book eight guests, get them there, brief them, rehearse them and keep the energy going the whole time. As well as this the wardrobe department had to prepare eight different outfits. A Polaroid of each of these outfits would then be pinned to the wall so we could attempt to match them up come the live show.

Ninety per cent of the time you saw me leave Gaby to go and join Zig and Zag in their bathroom, I was in fact just stepping off camera and going to have a cup of tea for the next ten minutes whilst the VT operator simply pressed the play button. By the way, the Zig and Zag outtakes tape is to this day the funniest thing I have ever seen. I still have a copy and watch it from time to time. It never fails to crack me up. I should put it on YouTube.

A person should always know their value in life and Mick and Keiron certainly knew theirs. Somehow they had managed to get the bosses to rent them an amazing warehouse apartment in Docklands for when they were over, even though that would only be for two days out of every fourteen. I am not exaggerating when I say that their apartment was the greatest living space I had ever seen.

It was two floors and almost completely open plan. At a guess I would say it was 4000 square feet with bare brick walls, a huge open fire and balconies onto the river. This was more James Bond than Planet Zog (Zig and Zag's native home), but good luck to the boys. Why not? When you're hot, milk things for everything they're worth – you can be a long time cold and then no one wants to know.

The bosses had the idea that I could move in with the guys whilst they found me a place of my own – if it was OK with Mick and Keiron that was.

They couldn't have been nicer about the situation; they could see I was in a fix and were happy to help. So that was it, for a while we were a half-puppet/half-human family except for one occasion when the puppets outnumbered the humans.

The apartment came fully furnished with a huge oak dining table next to the kitchen where, early on a Sunday morning following a pretty heavy night out, I staggered down the wrought-iron stairs to be confronted by not one Zig and one Zag but three of each, all sat down as if waiting for their breakfast. I thought I was seeing things and became even more confused when I noticed that two of the Zigs and two of the Zags looked considerably different to the Zig and Zag closest to me.

It was new puppet time!

The original Zig and Zag had come to the end of the line and now here they were being forced to sit face to face with not one but two each of their clean, fluffy, sparkly-eyed, slightly weird-looking replacements. What a terrible thing to do to my co-hosts. They had served their television show well and this was their reward. Not even the chance of a quick dry clean to see if they could scrub up a little and maybe last a few more weeks before being consigned to the scrapheap. It was already a sad scene and one made even sadder by the fact that because they were old, and less rigid compared to their new counterparts who seemed to be sat bolt upright ready for anything, my boys had slumped down in their chairs, looking almost as if they had suffered some kind of seizure, with their lifeless eyes staring blankly off into the distance and their mouths hanging open as if attempting to utter one final alien word.

That day at the pre-records I almost couldn't bear to look at the imposters – two of them having been drafted in straight away to take over. If they thought they were just going to pick up where the original Zig and Zag had left off, they had another think coming. These weren't my boys – I knew it, they knew it, the crew knew it and I wanted to make sure the viewers knew it. It wasn't long into the recording of that day's first segment that the opportunity to do so presented itself. Zig tried to pull one of his trademark comedy faces but it just didn't work, he couldn't do it, he was all new and stiff, like an ageing Hollywood actress who had had too much facial work. I was thrilled and didn't waste a second pouncing on Zig to ask if there was anything the matter as he didn't seem himself today.

Zig for once was lost for words and the new Zag, feeling obliged to defend him was about to speak when I turned around and scowled,

'And don't you look at me like that either!'

'Like what?' protested Zag.

'Like you have never looked at me before,' I declared triumphantly. 'Like all of a sudden you are different!'

By this time we were all in hysterics. I could feel Mick and Keiron killing themselves where they were lying down on the floor next to my feet.

After the recording session was over, we all had to admit the new puppets had come through their initiation with flying colours, providing us with endless new material. That night, however, my old pals, the first Zig and Zag, my buddies in *The Big Breakfast* bathroom for the last twelve months, were to pay me one last visit so they could say their goodbyes ...

I was fast asleep in bed when I felt a tap on my shoulder. I almost jumped out of my skin before turning round to see who it was. When I did so it was none other than the original Zig and Zag back for one last performance.

'Hey Chrissie,' Zig whispered, 'we just wanted to say thanks.'

'Yes – and that we'll miss you,' added Zag.

'And, and, and – and!' said Zig triumphantly.

'Oh yes, and!' confirmed Zag.

'Every speech deserves a nice big "and" somewhere in the middle of it, eh Zag?'

'Indeed, brother Zig, indeed.'

They both giggled.

'But hey, Chrissie, just one more thing,' Zig went on in an almost serious voice, as serious as I'd ever heard him, 'we just wanted to say – we love you.'

'Yeah – you silly old ginger-haired megalomaniac,' agreed Zag sincerely. I could feel myself welling up; I had genuine love for these puppets but of course they had to leave on a joke.

'And even though sometimes you think this apartment is yours now, and bring girls back and do things with them, we want you to know that we've seen you in the shower and you have our greatest sympathy.'

'Yeah, no man should have to make excuses for that.' Zag could barely get his words out for laughing.

It was both hilarious and poignant at the same time and at no stage did Mick and Keiron admit to being in the room. It was a moment that will stay with me for ever. That night, for both the first and the last time, it was just the three of us.

Mick and Keiron are still the funniest things on TV anywhere in the world. They host an entertainment show back over in Ireland with their new puppets Podge and Roge, two naughty old Catholic monks – go find it, it's all over YouTube and is as funny as anything I've ever seen.

top
10 Songs Regularly Murdered at Karaoke

10 'Angels'
9 'Dancing Queen'
8 'American Pie'
7 'Hi Ho Silver Lining'
6 'Paradise by the Dashboard Light'
5 'Love Shack'
4 'I Will Survive'
3 'Summer Nights'
2 'The Greatest Love of All'
1 'I Will Always Love You'

The Zig and Zag apartment was also the location of another extraordinary few hours in my young *Big Breakfast* 'celeb' days.

It was coming up to Christmas and I could not have been happier. I was twenty-seven years old, I was on a hit show which I loved, I was staying with the boys in their swish showbiz pad and I had just bought my first Ferrari – a Christmas present to myself.* And as if all that wasn't enough, I was also loved up with the amazing Kim Wilde whom I was now waiting to take to the staff Christmas party.

Because of the phenomenal success of the show Gaby and I thought it only right we pay for all of the crew to go out for a slap-up meal – it was the least we could do. The show was very much an ensemble piece, a huge team effort from which Gaby and I were turning out to be two of the main beneficiaries. We decided to hire the upstairs floor of my favourite Chinese restaurant and told the crew to eat and drink as much as they liked – tonight was on us ... let the revelry commence.

It was around six o'clock on the night of the party and I was sat at home in Docklands, anxiously awaiting the arrival of my superstar

---

* This was a huge big deal for me. I never thought for one second I would ever get such a car of my own – I paid cash for it (all the money I had in the world at the time – £47,000). On top of this, I also had to stump up the insurance premium which, because of my age and job, came in at a whacking fifteen grand a year, which I sorted out with instalments – but hey, I didn't care.

girlfriend. As I had a few moments spare, I walked out onto the balcony to have a think and a cigarette. I'm not a very good smoker but I've always had a go and have to admit I do enjoy the odd fag now and again – usually either when I'm either really happy or really drunk – preferably both.

It was December 1993 and there I was stood out in the cold fresh air, looking over the River Thames, black and deathly swirling menacingly below, as I contemplated what the heck had happened to me in the last few years and how on earth it was that I had come to find myself in such a ridiculously fortunate, almost make-believe, position. I was living the kind of lifestyle which I had only ever seen in the movies. This was one of those surreal moments where the more you dwell on something the less you understand it. It was just beginning to really mess with my head when the phone rang and snapped me out of the need to strain my brain any longer.

I presumed it was Kim to tell me she was outside. I was half right. It was Kim but she wasn't outside, she was nowhere near. In fact she was still at home in Hertfordshire. She was phoning to say she wasn't coming and not only was she not coming to the party, she was never coming again. She said she had been reconsidering our relationship and had come to the conclusion that, in the long term, it was never going to work.

Well, you can't have everything can you – where would you put it all for a start?

I have to admit, however, I was a little rocked by her announcement. Even though I, along with the rest of the world no doubt, secretly suspected I was living on borrowed time as far as being her boyfriend was concerned, I would have loved to take her out this one last time as it was such a special occasion. Having said that, I completely understood why she felt she couldn't come. She would be turning up under false pretences and it was better to be straight with me sooner rather than later. She knew the party was a big deal for me and didn't want to be there for the wrong reasons. I respected her for that.

After putting the phone down, and still in some degree of mild shock, my attention was immediately taken up by the need to order a taxi. Kim's driver was going to take us to the party but seeing as she was no longer coming, neither was he, I presumed. Luckily the local taxi company had a man free and only a few minutes behind schedule I was soon on my way.

I had plenty of time to 'grieve' on the way there. This had been a great year and as much as I might have wanted Kim to be there to share it with us, I couldn't let the news of the death of our relationship dictate the evening. I would go to the restaurant, tell everyone Kim was indisposed and get on with the night.

My friend Dan, a sound engineer at *The Big Breakfast*, called to ask where I was. I said I was en route and that Kim wouldn't be coming but I'd only just found out, which was why I was late. Dan said it was cool and that the restaurant was filling up nicely and that everyone was in a great mood and really excited. He said he would hang on for me in the pub next door so we could have a quick pint before joining the throng.

When I arrived Dan could see something was wrong.

'What's up?' he asked.

'Kim's just finished with me.'

'You're joking,' he said, trying not to laugh. I could see he thought it was hilarious.

'It's not funny,' I said but at the same time suddenly feeling I might start laughing too.

'Oh come on, you knew it was never meant to be. You took a chance in the tent and it paid off – well done. But you didn't think for one second it was going to last, did you? You had no chance.' By now Dan was rolling around on his chair he was laughing so much. Having said that, had things been the other way round I'm sure I would have found his predicament equally as amusing.

Of course he was right. I never had thought Kim and I would be together for very long but nevertheless he could have pretended, for a few minutes at least.

After two very quick pints, through most of which Dan kept bursting into laughter whilst at the same time apologising for doing so, we made our way to the restaurant. As we walked up the stairs we heard lots of loud whispering as if there were some plotting going on. We were right. As we rounded the stairs there was silence and then a crash as the karaoke machine struck up with the chorus of:

We're the kids in America, whoah oh
We're the kids in America, whoah oh

This was no doubt meant to be an overture to the imminent arrival of Kim and me, but upon seeing a severe lack of 'Kim' there was now an awkward scene to the backdrop of the continuing song.

But it was OK. Dan, still on form, declared, 'Look everyone, it is me, Kim Wilde, and I am now a man!'

Dan's witty line got everyone, including me, off the hook. Finally the party could get into full swing with Dan and me still the only two aware that Kim had come to her senses and dumped the ginger kid.

The evening went with a bang, in fact many bangs. It was as if we were a football team and we'd just won some championship or other. We had all worked extremely hard over the last year and now it was time to celebrate. It was going to be a long night.

The food and fizz kept on coming as did the karaoke with the usual mix of surprisingly good and ear-splittingly bad. As the party started to take care of itself I began to relax and my mind began to wander back to Kim and what might have been. I must have floated off into my own little world as after a few minutes I heard a voice saying.

'Chris ... are you OK?' When I realised it was someone talking to me, I looked around to see who. It was Rachel sat opposite me on the same table.

Rachel, as well as being a lovely human being, also happened to be drop-dead gorgeous and particularly so tonight. She was wearing a man's white shirt, open at the collar, cuffs folded back and tied in a knot at her waist, along with a short black skirt, black tights and black shoes. This, added to the fact that she was an ex model, stood close to six foot tall, with long blonde hair and blue eyes meant she was pretty much the hottest totty in town.

I had met her when she turned up to my radio show out of nowhere to enquire about some work experience. Who wouldn't want a girl like Rachel around? I took her on straight away and she proved to be a real grafter.

Rachel Tatton Brown came from a military family so the work and discipline ethic was part of her make-up – maybe this is why she had felt like such a square peg in a round hole when it came to modelling. She also drank pints, one of the many attractive twists to her personality. Rachel and I quickly became firm friends and, not surprisingly, drinking buddies, but never anything more than that. Even though she was absolutely gorgeous there never seemed to be a man around. When *The Big Breakfast* started I put a word in and Rachel got a job answering the phones, which was how she came to be at the party.

It was typically thoughtful of her to notice that I wasn't myself.

'I'm OK,' I mouthed in reply. Rachel frowned unconvinced. I smiled back as if to say don't worry but she was having none of it. She gestured for me to leave the table and join her for a chat. We ended up in a corner of the restaurant next to the loos.

'So come on, what's going on with you then? There's obviously something wrong.'

'Alright if you really want to know, Kim's finished with me.'

'What?'

'Kim's finished with me.'

'When did this happen?'

'Just before I came out, I was waiting for her at home and she called to say it was over.'

'Silly woman, what did she do that for?' She sounded almost as if she meant it.

'What do you mean – what did she do that for?'

'Well, where's she going to get someone as good as you?'

I actually burst out laughing at this point – I think I even may have spat my drink.

'Rachel, that is a lovely thing to say but she's Kim Wilde.' Rachel was having none of it.

'I'm serious, she must be mad.' Drink had obviously got the better of her.

'Don't be silly, Rachel.'

'What are you talking about?' I began to see she might be serious. 'Alright – cards on the table, you idiot. I would love to go out with a guy like you.'

Where the heck was this conversation going?

'A guy like me ... but not me?'

'Of course you. You included – definitely you, you would be my number one choice but you're not interested, you never have been ...'

I thought I was hearing things.

'Not interested,' I exclaimed. 'I had no idea it was an option. I've always thought you were amazing but ...'

'But ... you've never bloody done anything about it – why do you think I came to the radio show? Why do you think I'm always hanging about with you? I fancy the pants off you – I always have.'

At this point you could have knocked me over with a feather – a really small one from a chaffinch perhaps. Rachel was a goddess – the catch of a lifetime. She was nuclear in fanciability terms and what she had just said had left me completely stunned, although not stunned enough to see another glorious window of opportunity opening up. I seized the moment.

'So *you* would go out with *me*?' I recapped.

'Yes – I – would!' she confirmed.

'What, right now, you would be my proper ... full-on ... girlfriend?'

'*Yeeeesssss!!!*' She was becoming extremely animated.

I decided to challenge her. 'Well, kiss me then ...' I was actually going to add, 'in front of all these people,' but I didn't get the chance. She was in there like a shot.

Now this doesn't happen to a guy very often, as no doubt you can imagine. Sure, I was on the rebound and admittedly by only three or four hours to be precise but now I was going out with Rachel – that was fine by me. Had I known how she had felt, I would have asked her out months ago.

The other partygoers were equally as shocked as I was with regards to what was now taking place in the dimly lit corner by the loos but, hey, it was still Christmas and Christmas, as I had occasion to discover before, does funny things to people.

For the rest of the night Rachel and I were inseparable. When the whole group moved on to another party after the restaurant, we were like two kids at a school disco, we hardly came up for air. When we did it was only for a fag or a beer as well as several highly inadvisable tequila slammers dispensed by one of those mischievous hostesses who go round in a cowgirl outfit serving shot glasses from a gun belt.

This was all very well but what, I wondered, was going to happen when it came to home time. I decided to leave it up to the new boss.

'I'm coming home with you of course,' Rachel declared unblinkingly. She was adamant. I was ecstatic. My heart was singing. Happy Christmas!

It had been a highly unpredictable night and it wasn't over yet. In the taxi on the way home poor Rachel started to go the whiter shade of pale that tells you maybe the tequilas were one celebration too far – their evil suddenly beginning to catch up with her. It was now not a matter of *if* she was going to throw up but *when*.

'Can you hang on till we get home?' I enquired.

'How far is it?' she managed to reply, at the risk of the inevitable.

'About another mile,' I said hopefully.

'I think so,' she moaned.

I have to say, considering the situation, her efforts in holding down whatever it was that wanted to come up were nothing short of heroic and thankfully it was only a few minutes before we arrived outside the apartment. As I went to pay the driver, Rachel staggered past me on to the grass verge by the side of the road – it was time.

'Oh please, I really need to be sick,' she mumbled, as now free to do so, something was stopping her. I was holding her up from behind but she was becoming increasingly floppy. I feared she was about to pass out so I did the only thing a newly devoted boyfriend could do. I plunged two of my fingers down her throat.

Immediately they did the trick. Rachel took no time at all in projectile vomiting all over the place and very much all over me – her new beau. Another deal had been sealed. We were in love.

Rachel stayed in the spare room that night and left early the next day, but only to return a few hours later with a bunch of clothes. This would be the first of two Christmases we would spend together.

Another fabulous woman agrees to be in my life.

top
10 TV Shows

10 *Magnum*
9 *Starsky and Hutch*
8 *The Two Ronnies*
7 *The Professionals*
6 *Minder*
5 *Happy Days*
4 *Tiswas*
3 *Morecambe and Wise*
2 *Noel's House Party**
1 *Swap Shop*

The Big Breakfast was becoming the bigger and bigger breakfast by the programme. The day wasn't far off when we would eventually beat the powerhouse that was *GMTV* in the ratings war for viewers, something that had been inconceivable just a year before. After putting the wind up the opposition, our next target was to top the two million viewer mark. Could this really ever be done at breakfast time on a channel that twelve months previously had been watched by only 100,000 people? Thanks to an overwhelmingly ambitious undertaking – *The Big Breakfast* wedding – the answer was yes.

We ran a viewer competition for a couple to get married live on the show. The happy couple exchanged vows in the garden of the house next to a huge

---

* I was the subject of NTV, Noel's surprise bit when he would turn someone's television into a camera and suddenly they would find themselves live on the air in their living room. It was his last show of the series so they upped the ante by secretly setting me up. I was still with Carol at the time, who was completely in on it, and I honestly had no idea that our whole house had been rigged up for broadcast whilst we had been out for most of the day. There is an urban myth that whilst I was lying on the sofa watching *Baywatch* I was caught on videotape in a compromising position due to the onscreen charms of Pamela Anderson. Although a fabulous story, unfortunately this is not at all true, but I can understand why such a tale gathered momentum. I once threw out a million-pound challenge for anyone to produce such a tape but none was forthcoming. There is a very similar story concerning an audio tape and a famous female newsreader. This 'tape' has also strangely never seen the light of day.

marquee which had been erected for the reception. Friends and family plus the whole of *The Big Breakfast* cast and crew made up the congregation. There were tears from the girls and cheers from the boys, not to mention our bosses, as advertisers flocked to book spots on what was fast becoming one of the hottest shows television had seen in the last few years.

It was around this time that Channel 4 started to think about exploiting some of the new talent they'd helped discover. Having never been a primetime player on Saturday night, they thought I might hold the key to them breaking the two main channels' stranglehold on the slot.

They asked me if there was anything I'd like to do as well as *The BB* and perhaps on a Saturday night – which heralded the birth of *Don't Forget Your Toothbrush*. Although not until we had produced no fewer than four pilots at the cost of over a million pounds.

The first pilot was an unmitigated disaster, the second not much better. Now by this point most pilots would be shelved, but the thing was that Channel 4 couldn't walk away – they were too far in. The cost of the pilots had snowballed and there had to be something to show for it at the end. We had to keep on going until we struck oil, which eventually, thank heaven, we did. The ratings for *Toothbrush* reached a peak of four million, another first for the channel and for a while the show became the talk of the television world.

Now how did we come up with it again?

top
10 Expletives

10 Poo
 9 Bum
 8 Arse
 7 Titsville
 6 Arsehole
 5 Cock
 4 Nob cheese
 3 Shit
 2 Fuck
 1 Bollocks

What's wrong with swear words in the first place? More to the point, what's wrong with humans when it comes to swear words? How come we get so hot under the collar about them when it suits us, yet use them all the time on other occasions? We really are a strange lot.

I swear mostly to myself, mostly when I am writing. For the last few years I have been 'wondering', which is really just writing in your head as well as physically getting a lot of it down on paper, about the next big TV quiz format. I have come close several times but nothing that I could honestly say would set the world on fire.

Whatever it might be, it has to follow of course the mighty *Who Wants To Be A Millionaire?* – the most successful quiz show of all time. Sure, there have been others since, like *The Weakest Link* and *Deal or No Deal* for example, but as good as they are – and they have made hundreds of millions of pounds for the people involved with them – they pale in comparison to *Millionaire*.

I remember I was once shown the original pitch document for *Millionaire* that was sent to ITV. It is regarded as the Holy Grail of TV documents and made the hairs stand up on the back of my neck when I first set eyes upon it, almost like the original lyrics from a Lennon and McCartney song. Allow me to describe what it was like.

Created in the days way before coloured inkjets and fancy PC applications, it read from four simple white pages of A4 stapled together in the top left-hand corner. The only words on the first page were:

WHO WANTS TO BE A MILLIONAIRE?

(A stripped, ten-part primetime quiz show for ITV)

'Stripped' means it is broadcast over consecutive nights. The next page said:

ANSWER FIFTEEN QUESTIONS AND WIN A MILLION POUNDS

There was then a pyramid drawing of how the cash built up in fifteen lots from £100 to £1,000,000.

£1,000,000
£500,000
£250,000
£125,000
£64,000
£32,000
£16,000
£8,000
£4,000
£2,000
£1,000
£500
£300
£200
£100

Page 3 explained the nature of the multiple-choice questions.

And finally, Page 4 was the curve ball – there were these things called LIFELINES. In case a contestant wasn't sure about an answer he or she had three 'chances' to ask for help. These were:

FIFTY FIFTY
PHONE A FRIEND
ASK THE AUDIENCE

And that was that – it really is breathtakingly simple but there is genius running all the way through it.

For a start there is no fat, everything that's in there matters. Then there's the contestant selection process, where ten become one via the keypad round – again, quick, simple and highly effective. There's the junctions where on the journey to a million your money is safe and you get a free guess at £1000 and £32,000 – I think this is a particularly clever twist. And the best bit of all? The fact that there is no time limit on the game – so contestants can roll over from one show to the next, thus creating cliffhanger episodes ... unheard of in a quiz show before.

I think when it comes to the TV quiz format, *Who Wants To Be A Millionaire?* is perfect.

Don't Forget Your Toothbrush on the other hand was an 'entertainment' game show – an entirely different kind of animal. Whatever you do, be very wary if you're thinking about coming up with one of these, for they are the hungriest of beasts, devouring energy and ideas by the truckload. The 'entertainment' part is the nightmare because it has to be written and rehearsed every week, whereas the straight quiz or game show like *Millionaire* is more or less the same week in, week out. All you have to do is change the contestants and the questions.

Even though most of *Toothbrush* was unrecognisable from one show to the next, we did still have to invent a workable game which would become the show's regular finale, a mini *Who Wants To Be A Millionaire?*, if you like. In our case it was a thing called 'Light Your Lemon', and when I say 'we' I mean me and my writing partner Will MacDonald.

I first came across Will as a researcher on *The BB*. He was ex Eton and Oxford and yet had managed to retain much of the child in him, something that Walt Disney said was a very important thing for a man to do. Will had agreed to come and work with me and was very much the brains behind many of the ideas that made *Toothbrush* the hit that it became. Will and I sat for days trying to figure out what we could have as our end game.

'What is the most exciting climax to a competition?' we asked ourselves, 'one that already existed and how we could replicate that on television?'

After hundreds of cups of tea and countless bacon butties round at my house, we concluded that there was nothing more sudden death than the simple tossing of a coin – heads or tails, what are you going to go for? It was a tried and tested method of settling the score once and for all, swift, dramatic and guaranteed to produce a result.

Next we looked around for a parallel that used this philosophy but in a more physical sense, the point at which we turned to the wonderful world of football and the penalty shootout.

A penalty shootout, we realised, is basically heads or tails ten times with the goalie and the kicker representing the two players and left or right representing heads or tails.

So this is what we did:

Our contestant would be the goalie and the questions would be the kicker. The questions would be the equivalent of left or right with an A or B answer and the contestant would have to decide which way to go. Each time the contestant guessed correctly, they would light up one of five sections on a cocktail glass – get five right and the last correct answer would 'light up their lemon' and they would be a winner. For every question they got wrong we would light up a section of an ice-cream cone – get five wrong and the last wrong answer would 'flash their flake' and they would lose. *The Weakest Link* uses a similar football penalty shootout format for its final round – have a look next time it's on.

Will and I had come up with our end-game and if your end-game is good enough, it almost doesn't matter how you get there. We were now free to have some fun with the rest of the show.

Ah, the rest of the show!

This is the bit that nearly killed us. Thinking of new ways to surprise the audience every week was so difficult. Will came up with the genius idea of secretly bringing somebody's bedroom to the studio, which went down like a storm. Next we floated somebody else's bedroom out on a barge in the middle of the Thames. There was the week we turned a whole block of flats into a giant hoopla game and invited a pizza boy to throw pizzas through the windows to win himself a brand new Harley-Davidson. Or the time we drove a gay guy in a wardrobe on a forklift truck to Trafalgar Square so he could 'come out of the closet'. How about when we plucked a member of the audience out and then challenged them to run to a waiting helicopter and go and take a Polaroid of Big Ben to prove that our show was live? My favourite though, second only to when I gave my own car away, was when we sent the whole audience off to Disneyland. They all went that night, 400 of them! None of them had the first idea what we were going to do and we didn't have the first idea whether or not we could pull it off. We just went for it and thankfully it worked. Friendships were made for life that weekend – apparently some people who were there still have reunions.

Don't Forget Your Toothbrush did us all proud and it won every award in the world there was to win. It was also my ticket out of early mornings and *The Big Breakfast*. For a time I doubled up doing both, but once *Toothbrush* was a hit, it was time to say goodbye to Gaby and the gang. My last *BB* show would end with me wandering across the lock on my own, clutching a brown paper bag – it was meant to be funny but after crying for most of the show's previous two hours, laughing was the last thing any of us felt like doing. *The Big Breakfast* had set me well and truly on the way to stardom and a life full of all the things I'd ever dreamt about and now, with a deep and sincere sense of loss, it was time to leave it all behind. My departure from *The Big Breakfast* was one of the saddest things I've experienced.

top
10
Great Questions
to be Asked

10 Would you like salt and vinegar on that?
 9 Would you like a drink from the bar before we take off, Mr Evans?
 8 Would you like that wrapped?
 7 Would you mind if I stayed tonight?
 6 Would you mind if my friend also stayed tonight?
 5 Would you like them all in black?
 4 Would you prefer a coupé or a convertible?
 3 Would you like some of Minnie's hotpot?
 2 Would you like some more of Minnie's hotpot?
 1 Would you like to host the Radio 1 breakfast show?

It was a Saturday morning in the early spring of 1996 when Radio 1 came knocking on my door.

After my period lodging with the legendary Zig and Zag, I had moved into my own swanky top-floor penthouse south of the river Thames that the producers of *The Big Breakfast* had rented for me. Seeing as I was still in business with them and doing quite well, they thought it might be prudent to let me hang out there for a little while longer – a situation I was more than happy to take advantage of.

Number 801 Cinnamon Wharf was a magnificent four-bedroomed affair with a huge high-tech kitchen opening onto the grandest of living rooms, which was a vast space flanked with spectacular glass walls and countless sliding doors leading out on to not one, but two balconies on either side. The terraces must have been forty feet long – at least – each boasting breathtaking views across the London skyline with an impressive 270-degree panorama – Canary Wharf lay off in the distance to the east with Tower Bridge just a few hundred metres away to the west. I still think about Cinnamon Wharf from time to time. My mum still thinks about it every day.

'Nicest place you ever owned,' she goes on. Not that I did ever own it – although I could have done. After I'd been there for six months I was asked if I wanted to buy the apartment for £600,000 but said no. Big mistake, as its value today is well into the millions.

During this period *Toothbrush* was doing great business in the UK and it wasn't long before Will and I were being flown first-class over to the States – all expenses paid – to be asked if we fancied a crack at the US market. We went to this big meeting in Los Angeles at Brillstein-Grey Entertainment – the US production company responsible for hits such as *The Sopranos* and *The Larry Sanders Show*. They were based in a large, imposing building with palm trees and a waterfall outside, just down from Rodeo Drive – all very L.A.

The Brillstein of Brillstein-Grey was a Mr Bernie Brillstein, a true Hollywood legend now sadly no longer with us – his funeral saw the whole industry grind to a halt. Bernie was a huge hulk of a guy – the absolute double of Santa Claus – and in many ways that's what he was. Bernie made people's dreams come true. In the Sixties, for example, he met a young Jim Henson and asked him to write down on the back of a restaurant receipt what it was he wanted to achieve. Thirty years later every one of his ambitions had been ticked off that list and both Jim and his Muppets had become world famous.

Bernie's younger partner was a small jet-black haired fireball of a guy by the name of Brad Grey. Brad couldn't have been more different, he was the gunslinger, the deal maker – a fast-talking Joe Pesci type who later went on to become the head of Paramount Pictures.

These guys meant business and didn't waste any time in letting us know – we were hot and they wanted us and to prove it there was a firm offer of $11,000,000 on the table and I mean 'on the table', it was there in black and white for everyone to see. But it was for a minimum period of five years with twenty-two shows a year and would mean us having to move out to the US full time – not an option as far as we were concerned. We had plenty going on back home and on our own terms.

There was no doubt about it, when it came to television we were pretty much ruling the roost. Whereas most people didn't even realise I'd ever been involved in radio before, the irony was that I still had far more experience in radio than I did in television.

When it comes down to it, I am a radio man through and through. I always have been and always will be. There's something much more naked about working in radio that tends to attract very different people from those working in television. Put the majority of radio people in a television studio and they would wonder what all the fuss was about. Put the majority of people from television in a radio studio and their knees would start knocking, in need of a meeting and a cafe latte.

Radio is a much smaller boat all round – there are far fewer berths available – especially when it comes to presenting a daily breakfast show on one of the national networks, the job I was about to be offered. Not only this but seldom do such berths become vacant. If the current 'turn' is any good, he or she can hang on to their slot for years if they want to. As with many things in life – getting the right radio gig is all about the timing.

So what was the time?

It was about half past ten as it happens and I was busy going through that night's *Toothbrush* script before setting off for the studios to host the live show.

It was approximately this time in the morning when I would begin to feel the first nauseous pangs of show-day nerves beginning to rumble inside me. As the words of the script started to swim around on the page, a deep-seated sick feeling in the very pit of my stomach would remind me of all the things that could go wrong with a live show. A situation not helped by the fact that I would never learn a script fully. I don't know exactly why I did this, it was either some kind of masochism or a subconscious ploy to give the show more of an edge, but whatever the reason, it worked, for the show – if not for my well-being.

I was sitting in silence as is my ritual when I am trying to concentrate. I am so easily distracted and will look for any excuse to do something else rather than what I'm supposed to be doing. I have to instil this kind of strict regime on myself to stand any chance of processing even the slightest bits of information. I can also get very grouchy at such times and am best left alone for everyone's sake.

The one problem with absolute silence, however, is that when it's suddenly broken it can scare you half to death, which is exactly what was about to happen. When the telephone rang I nearly jumped out of my skin.

For a start I hardly ever received any phone calls as very few people had my number, and secondly my retro phone had a heart-stoppingly loud 'bring bring'.

After checking I was still alive and hadn't died of a seizure I picked up.

'Hello.'

'Er, hello is that Chris?'

'Yes it is, who's that?'

'Hi Chris, it's Matthew, Matthew Bannister.'

It was the same Matthew Bannister who had given me my first London big break in radio seven years earlier. He had now been drafted in to save the ailing Radio 1, the BBC's station for young people which was foundering due to an identity crisis. This was mainly because most of its DJs were now old enough to be granddads.

Matthew is an all-round top man who, if he hadn't worked for the BBC, would probably have worked for MI5. He is just the tiniest bit more posh than he'd have you know and although he speaks with an indigenous robust flat vowel there is ever such a slight trace of plum fighting to get out. He also has that weird habit of pronouncing words like tissue as 'tiss-yew' instead of the more normal 'tishoo' – something I've never understood but for some strange reason quite like.

Everything that had happened to me since the early Nineties was very much a result of Matthew's gut feeling with regards to my potential as a broadcaster. If you know anyone who doesn't like what I do, you can tell them it's mostly his fault.

'Hi Matthew, what's up?' I asked.

'Well, I just wondered if you fancied coming back on the wireless again to do our breakfast show?' he said cheerily.

'Ah, I see, I was wondering when you'd call,' I replied, half joking.

I say half-jokingly because the fact was I'd heard about Radio 1's problems and in the back of my mind I had secretly nurtured the idea of having a crack at turning things around. Not that I ever thought I'd get the chance. Like I said before, my life was now television – I'd generally accepted that my radio days were over but no, here was Matthew telephoning to offer me one of the biggest jobs in the land.

It was a no-brainer, I didn't hesitate. This was another of those moments in my life that I had to grab with both hands.

'I'd love to do it, when do I start?' I said.

'Are you serious?'

'Of course I'm serious.'

'Excellent, in that case as soon as possible. Can I come and see you today?' Matthew replied, now laughing, at the easy nature of the conversation.

'Alright but you'll have to meet me at the television studios. I'm just about to leave for tonight's show. I'll put your name on the door.'

'Perfect, see you there.'

And with that, basically, it was done.

How did I know it was the right move? Well, the truth is I didn't. I don't think anyone ever does, but it did make me want to go to the loo – immediately. I don't mean to be rude or crass but this is one of my litmus tests. I have a very receptive nervous system when it comes to excitement and if something gets me going, literally, then I always sit up and take note before having to sit down and take care.

With both parties in agreement the next issue (or iss-yew as Matthew might say) was one that I had come to realise as being very important.

If someone asks you to do something that you don't need to do – and that something involves any risk on your behalf – you must make sure the person asking you to do it is also exposed to an equal or preferably greater amount of risk. If they are not, they are in a no-lose situation and you are in a very dangerous one.

This imbalance means that if whatever you're doing together doesn't work, it is all too easy for them to walk away, leaving you high and dry to fight your own corner. This imbalance has to be redressed before any agreement can be reached. I now found myself in such a position. It was time for a little underwriting.

I asked my agent what he thought we should be charging for the contract – and then when he told me, I instructed him to double it.

This instruction wasn't about the money, this was purely about the risk. If Matthew wasn't willing to stump up the cash then I knew he was hedging his bets. I couldn't take a job of such magnitude and one that was bound to have an effect on my highly successful television career on that basis. It simply would not have been worth it.

Matthew said he would sort the money.

It was time for me to go to the toilet again.

top 10 Reasons to Stay Friends with Your Ex

10 You have a friend for the rest of your life
9 There is no bitterness
8 No one has to take sides during or after your break-up
7 When you think about them it will only make you smile
6 You look forward to hearing about them doing well
5 You can compare notes on new partners
4 Their mums don't hate you
3 Their dads don't feel the need to come round and 'have a word' with you
2 There's always the potential of 'one' for old time's sake
1 They might help you find your dream house

For a while now I had been looking for a place 'out of town', as they say. In fact Rachel and I had spent many of our weekends together doing just that – before we broke up.

We had this massive row in the car one Sunday afternoon just as we were coming back over Richmond Bridge from the south side of the river. It wasn't about anything in particular – which I suppose was the point. What I remember most about it is that I did the majority of the shouting while Rachel did the majority of the crying. It was a typical angry boy/upset girl situation. I was angry about nothing, she was upset about everything. After that, things were never really the same again ... we had burst our own bubble and there was no getting it back.

Rachel had left *The Big Breakfast* to come and work alongside me on the first series of *Toothbrush* as my on-screen co-host, and although she had more than held her own on screen it was a role she was never comfortable with. After all, she had spent years being stared at as a model and would rather do anything in the world but that again and yet here she was being thrust in front of not just one, but sometimes as many as ten television cameras and live on a Saturday night in front of the whole nation. Not the greatest decision by either of us.

Rachel longed for less of that and more of something else, something for her to claim as her own, something that would help her find out who she was and what she might want to do with her life, whilst mine was proving a big old shadow to live in. I'd always known what I wanted to do and in that lies a certain freedom, a freedom that must be so frustrating to be around if you're yet to find your own purpose.

As break-ups go, ours was pretty emotional.

It was my birthday and that evening we were due to meet some friends at a curry house in St Katherine's Dock, just over the river from the penthouse Planet 24 had rented for me. We both sensed that we were about to go out and fake it again. Faking the fact that we were happy and jolly for the sake of the party. But Rachel had had enough.

'You go without me,' she said with tears in her eyes.

Stop.

When any relationship breaks down, you can't help but ask yourself how does this kind of thing happen? How do two people who loved each other so much and fell in love for all the right reasons and had so much fun and cared for each other so genuinely end up at such a bleak crossroads?

Hopefully you have never been there but unfortunately most of us have. Other than death and illness, I think it's life's cruellest trick.

I feel sick just thinking about it.

I knew Rachel was doing the right thing by saying she shouldn't come but I also knew that if I did go without her this would be the end.

Stop again.

This is another of those moments in life that no one tells you about. The moment that two people who no longer want to be together suddenly realise that they still love each other deeply and completely but it's never going to work. How could they possibly not love each other? Too much love and laughter has passed under the bridge simply to disappear into thin air, yet there is an inevitable fatality about the situation.

Exactly as I had done the night Rachel and I had got together, the night of Kim and the Christmas party, I ended up going to the restaurant on my own. This time, however, I was not so circumspect when it came to explaining why I was without my partner – most of the guests were 'our' friends rather than my friends so I felt duty bound to tell them what had happened.

'Rachel and I are no more, that's the way it is, it's all very sad, she won't be coming.' How else do you say it?

I then proceeded to get smashed as quickly as I could, I didn't really know what else to do. If I hadn't, I imagined I might run back home into the arms of Rachel at any second only for us to find ourselves in the same heart-wrenching situation again in a few weeks' time. Bertrand Russell says drinking is temporary suicide – that evening I knew precisely what he meant.

Come the end of the night, I ended up staying at a friend's house – apparently, by the time I'd finished I really had no idea where I was. When I did finally come to the next morning I was in total denial. I went straight out again on the tear, right through until the next day. I was too scared to go back to the apartment. Not that it would have mattered – Rachel had gone, back to her old flat. Underneath the tears, she was the strong one – girls often are.

So what happened to Rachel?

Everything she wanted, thank the Lord, including: a fine husband (a huge strapping army officer), a career in television production and just to round it all off, kiddies. And I bet she's the most amazing mum.

All no less than she deserved. She is a truly beautiful human being. I am honoured to have known her and privileged to have been her partner. I wish we'd never had that row in the car on the bridge when she cried and cried and cried, when she cried so much there was no crying left but then we would have stayed together longer than perhaps we should have done. People who love each other do that kind of thing.

What excellent fun it is looking at big houses. Actually the houses Rachel and I looked at weren't *big*-big, those days were still to come, but they were *quite* big – maybe five or six bedrooms with a few acres of land.

Following our break-up, I continued to go 'out' for several weeks during which time the house-hunting was put on hold; however, unbeknownst to me, Rachel was still receiving brochures from the various estate agents she had been dealing with and there was one brochure in particular that caught her eye.

Rachel was so struck with the details of the house in question she took it upon herself to forward them on to me with a brief note saying that she hoped I was well and thought, if I was still looking, this property may well tick all the boxes we'd been after.

I told you she was amazing – how many people would be so thoughtful to do such a thing after they'd split up with someone?

I took one look at the brochure and immediately understood where she was coming from. The house was a perfectly symmetrical white, detached, four-bedroom Queen Anne-style rectory set in four acres of land with a stepped lawn at the back, a horseshoe drive at the front, a paddock and an orchard (both apple and nut!), plus a pond full of koi carp. It also had access to the graveyard and enjoyed a stretch of private fishing on the river that lay behind it.

I started to get butterflies. I had to organise a viewing as quickly as possible.

The property was much further away from London than I would have preferred, down the M20 just off the Brands Hatch junction, but when I arrived there on what was the sunniest of Kent summer days, the place was absolutely beautiful and it was love at first sight. I made my mind up there and then I would do all I could do to buy it.

The couple who owned the rectory were in their fifties and had really good energy. He was a real man's man, bearded with short, cropped silvery hair; he looked extremely fit and strong for his age, the kind of guy whose forearms are bigger than most people's thighs. He was a police dog handler by profession and had that permanent healthy glow of a good life, led mostly outdoors.

His wife was an equally refreshing individual and an international shooting champion of all things – she also happened to be absolutely stunning. She was tall and must have been close to five-foot-ten with an all-over tan and a mop of scraggy sexy blonde hair. When I arrived she was gardening in cut-off jeans, a pair of old trainers and a white vest – 'an outdoors Mrs Robinson,' I thought to myself. She was the kind of woman it's almost impossible to find unattractive. Something I thought it might be wise to try and do, judging by the size of her husband.

The lady and her shooting was a story in itself. The husband had always loved shooting, a sport he'd taken part in for years and whilst his wife hadn't shown the faintest interest in his passion this hadn't stopped him from encouraging her to have a go every now and again   just for a bit of fun more than anything. An invitation she'd thus far declined; however, one day she did decide to have a go and what do you know? She was, as they say, a natural – a crack shot. In fact so much of a natural that within twelve months she was shooting for the British ladies team.

After spending no more than a few minutes in the company of this enchanting couple in what had been their home for the last fifteen years or so, I was filled with one of those overwhelming feelings of how right this all seemed and how if I lived in this house for a while a bit of their magic might rub off on me and my life would be better.

I made them a cash offer of the asking price – on one condition. The condition that the wooden chair I was currently sitting on in the kitchen was part of the deal. It was nothing particularly special, a relatively plain old farmhouse pine kitchen chair with two little curly arms and a worn-down back but it felt so comfortable and would always remind me of the day I first saw my new home.

The chair was thrown in and the deal was done – £350,000 for my own little slice of heaven – a bargain.

To this day it's the best house I have ever owned, plus I still have the chair!

A few months later, Rachel came to see me after I'd completed on the house. I picked her up from the station and the second we turned into the drive she smiled and said,

'I had a feeling about this one.'

top
10 Memories
of Radio 1

10 The morning after I won a Bafta and bent it on the way home
– it was the morning of my first show and the bent Bafta
became the star

9 Taking the Radio 1 Road Show to the Yorkshire town of
Driffield

8 Vic Reeves falling through the floor of a local disco in Newquay

7 Being asked to listen to a group of girls who turned up to
sing in our office – they were called the Spice Girls

6 Tina Ritchie, our newsreader – she has the longest legs of
any newsroom

5 The documentary of our week on the road – *Five Go Mad in
Dorset*

4 The fact that I've just discovered that documentary was in
fact called *Six Go Mad in Somerset*

3 The day we had a brand new Beatles record to play – 'Free
as a Bird'

2 Oasis v Blur and the race to number one

1 The morning after the Christmas party and a phone call from
the boss

My time at Radio 1, like much of life, especially the really good bits, passed
by in a flash – almost like it never happened.

Our new breakfast show was an instant hit with the listeners. I put
together a team of old pals – Holly 'Hot Lips', the glamorous Greek with
the gorgeous voice who worked on *The Greenhouse* at GLR, Dan Dan the
soundman, he of the Kim Wilde dumping me story, and good old John
Revell, whom I met on that first day at Radio Radio, the owner of the
legendary 'lucky tie' that helped us both get our first jobs working for the
BBC.

We were all friends – Holly and I a little more than friends at times –
and all we did every day was go on the radio and have fun. It was a simple
formula but one that worked a treat.

Sometimes all you have to do is 'be' and that's enough, especially when
you are younger. It is the job of the young to write the tunes of the day

whilst the rest of the world looks on. And so it was with us, we just lived out our lives and then went on the radio the next morning and talked about what we'd been up to.

We were doing extraordinary things with extraordinary people and it all made for good listening. All we had to do was stay out for as long as our bodies would allow us, collecting stories and then manage to get up in the morning in time for the start of the show. Something which, contrary to popular belief, we only failed to do once and that was on purpose!

It was Christmas and we were on our Christmas night out. Without telling the team, I had booked them all rooms in a hotel for the night – a fact I gleefully revealed over dinner and one that seemed to go down very well, to say the least – suddenly, the celebrations seemed to go up a notch.

As the revelry went on I got to thinking about the next day's show and how we could best relate to our audience when it came to the infamous subject of the staff Christmas party. The listeners were aware we were going out that night and would want to know what shenanigans had taken place. After a few more beers and a bit more of a think, I declared a eureka moment. I called the troops together at the bar and informed them I had the perfect ruse for the next day's broadcast.

'Team,' I declared, 'I have decided it is our duty to the show, to our listeners and indeed to the country not to turn up for work tomorrow. That is what we must do, for that is real life. That is what happens when people have a Christmas do like we are having this evening and we are but a mirror to what goes on elsewhere. We must not turn up for work – to do so would be to not be doing our jobs properly!' There was also a caveat – for the idea to work properly, none of us was allowed to tell anyone, otherwise cover could be arranged and the impact of our absence would be lessened.

I admit, it sounds totally insane now, but back then, at that very moment, I was genuinely convinced it was the right thing to do – obviously I was very delusional.

At first the team thought I had gone nuts, which I probably had, but I was having none of it and proceeded to order them not to go in. Once they could see I was serious and realised they had no choice – I was the guy who paid their wages after all, as we were an independent production company – acceptance began to sink in and with it a strange euphoria came over the group. This was creative thinking at its most obtuse.

People still to this day don't believe we missed the show on purpose, but I promise you, that's what happened. How else would all of us have failed to turn up?

The morning after the night before I was woken up by a phone call from Matthew B. I was in the hotel room asleep when he called. He was not happy. In fact he was spitting feathers, especially when I told him that it had all been a plan and that there was a creative logic behind it and that he should be congratulating me instead of berating me as he was now.

Matthew said that, if it was a plan, which he still couldn't quite get his head around, then I should have at least warned him as a lot of very nice people had been put to a lot of trouble as a consequence of our no show. Of course he was quite right and being entirely reasonable.

He went on to add that in no way should I expect to be paid for that morning. A little unfair, I felt at the time, as I honestly thought I was doing what was right for the show and especially seeing as the next day we were front-page news – publicity money couldn't buy!

There was no doubt about it, I was beginning to display the first signs of potty-ness.

top
10 Bands on Radio 1
During Our Watch

10 The Boo Radleys
9 Dodgy
8 Cast
7 Space
6 Shed 7
5 Black Grape
4 Blur
3 Oasis
2 Ocean Colour Scene
1 Texas

The figures for *The Breakfast Show* had been on the up almost since the day we'd arrived on the air but more importantly the whole perception of the station had also changed. As a result of our show, and its ripple effect throughout the rest of the station, almost overnight Radio 1 had gone from a museum piece to the heart of the here and now.

The old guard had clung to the wreckage for as long as they could but finally their fingers had been prised away from the driftwood and they were sent floating off to die. Or at least that's how we saw it. This was the Nineties, Britpop was on fire and the new Radio 1 was smack bang in the middle of it.

Every decade needs to define itself but first it has to decide how and it can't do that until it's at least halfway through. This is what had now happened. We all knew exactly what was going on – guitars were back, Britain was the coolest it had been since the Sixties and there wasn't a big hairdo or a shoulder pad in sight. Energy was everything. After the financial boom of the Eighties, bust had given rise to the need for a new generation to assume control. The grown-ups had messed things up: it was time for the kids to take over.

Remind you of anything?

I don't think I'll ever be as excited again in my time on Planet Earth as I was back then. Jesus, it was like a real-life rollercoaster ride that none of us wanted to get off – just thinking about it now makes my pulse race. There was one thing missing, however. We didn't have our own television show.

In television terms every generation gets what that generation deserves, which incidentally says a lot about the last decade with the dominance of *Big Brother*. Back then we wanted our version of the shows that had helped shape the more inspirational things in life: *Ready Steady Go*, *The Old Grey Whistle Test*, *The Tube*, *The Word*, and seeing as no one else seemed set to come up with anything soon, we decided we would have to come up with something ourselves.

I have no idea, not a single clue, how, when, or where we came up with *TFI Friday*. All I remember is that it was 1996 and we needed a place to play.

That place turned out to be a famous old television venue called Riverside Studios.

Located on the north bank of the River Thames no more than a couple of hundred yards from Hammersmith Bridge, Riverside Studios came with an impressive pedigree – there was magic in them there walls. *Top of The Pops*, *Dr Who*, *Dad's Army*, to name but a few, had all been filmed there.

Round the back of the building there was a terrace that looked out onto the water whilst inside there was one cavernous main studio simply begging to be filled with the energy of entertainment again. There were rooms we could use for production offices and four rooms next to the main studio that served as dressing rooms.

It was perfect.

Again, however – just like *Toothbrush* had been – when it came to the pilot, *TFI* was a disaster.

In the pilot the interviews took place downstairs, alongside where the bands played; the upstairs bar was meant merely as a 'star bar' for the guests to hang out in while waiting to appear. As I watched the pilot back it became obvious that the place to have fun was the more intimate atmosphere of the star bar and not the abyss of the main studio.

The upstairs bar was much more conducive to what we needed for our non-music segments, plus it meant the audience would be within just a few feet of all the guests, which would hopefully heighten the excitement on a show where the atmosphere was going to be paramount to its success. With the guest walk-on also passing through the audience, there was a good chance if you were in the bar, you would almost certainly be on camera – this should help charge the atmosphere even further. The bar's low roof would also be much more efficient when it came to holding in the laughter, applause and other audience reaction.

Then when it was time for a song, the handheld camera could whip 180 degrees – leaving me at my desk to go and 'find' the band by diving downstairs into a frenzied mass of people as the band exploded into action.

This one simple change sorted out the whole problem of our lacklustre and confused pilot. From that point on we were good to go and looking at a run of close to two hundred shows over the next five years.

To have an entertainment show is one thing but to have an entertainment show with music is entirely another. If you can get it right and make it work there is no more fulfilling combination. Each week has its own soundtrack – a new moment in time in which to exist – like a mini movie.

There is one major problem, however: music on its own doesn't rate on television. It never has done, with the one exception of *Top of The Pops* in its heyday. This is why TV producers have to wrap the music up in something else. For us on TFI we chose jokes, stunts and guests but we loved our music and we loved our bands so we stuck them in right at the top, then again in the middle – as well as at the end – and with the help of all the nonsense in between people did stay tuned. Praise the Lord, we had another big fat hit on our hands.

All the music on *TFI* was always 100 per cent live and we only ever had bands on that we liked – they were glad to be there, we were glad to be there – and as a result we hoped the viewers would be too. The central philosophy behind the show was that everyone watching would be in a great mood already as it was Friday night and time for some fun. All we really had to do was help them on their way.

TFI would be screened twice a week within a few hours every Friday night. First of all at teatime for those just arriving home and getting ready to go out and again later at around 10.30 for those who had decided to stay in or were returning from their own night of partying. This nightly repeat gave the show and the acts double the exposure as well as giving Channel 4 double the value – two shows for the price of one. Everyone was happy – everyone was rocking.

Would I bring it back tomorrow? Absolutely.

Would it work? Probably not. Ha ha!

top
10 *TFI* Moments

10 Puff Daddy turning up with his new girlfriend
a sweet young thing called Jennifer Lopez. I talked to P. Diddy at the desk while J Lo stood at the bar having a beer, none of us – including her – had any idea she was ever going to be the big star she became in her own right.

9 David Bowie coming to perform
and having so much fun he stuck around and played for half an hour after we had gone off the air.

8 St Patrick's Day live from Dublin
while hundreds of people were packed inside the venue and thousands cheered outside in the street, U2 came and played acoustically at the desk.

7 Tara Reid when she came on to promote the first *American Pie* movie
Tara ended up staying at my apartment for the rest of the weekend after casually asking me in the dressing room, 'Do you know any good pubs?' I couldn't believe my ears.

6 Comic Relief – our red nose special
the night when we didn't go on the air until after midnight – the only time a rival channel has shared their airtime for the Red Nose event. We simulcast the show on both BBC 1 and Channel 4 and had close to seven million people watching, achieving an audience share of 66 per cent – still a record as far as I am aware.

5 McCartney taking over the whole show
and then running off stage at the end out to the terrace and down a gangway we had built so he could jump straight into a waiting speed boat to shoot off down the Thames back to Rockstarland.

4 The night we gave away a million pounds
we became the first TV show in the world to give away £1,000,000. It was to a bloke called Ian. I had to get one up on the brilliant Who Wants to Be a Millionaire? somehow!

3 When Geri kissed Kylie
Geri (Halliwell) snogged Kylie (Minogue). 'Have Kylie and I

got something special for you,' Geri assured me before the show. Of course it's on YouTube.

2 New Oasis album officially dead
we opened one episode of our show by trying to resuscitate the new Oasis album Be Here Now. *It was not a good album. Danny wrote this skit where I would have a defibrillator held against the album in an attempt to bring it back to life as if it were a heart attack victim.* Be Here Now – *which is the last thing the album appeared to want to do – was a dog in my opinion and as nobody would say a word against Oasis at the time, what we did was all the funnier in my eyes. Noel Gallagher hasn't spoken to me since. His brother Liam and I, on the other hand, get along fine – a far more convivial individual altogether.*

1 The *Lock, Stock and Two Smoking Barrels* special
my personal favourite.

The *Lock, Stock and Two Smoking Barrels* special was one of those things that was just meant to be. It was entirely unplanned and all came about as a result of us booking a particularly 'difficult' songstress.

Frankly, from the moment she arrived at Riverside Studios she was a complete pain in the arse – like not just a bit of a pain in the arse but a massive pain in the arse – so much so that in the end I felt duty bound to tell 'my people' to tell 'her people' she had to go.

One minute she did want to perform, the next minute she didn't want to perform and then she was willing to be interviewed and the next minute she wasn't. She spent the whole of the afternoon changing her mind whilst the rest of us waited around trying to finalise a running order – something she was making it increasingly difficult for us to do. In the end I'd simply had enough.

'Tell her thank you very much but we won't be needing her any more – tell her she can have the rest of the day off,' I said to Suzi, our music producer who also happened to be my girlfriend at the time. We'd met on *The Big Breakfast*, and had got it together after I'd split up with Rachel.

'Really?' said Suzi.

'Absolutely – tell her to go and bother some other TV show. This one has had enough of her.'

'If you're sure,' she smiled.

I couldn't help feeling like Suzi had been waiting to do something like this for years. In her time as a music producer and before that as a guest booker she had been made to suffer this type of precious luvvy behaviour on far too many occasions. I could swear I almost saw her salivating upon hearing that she now had full permission to tell one of them where to get off.

When news of our desire for her to depart first reached the particular diva in question, apparently she didn't believe it, thinking it was some kind of joke – who would dare throw her off any show? Ultimately I had to go and tell her myself, whereupon she apologised but it was too late – she had caused far too much trouble and we had all had more than enough of her.

Now although this briefly painted me as the hero to my team, it also left us with a fourteen-minute gap in our programme – not an ideal situation as we were due on the air in under three hours.

So what did we do?

We had no choice but to look at what we had left, and see if there was anything more we could do with it.

We were due to have Vinnie Jones on to talk about a new British film he was in. Everyone was getting very excited about this new movie along with its young director – a kid called Guy Ritchie. Guy was coming along with Vinnie as well as half of the cast. In the end, this was all the material we needed.

There were potential guests everywhere if we wanted them so we immediately declared a *Lock, Stock and Two Smoking Barrels* special. The film, the cast and Mr Ritchie dominated that night's proceedings and it ended up being one of our best ever shows. When we went to air it looked like we'd been planning it for weeks – the karma police were on our side that night.

Ultimately though I think *TFI* will always be remembered for the music, as it should be. The music was the furnace that fired the rest of the machine.

It's amazing how many musicians I still meet today who cite their inspiration as watching *TFI* every week as a kid. Kids want to be what they see on TV. When they watched our show they wanted to be in a band, and there's nothing wrong with that.

10 There are several renowned wig wearers
9 Famous people act like friends when they've only just met
8 The lesser the talent, the bigger the ego
7 The more famous they become, the less they want to pay for things
6 Chauffeurs know almost everything
5 Make-up artists know the rest
4 The only thing celebs hate more than being chased by photographers is not being chased by photographers
3 You have no idea who really likes you
2 All comedians are mad
1 Everyone loves Kylie

The combination of a national breakfast show on the Beeb and the hippest music/entertainment show on the box had turned into a formidable and powerful combination which ensured us all the best guests, all the best bands and more press than we knew what to do with.

The press was both good, bad and in between. 'All publicity is good publicity', as the saying goes, but bad publicity was way better as far as we were concerned.

For a while the BBC liked their new spiky image and so did I – it was helping haul the previously dust-covered lurching giant back into the present day while making me feel like a rock star in the process.

Nobody really minded that we were being 'naughty' – at least if they did they never said anything. I wasn't a bad kid after all and most people knew that in my heart of hearts I had a genuine love for what I was doing. Although admittedly I was acting a little more strangely of late, I was still breaking new ground and for now that was enough … just.

Things were definitely changing though. I was changing. Those oh so important lines of what's real and what's not were becoming increasingly blurred. Writers may inhabit the lives of their characters for a while but only for as long as they need to, a lesson I was yet to learn as I continued to get lost in my world of make-believe.

Take my thirtieth birthday, for example.

We finished the breakfast show and immediately hot footed it over to the Langham Hilton Hotel which was opposite Radio 1. I had hired a suite for the day. This is where my party would take place.

The 'celebration' started at around five past nine in the morning, straight after the show.

Whatever anyone wanted they could have, which is probably why so many people turned up. By lunchtime it was like midnight – there's something far more rebellious about starting drinking earlier on in the day. Suddenly the clocks didn't matter – the world was on our time. New arrivals greeted this daylight mayhem with shock, but that soon gave way to excitement as they quickly decided to throw caution to the wind and pile in themselves to play catch up.

I set myself up in the drawing room to play cards with a couple of pals, helped along with a bottle of whisky, several packets of cigarettes and a case of beer. I don't think I left the table, other than for toilet breaks, until well into the evening. All day I remember the flow of human traffic was non-stop; people came and went constantly, some of them popping in during their lunch break and then coming back again once they had finished work. Several presents arrived from various newspapers as they heard what was going on and were desperate to get in the door.

By the end of the night there were corpses everywhere. I have no idea what the final body count was but my last vision of the scene was of me stumbling out of my bedroom in the early hours of the next morning to go and do the show. I had to carefully step over some additional 'guests', the majority of whom looked like they might never wake up again.

There was no doubt about it, we were having 'fun' and lots of it. But whereas a couple of years before when in between the fun I would sit at home quietly figuring out the next big idea, now I was just out – all the time. Sure I was turning up for work every day but the fuel gauge started to register dangerously low.

Energy wasn't the issue. I was young and relatively fit, plus, as the breakfast show was so early in the morning, I was still generally on a buzz from the night before whilst we were on the air: anyone who knows will tell you a hangover doesn't properly kick in until lunchtime and by then I would be at the gym.

The problem was more about creativity. The ideas machine had stopped because I had stopped. As a person I had ceased to be. I had vanished into thin air and been replaced by a made-up character surrounded by other made-up characters.

The problem was that we no longer had a script and when the actors start making up the words it's time to run for the hills.

top
10
Signs You Are
Losing the Plot

10 You stop looking at bills in bars and restaurants, just handing over your card instead. You pay for everything for everyone all the time
9   Everyone you call a friend is on your payroll
8   You stay in hotels because it's easier than getting a taxi home
7   When you're in a bar, tired, you order another drink instead of going to bed
6   You think it's alright to wear sunglasses any time of the day or night inside or out
5   You start to call people 'man'
4   You look for yourself first in the papers before considering what might be happening in the rest of the world
3   You think you are as talented as the artists you interview
2   You contemplate there may be at least one comedian in the world that might not be insane
1   You advise your boss to fire you as the best way forward from a job you love and have dreamt about doing since you were a kid

The day after my thirtieth birthday party, Matthew asked if he could see me. He asked me to meet him at a restaurant called The Heights – an establishment no more than half a minute's walk from Broadcasting House and, as its name suggests, it's pretty high – high enough to see a spectacular view of the north-London skyline.

Matthew smiled nervously – he was obviously concerned and wanted to discuss something. He asked me how that morning's show had gone.

'Fine, it was fine, thanks, now what's up ?' I thought it best to cut to the chase as I could see his mind was elsewhere

'Alright, well, seeing as you ask ...'

'Here it comes,' I thought.

'Look, Chris, we have a situation and that situation is that things are becoming difficult to say the least with the powers that be.' The powers that be that he was referring to I presumed to be the BBC's board of governors.

'What do you mean?' I enquired.

'Well, Chris, you're in the papers every day ...' This was true – there had been a recent report out that the three most written about people in the UK with regards to column inches were Princess Di, me and then the Prime Minister.

'... and not always for the right reasons,' he continued, 'things have been fun for a while but there is growing concern that maybe we should be reining things in a little – i.e. reining you in a little. All I'm really asking is that you give me a chance to defend you, something I'm finding it increasingly difficult to do.'

I could completely see where Matthew was coming from. The lack of ideas on the show meant that I had begun to become more self-indulgent on the air – all I ended up talking about was myself. When I wasn't doing that I was talking about things that had little or no place on a national breakfast show. I was playing fewer and fewer records – one morning I went almost an hour without playing a single song at all, thinking that what I had to say was far too important and interesting to be interrupted by something so trivial as music. In short, I had lost all perspective.

As well as that, the shape of the show had all but disappeared – something I used to pride myself on.

I was also becoming more 'outrageous', another euphemism for someone running out of steam. Outrageousness, unless you're nineteen and in a band, is no substitute for creativity – it never has been and never will be. When outrageousness begins to creep in, everyone should sit up and switch to code red because unless somebody does something about it – and quickly – time will be called and everyone will be asked to leave.

Both Matthew and I knew this but whereas Matthew was trying to do something about it – for all our sakes – I was still very much away with the fairies.

'You know what you should do, Matt?' I suggested excitedly.

He looked at me almost shocked that such a grave topic of conversation could elicit this kind of frenzied reaction.

'No, I don't actually,' he said, almost indignantly, 'please – do tell.'

He was now looking at me as if he didn't recognise me, like I might be ever so slightly insane. He wasn't far off the mark. No sleep and twelve months of going out does that to a person, but no matter – I had big news for him.

'You should sack me,' I declared triumphantly.

'What?'

'You should sack me,' I repeated with the glee of the crazy man who'd taken up residence in my head.

Matthew was speechless – had I just said what he thought I'd said?

'I don't understand,' he remarked, but there was more, I hadn't finished yet.

'Come on, if you think about it, it's simple,' I went on. 'You had the balls to bring me here – it worked – everyone acknowledges that. Now if you further have the balls to dispense with my services – you'll be the complete hero. He knows when to hire and he knows when to fire.'

What on earth was I rabbiting on about? I must have been so far gone. I honestly thought it was a brilliant idea – like when The KLF burnt a million pounds in cash in the name of art – filmed it and then nobody gave a hoot. D'oh!

I hadn't for one second contemplated that there wasn't another Radio 1 for me to go to if Matthew did take up my idea. I had forgotten that this was the job I had always dreamt of having – the show I used to listen to while driving in the Mini my mum bought me to go to work collecting trolleys at the local supermarket for £40 a week. The very same show I was now recommending I be relieved from – and by a very nice man to whom I owed a good chunk of my career.

I even went on to suggest to Matthew who he might want to replace me with!

'Chris, have you considered taking a holiday?' he sighed.

top
10 Things a Celeb Should Never Do

10 Forget about the things that made them famous
9 Fight their battles in public
8 Forget those who helped put them where they are
7 Forget it's the public who keep them there
6 Fall in love with the press
5 Disrespect the old-timers
4 Refuse to sign an autograph if they have time – ever
3 Google themselves
2 Appear smiling in a picture with a politician*
1 Complain about anything – celebrities are the luckiest people on God's earth and can bow out any time if they want to

The situation at Radio 1 was clearly no longer sustainable – and sustainability along with consistency, I have come to realise, is what real success is about. Anyone can make a splash in even the biggest of pools but not many of them stick around to see if they can swim.

*

It was now evident to all concerned that this particular incarnation of Britain at breakfast was living on borrowed time. We had set the bar too high. This kind of show is a marathon and we had committed the fatal error of setting off at a sprint, and we were quickly running out of legs. For me the writing was on the wall – all good movies must end but if they take too long to do so, the audience will already have gone home.

And so it was.

I decided to force the issue and asked Matthew if I could have Fridays off – a ridiculous request and one that I knew was bound to end in tears.

My reasoning behind the plea (as if reasoning was any part of my world at all by now) would be that *TFI* was causing me to hold back my energy on the breakfast show in the morning and yet when I arrived at the television studio in the afternoon I was so tired anyway I was unable to do either job sufficiently well – so why not let me have the radio off so I could concentrate on TV?

Matthew responded in the only way he could. He said the request was highly unreasonable and smacked of disrespect and ingratitude. The same breakfast show had to run five days a week – no question. This was not now, nor had it ever been, negotiable. He stated in no uncertain terms that I was backing him into a corner and, if I continued to do so, there was only one course of action available to him. If I persisted with such a ludicrous demand we would have to part company.

This was all I needed.

I decided to jump before I was pushed but I did what you should never do.

I resigned on the air.

When it comes to being a DJ, resigning on the air is the single most defining quality of the loser – the drama queen – the coward – the desperate individual so consumed with his own hubris he decides to drag us all through his turgid suicide in the hope of gaining some kind of sympathy in the process.

I remember listening to a DJ who had done exactly the same thing several years before. I had the radio on in my car and had to pull over to fully appreciate what I was hearing. He was pompously declaring how his situation on one of the greatest radio stations that had ever existed had now become untenable and how the management no longer 'understood' him. I remember thinking that he sounded like the most ungrateful sanctimonious prick I had ever heard.

What he was saying was bordering on fantasy – was this guy for real? The more he droned on and on and on, the more excruciating and unbelievable it became.

'Hey pal! Like any of us give a damn.'

'Who would think to do such a thing?' I felt like shouting at the radio. 'When exactly did you have your brain removed? Precisely how far up your own rectum have you disappeared?'

The misunderstood DJ – please, do us all a favour. Has there ever been a less worthy cause on Planet Earth?

When it comes to being a DJ there is no message, there is no art – sure there is a connection with his/her audience and there is a lot of hard work (sometimes) but it's not art, it never has been and it never will be.

What it is is one of the greatest jobs in the world and the lucky buggers who get to do it should be on their knees from morning till night giving thanks, not bleating about how they can no longer go on.

For Socrates the hemlock, for George Best the bottle, for Hemingway the barrel of a shotgun, but seriously – a DJ!!! And this guy wasn't even threatening to kill himself, more's the pity, he was merely informing us that he was not going to be on the air any more!

And yet here was I, the same prize penis, the same high-falutin phallus, about to do exactly the same thing.

'Please somebody stop me from sounding like a total cretin and throwing away one of the best jobs on the planet,' I should have begged. But it was too late, for now I had also disappeared all the way up my own back passage.

CHRIS EVANS 1996–1997: A NATION YAWNS

That's how *Private Eye* put it. How right they were.

So.

Brilliant.

What a genius.

I now had Fridays off.

In fact I had the whole week off.

All supposedly to get ready for just '48' minutes of television. 'Oh my art.'

As a result of my 'resignation' I had caused absolute carnage, lost much of the respect I had worked so hard to build up over the years as well as a whacking great pay cheque in the process. And the worst thing of all? I had acted like a spoilt child – something I had never been and something that inherently represented everything I was against.

In short, I think we could safely say I had lost the plot, like when the participants of reality shows burst into tears because they haven't seen their family for three days whilst there are soldiers that haven't seen their family for months getting shot at in Afghanistan – that sort of thing.

And you know when you get that feeling deep down inside that tells you you 'know' you've made a grave error?

Well – I knew. I knew for sure. I knew that I had made the most colossal, misguided error of judgement. I didn't let on of course, not to anyone, but inside I was already dying.

I was dying because I knew that for the first time in my career, for the first time since asking Ralph for a paper round, for the first time since finishing with Tina for a quick snog with the captain of netball team, for the first time since walking out of the miserable git's shop after he confiscated my radio, for the first time since dropping a fat fryer on Bill's car when I was a forklift truck driver, for the first time since setting fire to the OB truck at Piccadilly Radio, for the first time since recording over the Geldof tape, for the first time since kissing Kim in the tent on *The Big Breakfast*, for the first time since I bought my first flash car, for the first time since I had been married to Carol, for the first time since having the conversation in the pub with Alison about Jade, for the first time since I made all those mistakes along with the countless others that you are bound to make if you dare to get out of bed in the morning and live this thing called life – for the first time since all of those things, I had *really* messed up and although I had messed up many times before, the thing was – on this occasion – I should have known better. Therein lay the difference.

Everything that I had experienced up until this point I could square with myself one way or another. Regardless of whether it ended up being right or wrong – I could reason in my head as to why or why not it may have happened. But this was not like that.

Success, once achieved, exists, whereas before it did not. Therefore it can no longer be ignored – hoping it won't have an effect, hoping it won't change things. Success has to be dealt with, it has to be fed and watered and looked after and given a place to sleep. Success is a wonderful thing, in the right hands – it is wholly good and can achieve many things if harnessed and exploited in the right way. But if abused, it can be lethal, a ferociously powerful racing car on a wet road being driven by a blind man wearing lead boots.

In the last four years I had undoubtedly achieved 'success', success beyond my wildest dreams, but it was obvious I didn't have the first clue what to do with it.

It was time for a think.

top
10
Things I Think About –
Other than My Wife and Family

10 Life
9 Death
8 Flying
7 Number plates
6 Cars
5 Getting old
4 Sex
3 Work
2 Food
1 My belly

I'm very happy when I am thinking. I often wonder how other people think. Do they think quickly or do they think slowly? Do they think only when they have to? Do some people not think at all – scared of what their thoughts tell them? Are these the sort of people who deal with life by 'getting on with things' to occupy their mind?

TFI was still on the air and was now more of a priority than it had ever been. After having made such an unnecessary fuss about how much effort it took to make, I was now thinking how I needed to ensure the next few episodes were up there with the best.

Cut to:

My house in Kent.

As soon as the house in Kent was mine I spent as much time there as I possibly could. The commute to work was a long way – especially at four in the morning – but whenever I returned after the radio show around lunchtime, it was always worth it. It didn't hurt that I was also now travelling to and from London in a sparkling black Bentley complete with tinted windows and a dark green leather interior – the next little beauty in my life-line of automobiles.

As soon as I laid eyes on it, I thought it was such a special car, or 'motor car' as Bentley refer to them. It was also the first car to which I had a carphone fitted. This phone, although cutting edge at the time, was a big old brick of a thing that somehow managed to fit into the central console. I remember being highly amused when I had to record the answer phone message, which was the opposite of the one I had on the phone indoors:

'Hello, this is Chris. I'm at home right now but leave a message and I'll call you as soon as I go out.'

The most important phone call I took on this revolutionary new innovation was from none other than Michael Grade during the second series of *Toothbrush* when the BBC were after me to sign an exclusive television contract with them. I was on the M20 when Michael, still in charge of Channel 4, rang to tell me in no uncertain terms that this was not something that was going to happen and he had a cheque for £500,000 waiting on his desk for me that said so.

'So, Michael, let's be clear about this,' I shouted into a microphone, the location of which I had no idea, 'what do I have to do to get that cheque again?'

'You have to sign a piece of paper with us that says you won't sign a piece of paper with anyone else,' echoed his reply.

'That's it?'

'That's it.'

'Cool.'

Having the carphone fitted to my marvellous new Bentley was one of my better decisions.

By now I had left the penthouse and bought myself a new place in London back in my old manor of Belsize Park, where my first little studio house was and where Carol and I had enjoyed all those crazy times when I first moved down to London. This latest place was a modern two-bed flat but set in a period building. It was very 'of the moment'. I bought it off a woman who seemed to become agitated every time any men were around her. At first I thought she 'batted for the other team' until I learnt that she used to be married to a bloke in a well-known band who had ended up running off with the female lead singer. As a result she had decided to hate all men for the rest of her life, and she could barely bring herself to speak to me.

As much as I loved my new little crash pad, after Radio 1 – The End, I decided it was probably a good idea if I holed up in Kent more permanently for a while. It was the secure gated fortress that I needed. The press were intent on following me everywhere and although I was more than used to this 'intrusion' (if you don't want to be intruded upon don't become famous), I hadn't yet decided where my story was going to go from here and I didn't want to give them the chance to write the next chapter.

It was now the following Tuesday after the Friday I walked out of Radio 1. Tuesday was always the day we would get together to talk about *TFI Friday* and this was to be no exception. Myself, the producers, who consisted of Will and another couple of characters – Dave and Stephen – and our writer, none other than Mr Danny Baker himself, would meet up at wherever I was staying and after an hour or two of shooting the breeze, we would eventually turn our attentions to what we thought might be interesting and fun to put on that week's show.

We would draw up a wish list of ideas that the producers would then research while Danny would go off and conjure up a script. Thursday would see the script emerge – hopefully – and then we would be all set for rehearsals on Friday.

As the script often made reference to some of the week's more popular news stories, we were first faced with the question of whether to include anything with regards to what had happened between myself and Radio 1 as it had been the story on many of the front pages.

We decided I would acknowledge it at the top with a quick remark or gesture but other than that we would steer clear. Instead we would concentrate on what was going on in the rest of the world and the guests we had already booked – one of whom just happened to be the legend that is John Cleese.

John Cleese rarely appeared on chat shows and had only agreed to appear on ours if he could help write his part of the script. We had no problem with this – on the contrary, we were very much looking forward to working with a real-life Python and co-writer of the great *Fawlty Towers*.

Now what you need to know next is that John is a perfectionist and is renowned for his attention to detail. He had acquired my home number and had already been on the phone the week before, enquiring as to how the script was going and when he could have a copy. After several minutes of my explaining to John that this wasn't how *TFI* worked and how we didn't write the script until a couple of days before the show to keep it fresh and current, he said he understood and was happy. In the course of our conversation I also told him that we would begin writing his show on the following Tuesday morning and assured him that as soon as we had anything worth reading he would be the first to know.

So, one hour into the *TFI* meeting at my house in Kent, with the press still camped outside the main gates and us scratching our heads inside over ideas for the show, the phone rang. After excusing myself from the meeting, I went to answer.

'Hello,' I said.

'Ah, hello, Chris, John here, John Cleese. Hope I'm not interrupting – how's the writing going?'

Fair enough, I suppose, it may have only been mid morning but it was Tuesday after all and Tuesday is the day I had told him we would be working on his script.

'Ah, hello, John … we're just getting on to your bit now,' which we were – sort of. 'As soon as we have something I'll get it to you.'

'Ah, good, good, that's excellent. Now the thing is I'm on a plane, you see.'

He was calling me from a plane! I had no idea that was possible.

'Really?'

'Yes, I'm calling you from a plane on my way to my apartment in New York.'

This was cool; a little mad – but cool.

'Do you think you could fax whatever you have to me there so I can get to work adding my bits and bobs when I get home?'

'Yes John, of course, sure thing.'

I took down his fax number, said goodbye and returned to the boys.

'It was Mr Cleese,' I offered. 'I don't know what he's expecting from us but it'd better be good. He wants us to send whatever we come up with to him in New York to his apartment so he can add his "bits and bobs". He's on a plane by the way.'

'He called you from a plane!' remarked Danny.

'Yeah – I know, how cool is that?'

'Man – you've got to love The Pythons.'

After talking about the plane aspect of the scenario for a while (on script day we loved to talk about anything but the script until we absolutely had to) there was now ever such a slight note of tension creeping into our meeting.

What could we offer John that was different? What kind of thing was he expecting from us?

After a few minutes of chin stroking and temple thumbing, I suddenly had a lightbulb moment. The kind that comes out of nowhere but seems to solve all your problems at once as if someone's been working on them secretly for years on your behalf.

'How about John wanting the script so badly and us getting it to him is the thing?' I suggested.

'Go on,' said Danny, intrigued.

'Well, how about I tell the story of how it's such a big deal to have John Cleese on the show and how we didn't want to upset him and how much he wanted to see the script and how we decided, in the end, the best thing for us to do was hand deliver the script to John himself at his apartment in New York.'

'And so?'

'And so – we go to New York.'

'What do you mean we go to New York?'

'We all go to New York to do what I just said.'

'When?'

'Today – and we film it. That's the joke. We play in the film and on walks John with the script in his hand and we start the interview.'

'Marvellous!' declared Danny.

The producers giggled nervously, wondering whether we were joking. One hour later with the six of us hurtling towards Heathrow in the Bentley, they realised we were not.

The budget for *TFI* was very healthy to say the least, although naturally some weeks we spent less than others. This was not going to be one of those weeks. In fact we were on our way to film what is probably the most expensive thirty seconds of video footage in the history of light entertainment television.

As we made our way from Kent to the airport, the press, whom we'd all but forgotten about, were back, hot on our heels, bless them. We thought it was hilarious that they had no idea we were off to New York and if they wanted to stick with us they were going to need more than a car – namely:

A. Their passports
B. A return ticket on Concorde.

No sooner had we convinced the producers that this idea was a runner and that we were serious than the great wheels of television production started to swing into action – an impressive machine when firing on all cylinders.

Motorcycle couriers were dispatched to retrieve various passports from incredulous wives and girlfriends. Travel agents were deployed to organise airline tickets. Cars were booked on both sides of the Atlantic and a laptop computer and printer was being delivered to Heathrow's Concorde Lounge. The Concorde aspect of the ruse was what took the whole episode on to a different level and one that would provide our adventure with a twist all of its own even before we took off.

We had discussed 'briefly' the cost of what we were about to do and had somewhere along the line managed to convince the production manager that Concorde was a necessity if we were to get there and back in time.

There – in time to deliver Mr Cleese his script.

Back – in time to prepare the rest of the show for Friday.

It was a distinct advantage that I also owned the company, of course.

Six tickets for Concorde at £7000 each – that was £42,000 – plus a further couple of thousand on top for who knows what.

New York, here we come.

But not so fast, sonny, it was time for the twist.

top
10
Offers I
Have Declined

10 To appear on practically every celeb-based reality show you
    have ever heard of – not in a million years would I even
    consider it

9   To appear on *Question Time* – one of my fave shows but no
    way would I ever go on

8   To appear on *Newsnight* – as a result of several news stories,
    the biggest of which was losing my court case against the
    Scottish M… (sorry can't bring myself to say the name)

7   To host *Deal or No Deal* – Noel was welcome to that one;
    though I'm not a fan of the show I think he does a sterling job

6   To listen to the Spice Girls back at Radio 1 – Simon Fuller
    didn't forgive me for that for years, saying I was needlessly
    rude, which I was and I apologise

5   To host a new version of *The Generation Game* – nearly did
    but just didn't feel right in the end

4   To buy a 1960s Ferrari GTO when they were still in my price
    range – they arc now £15,000,000!

3   To be the subject of *This is Your Life* – twice!

2   To sell my shares in that company that I can't bring myself to
    say the name of, when they were worth £37,000,000. The same
    shares eventually fell to the value of just under £300,000 and,
    yes, I still owned them. I rationalise it as God's way of letting me
    know how big and ungrateful a schmuck I had become

1   To host the Virgin Radio drivetime show – before I went on to
    own the station; not the best offer but by far the best story

On the way to the airport I received a telephone call. It was from my good
friend and agent, Michael Foster. Michael is a very small Jewish man, as
equally proud of his heritage as he is unphased by his lack of height.

'Chris, Richard Branson just rang – he wants you to sign for Virgin
Radio and he wants you to sign now.'

'What?' I replied. My life has been full of these kind of 'whats'.

'He says it's the perfect time to capitalise on what's happened over the
last few days with Radio 1 and that you still belong on the radio and you
sound like more of a Virgin man than a BBC man.'

'Wow.'

'Oh, and he says you can have Fridays off as well.'

The guys in the car could hear what was going on and were nodding their approval.

'So what do I have to do?'

'He wants you to go and see him this afternoon to do the deal.'

'Er ... I can't do that.'

'Why not?'

'I'm going to New York.'

'I'm sorry it sounded like you just said you were going to New York.'

'I am.'

'You are.'

'Yes.'

'When?'

'Now.'

'Why?'

'To deliver a script to John Cleese.'

'What?'

After I explained, or rather attempted to explain to my agent what we were doing and why we were doing it, there was a brief moment of silence at the other end of the line ...

'I'll get back to you. Make sure you stay near a phone,' he snapped.

No more than three or four minutes later the phone rang again. When Branson sees an opportunity he likes to move fast, as does Michael. He had further news.

'Branson says he has reserved twelve upper-class seats for you on the next Virgin flight to New York free of charge. He says you can invite eleven mates and he will pick up the tab for everything – he and I will be joining you on the plane and we will do the deal there.'

This single statement confirmed everything I hoped was true about Branson. What an operator. How exciting must it be to be able to call the shots like that and all in the name of a bona fide business deal.

Unfortunately though ...

'Michael, that sounds amazing, more than amazing, it makes me want to scream it's so amazing but—'

'But what, there are no buts, how can there be any buts, this is not a but situation.' Michael was incredulous.

'No you don't understand,' I implored, 'taking a Virgin flight is not an option. We have to fly on Concorde to make all the timings work and besides we have already paid almost fifty grand for the tickets. If he wants a meeting *he's* going to have to come with *us*, tell him.'

'What?'

It was the only thing I could think to say. Branson's offer was straight from a movie script but, as flattering as it had been, I was more concerned about Mr Cleese and his script than Mr Branson and his radio station.

'Stay by that phone,' snapped Michael again. He was pumping on gas now. He could smell the fresh ink of a new contract in the air, like a tracker catching the faint whiff of some far-off prey. He wasn't going to let an opportunity like this pass by if there was anything he could do about it.

With Heathrow airport now in sight, the phone rang again.

'It's me – Branson says there is no way he can be seen getting on a BA flight – especially Concorde. He says the press would have a field day.'

Of course this was true – it was the kind of story the press would kill for. Branson hated BA and understandably so. They had tried to put him out of business almost since the day he had set up his airline – most infamously with their illegal dirty tricks campaign. And as much as I would have loved the service, movies, booze and snooze of a luxurious Virgin long-haul flight, I was in a fix. There was a genuine time issue that was proving to be a deal breaker.

'Michael, seriously, we have to take this flight. You're gonna have to tell Branson that this time, regrettably – it's going to have to be a no.'

The silence on the other end of the phone was deafening ...

'Are you sure?'

'Yes.'

'Are you sure you're sure – we could be talking millions here?'

'Michael, I'm sure.'

'OK – your call. I'm just the agent.'

'Thank you.'

And with that he was gone.

* * *

267

The Concorde Lounge was a most magnificent place, situated just beyond the already impressive BA first-class lounge. The best thing about the positioning of the two lounges was that when you walked past the first-class lounge, everyone knew where you were heading. Everyone knew you were one of the supersonic set – suddenly you were regarded as an entirely different commodity. You were one of the special ones.

What must we six have looked like walking into that place? Two hours before we were having a cup of tea in my living room and now here we were about to board the most prestigious aircraft in the world and to deliver a nonexistent script (as we had still yet to write it) to a real live Python.

Champagne was the order of the day.

'Cheers,' I offered up.

'Good health,' said Danny.

'How mad is this?' said Will.*

I was about to take my first sip when my phone rang again. It was Michael back on the line.

'Branson says he wants this deal and if he has to fly on Concorde to make it happen then so be it. He refuses, however, to give BA a cent of his money – point blank – so he says you're gonna have to pay for his ticket … oh, and mine by the way.'

'He said I have to pay for yours too?'

'No – I added that last bit, but that would be nice.'

Now, it could be argued that because R.B. was the one who called the meeting, he should bear the cost of any expenses incurred as a result, regardless of who his money was going to, but to be honest I was blown away by the fact that he was prepared to surrender such a huge slice of his personal principles to meet with me. I was more than happy to fork out for a ticket for him as I was for Michael's – only a fool leaves his agent behind when thrashing it out with a player like Branson.

I informed the guys that we were about to become two more.

'Could this day get any crazier?' I thought. Yes, was the answer.

The brief half hour it took Branson to arrive at Heathrow on the back of one of his Virgin limo-bikes seemed to take forever. We couldn't wait for

---

* Will has since told me he did not come on this trip as it was he who had to go back to the office to sort the script out!

him to walk in so we could see the expression on the faces of the BA staff as he entered the elite palace of his sworn arch enemy.

When he did finally show, we weren't disappointed – you could almost hear the sound of jaws hitting the floor one by one as each uniformed member of BA staff realised who had just walked into their lounge. Everyone was mystified as to what was going on. Why on earth would Richard Branson even consider flying with British Airways?

The shock lasted right up until we boarded the plane, manifesting itself in the most colourful display of nerves and excitement – the male members of staff trying to be respectfully cool, almost as if nothing out of the ordinary had happened at all – whilst the female members of staff were altogether more honest with their emotions, giggling like schoolgirls and fluttering around the great maverick vying for their 'moment'.

As the countdown to launch continued, our original group of six – now eight – was about to be joined by an unofficial ninth – a reporter from the *Sun* newspaper.

The *Sun* had caught wind of the fact that there was something going down between Branson and the newly ex-Radio 1 Breakfast Show host, and had sent Andy Coulson along to find out more. Andy, later to become an infamous editor of the *News of the World* before being appointed the head of press and communications for the Tory Party, was at that time editor of the Bizarre column, the paper's showbiz gossip page. Somehow he had persuaded his bosses to part with seven grand so he could 'cover our story'.

Andy was the happiest person on the plane and no wonder. This was no minibus trip to Blackpool – this was New 'bloody' York on Concorde my son. Andy would, of course, get his balls chopped off if he didn't come back with a story but for the time being he was going to enjoy every second of this wonderful aircraft.

Not that we minded him being there – not for a second. Someone had to tell this story and it might as well be Coulson – he was a smart boy who knew the score. He promised to keep a respectful distance in exchange for a heads up on any potential headline-grabbing developments. I ran it past R.B. who said if it was fine by me if it was fine by him. Andy had a deal – off the record of course.

Papers can make you and they can break you, but they only usually do the second bit if you've done something wrong in the first place – very rarely do they go after someone for no reason at all. And even if they do nail you, as long as you take it on the chin and are prepared to climb straight back on the horse, they'll pretty much back off until 'the next time'. They generally know when someone is good for business.

Meanwhile, back on board, all I can say is that if you want to know what it's like to receive the absolute best in-flight service possible, I recommend you travel in the company of someone who owns their own airline and if possible Richard Branson – the heroic privateer. Most people love Branson and when you see him in the flesh he definitely has that indefinable charisma people talk about. His effect on the BA crew during the ensuing three hours thirty-seven minutes was nothing short of mystical – in fact the whole plane was buzzing as a result of his presence.

There were only one hundred seats on Concorde – twenty-five rows of four, two either side of the aisle which made it a surprisingly poky aircraft. It is much smaller than people think, like a sports car compared to a coach. There were also no movies, no screens of any kind, in fact, just a speedometer readout of how fast we were going and to inform us when we were supersonic. I found myself seated towards the middle of the cabin next to my agent while Richard was sat at the front, no surprise there – I'm sure he could have had the pilot's seat if he'd asked for it!

Once off the ground, about 20 minutes into the flight when the plane was about to enter the speed of sound, the pilot let us know via a brief announcement. We waited expectantly for something to happen but nothing did, or at least nothing seemed to. As we looked at each other the pilot came back on the speaker to confirm that we were indeed now beyond the speed of sound and quickly heading towards 2000 km per hour – twice the speed of sound and Concorde's normal cruising speed. So with that stultifying event over, it was time to enjoy the rest of the flight. The seatbelt signs were turned off accordingly and it was time for food, fine wines and free gifts.

I was just settling in when one of the stewardesses approached me.

'Mr Evans, Mr Branson has asked if you would like to join him up at the front.'

This spoke volumes about the situation. Here was I effectively having paid for all the tickets – a mind-blowing £56,000 and suddenly I was at someone else's party. I have discovered over the years that there are many things money cannot buy and pulling rank over Richard Branson on an aircraft – regardless of whether it's one of his or not – is definitely one of them.

'Oh yes, of course, tell him I'll be right there,' I replied to the nice lady.

As she turned to go back up the aisle, I went to get out of my seat, but suddenly felt a vicelike grip on my arm dragging me back down. It was the hand of a very determined and surprisingly strong agent.

'Ow, Michael, what are you doing?'

'You're not going up there.'

'What are you talking about, you madman, of course I am, let go of my arm!'

'No.'

'Michael – let – go – of – my – arm ... now.'

'No, fuck off and stay there.'

'How on earth does a person begin to do that?' I thought to myself.

Michael then did that anxious whisper thing through gritted teeth.

'Richard Branson is the sharpest knife in the drawer. On no account am I allowing you to enter into any space where there is just you and him and where there might be a pen and a piece of paper around. He has done some legendary deals on the back of envelopes and I don't want you to be the next one.'

By now one could have been forgiven for thinking Michael and I were having a fight as there was an audible scuffle going on. I was just about to break free of Michael's clutches when, in a deft reversal of momentum, the little fellow somehow managed to thrust himself forward up and over me into the aisle leaving me alone in my seat.

R.B. would indeed be joined by a guest, albeit not the one he had invited.

I felt like I should protest, but seeing as there was now no one sat next to me to protest to, I decided I would let Michael get on with whatever he thought best and comforted myself instead by ordering a rather large glass of Krug champagne.

Several further large glasses of fizz later and who should return but none other than my trusty agent having smoothed the way for his client to have 'talks'.

'Right, it's safe for you to go,' declared Michael.

'Oh thanks,' I replied, knowing it was anything but, as I was half sloshed.

I don't know about you but I have a sliding scale of who I can and can't be myself in front of, especially when I've had a drink. When I'm operating in the 'can't' mode I am hopeless at best. My words escape me, my brain turns to fudge, I begin to sweat and I end up saying things I don't mean and would never normally say.

The thing was, though, all I had to do was reason with myself. I didn't want anything from this guy – and after all, that's all he is, just another guy. I hadn't done anything wrong and I didn't owe him anything – so what was I getting all worked up about? Before Richard had arrived on the scene that day I had been perfectly happy – I had come up with an excuse for us all to have a flight on Concorde to the Big Apple and yet now here I was, Percy Paranoia, pouring with perspiration and wondering what the heck I was going to say to the Virgin boss.

Once in the seat next to him, I really didn't feel very well – 'a little queer', as my mum would say. I decided the best thing for me to do would be to try to say as little as possible, be polite and just try not to pass out – I was suddenly becoming very light-headed. If I could remain conscious and not embarrass myself that would do, but the more I thought about doing this, the more my heart began pounding and the more panicky I became.

Richard grasped the nettle, thank God, and took no time at all in getting down to business. The more he talked, the more I relaxed. He ordered himself a drink and asked me if I would like another glass of bubbles.

'Ooh, yes please,' I replied, a little too excitedly.

Somewhere in the mix, Richard explained how he wanted me to host the drivetime show on his Virgin Radio station. I was happy talking radio stations and with the help of Monsieur Krug, didn't hold back in telling him what I thought he needed to do with his. I also made no bones about the fact that the only show I would consider taking on would be another breakfast show, anything other than that would not be a prospect I would be willing to entertain.

Richard listened intently as I spoke, pausing for a moment after I had finished before motioning to gain the attention of a stewardess.

'Yes, Mr Branson, what I can I do for you sir?'

'You don't have a pen I could borrow do you?' came his reply.

'Oh oh,' said a voice in my head.

I don't know how long it took but gradually there before my eyes a handwritten contract began to evolve in front of me. Richard would write something down, show it to me and then say, 'So how does that look?'

If I agreed he would move on, if I didn't – he would cross it out and start that bit again.

This was it – this was one of those moments I had heard so much about – the stuff of legend. I was witnessing one of his infamous 'deals on the back of an envelope', except this time it was on the back of a Concorde dinner menu.

I was transfixed with what was happening, his attention to detail was fascinating. The questions, crossings out and rewriting continued for twenty or thirty minutes until, satisfied, Richard declared the agreement complete.

I could now also see there was very clearly a place for my signature.

'There you go,' said Richard, 'why don't you put your name to that?'

top
10 Best Bits of Advice

10 See below
9 See below
8 See below
7 See below
6 See below
5 See below
4 See below
3 See below
2 See below
1 Don't sign it

Don't sign it – the only piece of advice I would ever give to anyone. No matter what 'it' is – unless you have thought it through and you are one gazillion per cent sure it is what you 'want' or what you 'need' – there is no sense in signing anything.

Things can always be signed but they can never be unsigned.

Thankfully, despite the bubbles of loveliness bouncing around in my head, Richard's persuasiveness and the general madness of the whole situation that day, I could still just about manage to hear my own mantra screaming back at me somewhere far off in the distance.

'Er, excuse me one moment, Richard – just give me a second,' I mumbled as I lifted myself up out of my seat to get past him.

I staggered back towards Michael and slumped back down next to him. He could see I was now even more bleary-eyed than before.

'What happened?'

'Oh, he wants me to sign a menu.'

'What!'

'Richard Branson, he wants me to sign a menu.'

'What for?'

'For a job – it had lots of other writing on it as well. Not just what there is to eat.'

'What do you mean?'

'He'd written lots of other things on it with a pen – sort of like a contract.'

'Shit – sit there and don't move,' and with that Michael was off again.

As for me, I couldn't have moved if I'd wanted to. I was done, I wasn't going anywhere except to sleep. I was 'emotionally exhausted'.

Michael, for his part, resumed his position next to the tycoon and for the rest of the flight attempted to continue with a more 'formal' style of negotiations. In the end, however, there was no deal done, it was all too frantic and there would be no need for anyone to sign anything.

When the plane landed, R.B. vanished into the New York night as swiftly as he had arrived at Heathrow, like a business superhero in search of his next financial adventure. On this occasion he had left empty-handed but he needn't have worried. We were destined to meet again six months later at his home in Holland Park in West London and this time I would have a signature for him.

It would be on the bottom of a contract for £87 million.

So how did the gag with Mr Cleese go?

Well, here's the thing, it didn't.

When we arrived at his New York apartment mob-handed and by this time with something that just about passed for a script which Danny had managed to cobble together on the plane, we were told by the concierge that Mr Cleese had left a few hours earlier – for Paris!

Paris, what the heck was he doing in Paris?

'Shit, what are we going to do now?' said Will.*

'Presumably go to Paris, I would imagine,' pronounced Danny, looking in my direction.

'Absolutely,' I replied, trying to appear nonchalant.

This trip had now evolved into a full-on caper. Of course we *had* to go to Paris. We had to tell this story somehow and if it meant another unscheduled whistle-stop trip then so be it. More calls followed back to the production office. There was only one aircraft in the world more glamorous than the British Airways Concorde and that was Air France Concorde. The plane we would have to take in order to get to our next destination in time but not before ... Danny broke his ankle.

---

* Will still wasn't there he assures me, so this must have been Dave Granger – or Grave Danger as we sometimes referred to him – one of the other producers.

We decided to go to a bar to kick back whilst things were being organised and take a moment to reflect upon what had happened in the last twelve hours or so. The bar we chose was a typical New York long-style bar that Danny had been to before – he knows New York like the back of his hand and wanted us to have a taste of the real thing.

The bar was daylight bright at the front, due to the huge window that looked out on to the street and then grew ever more mysterious as it stretched deeper and deeper into the shadows. It was a music venue at night and had an extremely cool vibe about it. American football was playing on the TV and there was a jukebox flashing away in the corner. We ordered a round of Bud Lights – how could we not?

We were all still reeling from the last few hours and were more dazed than anything. Conversation was slow to say the least, even with Danny around, which was a first in my book. After extraordinary things happen there is often little to say. This is probably why we sat there in relative silence for the first couple of rounds.

'I'm just gonna shoot out to a record shop I know,' said Danny after a while. When Danny's not working or with his family or talking, he buys records. These are the only four things he does.

'Alright, good luck,' I said.

'Yeah, see you in a bit, Danny,' said the others.

It couldn't have been three or four minutes later when Danny returned in what looked like total agony with his left leg dragging behind him. Upon seeing a big man close to tears I did what all good friends at such times do and started to kill myself laughing.

'What in God's name happened here?' I just about managed to get out.

'Fuck off – it's not fucking funny.' Danny was properly helpless and obviously in real pain but this just made me laugh even more. I was now dying.

It transpired that he had stepped off the kerb right outside the bar, turned his ankle and that was it. It was broken. For the last couple of minutes he had been attempting to shout back in to us for help but we hadn't been able to hear him. This last bit of information pushed me over the edge. I had to go outside to calm down.

Poor Danny's injury meant that he had to travel back to England on his own with his lower left leg now in a cast whilst the rest of us boarded the

Air France flight to Paris – we were one man down but we had to carry on. Our mission was incomplete.

Flying BA Concorde was amazing but Air France Concorde was even better. In their wisdom the French had taken out several rows of seats so there was more room and comfort for the supersonic commuter to enjoy. They had also replaced the cold leather material of the chairs with a softer, more luxurious fabric. The gimmicky gifts of BA had been forsaken by the French in preference of focusing instead on the service, the wine and the food. A far more sensible idea as far as I could see and one that we would happily indulge in during our flight.

As the arrival time to Paris drew ever nearer our attentions turned once again back to 'the most expensive joke in the history of light entertainment television' and the great John Cleese, who was staying at a hotel in Paris – except not by the time we got there.

When we arrived we were curtly told that Monsieur Cleese had checked out and was currently on his way back to London to appear on a television show.

I promise you that is exactly what happened.

We had left for New York on the Tuesday afternoon; it was now Wednesday evening and we were in Paris. We had spent close to £70,000 and here's what we ended up with – a twenty-second piece of film that showed me with a script outside John's New York apartment being told by the concierge he had left for Paris and then a 'wipe' (TV term for a fancy cut) to me in Paris in front of the Arc de Triomphe still holding the same script and stating that once again we had missed our intended target.

When we played it out on the night of the show as an intro to bringing John on there were audible gasps from the audience as they realised the extent of our endeavour. In the end it was more dramatic than comedic and as every television producer will tell you, drama is much more expensive than light entertainment, although maybe not normally several thousand pounds per second.

Yes it was decadent and yes that money could have been spent infinitely better, but those were the times, crazy, crazy times, and they were about to get crazier.

top

10 Most Useless States of Mind

10 Self pitiful
9 Jealous
8 Envious
7 Anxious
6 Greedy
5 Boastful
4 Ungrateful
3 Malicious
2 Bitter
1 In denial

It has been proven, apparently, that 90 per cent of what we do with our brain is unconscious. That is to say information is fed in by our consciousness and then worked on and figured out whilst we are doing other things. Then when we come across future situations where we are made to draw on some of our 'experience', the unconscious is waiting in the wings to spring forth with whatever it is we might need.

Many philosophers believe that if you have a problem and 'consciously' feed it into your 'unconscious', you can then forget about it for a while and fully expect the answer to pop up one day. They also cite this as being one of the reasons we dream.

I think this may go a long way to explaining how many of the things that have happened to me seemed to have come about almost by chance when in fact there has probably been a grand plan all along. Maybe this is how what happened next came about.

TFI only came off the air for twelve weeks of the year, two weeks at Christmas and for ten weeks in the summer. It was 1997, the summer after I walked out of Radio 1, when I went to Ireland where I would set about attempting to do two things:

1. Catch my first salmon.
2. Get back on the radio.

It was a beautiful August summer's morning when I found myself sat in the peace and tranquillity of the occupation that man has come to know as angling.

I was set up with my rod on the bank of the River Laune in an area called Killarney on the west coast of the Emerald Isle. I was holidaying there in a country house with Suzi.

Suzi and I had got together after Rachel and I parted company – something that didn't go down too well at first as Rachel and Suzi were good friends, having met on *The Big Breakfast*. Since then, however, Suzi and I had been an item for over two years and were now enjoying as good a relationship as either of us could ever imagine. I must also point out at this juncture that when it came to the trials and tribulations of living with a half-mad television and radio presenter by the name of Evans, Suzi definitely took the lion's share of the fallout. To say she was a saint would not be overstating the point. Especially seeing as she stuck it out for the next five years.

After enjoying breakfast this particular morning, Suzi had gone back to the room while I went to enquire about the possibility of borrowing some tackle to try my luck down by the waterside.

The owner of the house pointed me in the direction of the rods, wished me luck and sent me on my way. I had little or no idea what I was doing but was drawn to the romance of the river.

The house rods were old and tatty and were kept more for effect than competition, but after optimistically bouncing down to the water's edge I was now awaiting the arrival of a sympathetic fish that might afford me the generosity of attaching itself to my line. Not for one second did I think I might actually catch one, although incredibly this did turn out to be the case – not only that, but we ate the poor creature. The owner couldn't believe it, he said people had been coming years and not caught a thing! But the poor salmon wasn't the only thing I caught that day. I was about to catch the radio bug again but this time bigger than ever before.

Back in England I had placed myself under a self-imposed curfew of not listening to the radio. I knew I had majorly screwed up and this was the only way I could stop myself feeling sick at what an amazing opportunity I had blown. I knew that hearing other broadcasters having fun and enjoying that buzz that you can only get by being live on the air would have been too much for me. By not listening to the radio at all I could almost forget it even existed. What a total fruitcake – I think this is what the shrinks refer to as being in denial.

This extreme theory worked for a while, but like all curfews, in the end it was no match for the person it was designed to suppress. I decided the no-listening rule only applied to UK radio stations. Ireland is, of course, not part of the UK, so together with my rod, reel and tackle box, down to the river came my beloved Roberts radio.

Big mistake – *huge* (another one!).

If you're a drug addict it doesn't matter which country you are in when you have your next fix, it's still going to get you hooked again – and so it was with me and the wonderful world of the wireless.

The Irish are amongst the greatest talkers in the world. Not because they talk a lot – many Irish people hardly ever say a word – but when they do say something, they can throw a sentence on its back making the words sit up and beg like a well-trained dog. Add to this their voices are usually soft, with engaging tones and a teasing lilt. As you can no doubt imagine, if I was looking to escape the magic of radio, I had chosen entirely the wrong country to do it in.

A short film

CUT TO: EXTERIOR, DAY

> *Tight on a close-up of a classic Roberts radio. We can hear the voice of Gerry Ryan, Ireland's premier radio broadcaster.*

GERRY: Good morning to you boys and girls – it's your uncle Ger' here. Did you have a good weekend, did ya'? Sure enough it was heaven sent alright …

> *As Gerry continues we slowly pull out to reveal a man fishing on the bank of a river in spate. We cut to his eyes, they are listening more than looking – to what Gerry is saying.*

GERRY: … I heard lots of ya' went to der park wich yer kids, yer cats and yer dogs – no doubt yer donkeys some of yer and uncle Tom – and all dee udder lot. Well if yer interested, and I don't presume for one second you are, but it's me job to tell ya, so tell ya' I will. I heard rumours of sunshine afoot so I kept me curtains firmly drawn on der good Lord's day and went and poured meself a large whiskey, followed by anudder and anudder all t'roughout der day – if the truth be told. And there were cigars too, six or seven at least … and why – why? Because I'll tell you this and I'll tell you no more – I have to do dis' broadcast five days a week and as easy as it may sound – whilst you're out there frolicking in yer Sund'y best your man Ger' is sat all alone contemplating what rubbish he's goin' to illuminate yer' little lives with come the reluctant dawn of anudder five days of this bloomin' show.

The fisherman smiles – Gerry is on form again. During the next three hours Gerry will help the police with a day-old murder investigation which is crucially going cold. He will invite callers to ring in and talk about which fan clubs they were members of as kids. The highlight of this segment is one man who phones up to announce he is a member of The Captain Scarlet fan club and after Gerry has pushed for a while, he admits that he is the only member and that he knows very little about Captain Scarlet in the first place. Gerry starts laughing at this so much that he struggles to speak for a good two to three minutes. Gerry then invites listeners to advertise items they may have for sale and at one point lambasts a woman for 'trying to get rid of such crap via his show'. His last hour is a phone-the-expert section – a solicitor – and then he rounds off the show with a competition for older listeners to call in and sing old classics but without their false teeth in – the winner receiving a bag of chewy toffee …

As I listened to Gerry that morning I was in awe of what a radio show could achieve. His show was my mum and dad's corner shop – it had everything. This is the power of radio over television – it can achieve more and can do it better for longer. A radio show is more sustainable because it has to be. It has to find a way to breathe every day otherwise it will die. Gerry's show was on fire.

A radio show also has a unique relationship with its audience, it is a two-way street that's all about a connection born out of a mutual understanding and from what I could hear Gerry and his audience were one big team creating a daily masterpiece.

After just one morning's listening, the reason for my self-imposed exile became glaringly obvious. There was more work to be done and deep down inside I knew I had jumped ship too soon. The frustration I had felt before I left was because I didn't know what to do next, when the next thing to do was simply knuckle down, and take the audience with me. As I listened further I was bristling at the prospect of what a radio show could achieve. The kind of intuition this man had with his listeners was something I hadn't even come close to achieving during my time at Radio 1.

It was not yet midday and already Gerry and his listeners were weaving their magic, having just the most fun. Who wouldn't want to do that for a living?

I ran up the hill back to the main house.

'Could I borrow your phone, please, I need to call London,' I asked the gentleman owner.

'Sure, it'll be through there in the kitchen,' he kindly obliged.

I had to get back on the air.

'Michael, it's me ... I'm in Ireland.'

'You're in Ireland?'

'Yes, I came here so I could listen to the radio.'

'What? ...'

'Never mind.'

'Did you say you went to Ireland so you could listen to the radio?'

'Yes. Now, can you please get me back on it?'

'But you had the best job on radio there is and you said you didn't want to do it any more.'

'I know, but that is because I'm an idiot and I was lying to myself, please can you try?'

Michael said he'd have a ring round and get back to me, which he did later that day.

He called me back towards teatime the same day and said there was no chance, all the major slots were filled, and anyhow, the general vibe was that people were worried about my unpredictability and whether I was worth the risk any more.

'Shit.'

'The only way you could get a gig at the moment would be if you owned your own radio station.' He was joking of course, but I was desperate.

'Michael, you're a genius,' I screamed, 'that's what we'll do. How do we do that Michael?'

'Chris, you're not serious?'

Of course I was serious. For the next few days the owner of the house we were staying at would make more money from my phone calls back and forth to England than he would from the rest of his business.

Michael tore at the project like a rabid dog and within twenty-four hours, with the help of John Revell, who was now a partner in my company Ginger and was always on the look out for opportunities, they together discovered that Talk Radio, a medium-wave national station, was vulnerable and might be up for grabs. In fact it was more than vulnerable – Talk could not decide whether it wanted to be a news station or a sports station and was currently falling somewhere in between the two whilst not being particularly adept at either.

It was also losing money hand over fist as lowly listening figures were failing to attract enough advertising. Listeners were confused by its mixed message and already had something similar available over on BBC's Five Live. Five Live's formidably professional operation was steeped in resources and had a depth of experience coursing through its veins which left Talk Radio like a lamb to the slaughter. Due to the overblown price the owners had paid for the franchise in the first place, it was hard to see how it was going to survive.

Again very much with John's help, we suddenly found ourselves in the thick of takeover negotiations. It was all going promisingly until one of the shareholders dug his heels in and pushed the price up to a figure that was unjustifiable as far as we were concerned. It was time to say goodbye to Talk.

The next significant thing that happened was that Zoe Ball was signed up to re-save Radio 1, which was already back in the doldrums again. The breakfast show that had replaced mine was not, as it transpired, what the nation wanted to wake up to – in fact it wasn't even what the new hosts wanted to wake up to. They didn't like 'breakfast' and 'breakfast' didn't like them. So, 'Bring on Ms Ball,' came the cry, 'your effervescence is required.'

Getting Zoe to sign up was a smart move by the BBC. She is hugely likeable and had a sizable following as a result of her massively successful partnership on the telly with Jamie Theakston and their Saturday morning show *Going Live*. She was sexy yet sophisticated, the darling of the tabloids, loved by kids, fancied by dads and admired by mums – the perfect combination. Her arrival would be a welcome tonic, nobody doubted that, but nor did anybody have any idea just how explosive her arrival would be.

For whilst Radio 1 were polishing Zoe's new microphone in readiness for her first day, a whole set of extraordinary circumstances were playing out at No. 1 Golden Square, in the heart of London's Soho, the home of Richard Branson's Virgin Radio.

top 10 Things that Help Get a Deal Done

10 Timing

 9 Groundwork

 8 Energy

 7 Honesty

 6 Holding your nerve

 5 Two willing parties

 4 Money in place

 3 A man on the inside

 2 Two men on the inside

 1 A pen

Richard Branson had set up Virgin Radio some four years before at a cost of around £7 million. He was now poised to sell the station to the mighty Capital group for a whacking £90 million – not a bad bit of business. The sale, however, had temporarily been put on hold pending a ruling by the Monopolies and Mergers Commission with regards to how this acquisition would affect Capital's strength in the market, especially in London where they were already dominant.

The financial situation was that no money had yet changed hands but the two parties had signed an exclusivity agreement stating that Virgin was bound to sell to Capital regardless of any other offers it might receive for the duration of the agreement. Should that agreement lapse, of course, then all bets were off, leaving the door open for anyone else who may be interested.

Well, here's the thing: the ruling was taking longer than anyone had predicted and the exclusivity contract was teetering ever closer to becoming null and void. Not that this should have mattered, as Virgin were way down the 'procedures' route with Capital and anyone else who did throw their hat into the ring would have an awful lot of catching up to do.

All Capital had to do to further protect their position was place an extension on the exclusivity agreement, something Virgin would more than likely have been happy to comply with. Surely Capital would do this 'just in case'. Well, actually, no they wouldn't, not if either:

A. They didn't realise the clause had lapsed.
B. They didn't believe anyone else had £90 million cash to spend on a radio station.

(Incredibly both these things would later turn out to be true.)

Although the Virgin Group were keen to sell, the current management of Virgin Radio were not fans of the potential new owners, to put it mildly. They had built Virgin Radio from literally nothing into what it was today and despite the fact they were all in line for a big pay day come the sale, it was a surefire bet that once Capital took over, they would most likely be out on their ears. Capital were renowned for doing things their own way with their own people.

'Thanks a lot, here's a cheque, see you in another life' – you know, that kind of thing.

Virgin Radio had grown like one big, happy, slightly rebellious family that had been together from day one. There had been exceptionally few staff changes, the true mark of a well-run company. And like all good families, a lot of the credit was down to the parents – both Dads in this case!

There was Andy Mollet, the finance guy, an aquiline-looking thirtysomething, who was a lifelong Fulham fan – sharp as a razor and as straight a guy as you could hope to find. Then there was D.C. – David Campbell, the big boss. Imagine a huge bear, a big huge smiley bear, a bear whose favourite thing in the world is Guinness and then give that bear as much Guinness as there is in the world. Next watch as the bear's smile grows wider and wider until eventually he falls asleep, usually stood up, usually in the corner of a pub somewhere, that was D.C. – still is on a good day.

The Virgin Radio culture was work hard and play hard. Their parties were legendary. If targets were reached – it was down to the pub for an almighty beer bust; if targets weren't reached – it was still down to the pub for an almighty beer bust. There was always the next quarter.

The whole company prided itself on being part of the non-establishment Virgin empire. Working for a Virgin company does that to you – all those neverending days of publicity that Richard has carefully manipulated over the years having paid off. If you are a Virgin employee it's just that little bit sexier than if you work some place else for a similar company.

It was this mentality that would be vitally instrumental when it came to scuppering the Capital deal. For the current management to be sucked up, paid off and spat out was not a prospect they were looking forward to. If there was any way on earth they could break off their engagement with Capital whilst in the process also keeping their jobs, it wasn't difficult to conceive they would be more than willing to help any potential alternative suitors sneak in the back door.

David and Andy were actively on the lookout for some kind of lifeline and had been for the last couple of months but there seemed to be little hope. Everyone had generally accepted that the Capital Group were the new owners in all but name and it was only a matter of time before the Monopolies and Mergers Commission ruled in their favour and contracts were exchanged.

Dave and Andy had begun to count the days, until, that is, Radio 1 announced the appointment of Zoe Ball to host its breakfast show.

Virgin's current breakfast show had been treading water for a couple of years by now and although there was nothing particularly wrong with it, it had just become a bit staid. With an imminent takeover looming, there was little incentive for anyone to do anything to change it; but now Zoe and her new breakfast show were around the corner, and the Virgin guys thought it was too good a chance to miss to have one last bit of fun.

How about they put me up against her, to start on the same day at the same time? Capital were due to take over in ten weeks anyhow, so what the heck?

Radio Wars, the newspapers would call it.

No sooner had D.C. contacted Michael, he was straight on the phone to me.

'Chris, it's Michael here. Virgin Radio have been in contact. They are aware you have been sniffing around for a gig back on the air and would like to offer you the breakfast show, but *it's not what you think* – in fact, to be frank, it's a bit weird.'

'Michael, life is weird – get on with it.'

'No Chris, this is *really* weird.'

'Michael, weird is what we do, come on tell me.'

'They want you to do the breakfast show and they want you to start on the same day and at the same time Zoe Ball starts on Radio 1.'

'But that's fantastic, that's amazing, are you serious? This is the greatest news ever, that's not weird at all.'

'But—'

'But what?'

'That's not the weird bit – you can only do it for ten weeks until they sell the station. Then you'll have to leave.'

'That *is* weird.'

As weird as it may have been, it sounded like it was going to be fun and once I was back on the air, who knows what might happen?

The press fell in love with the story of 'the big fight'. The tabloids stuck both Zoe and me on their front pages, while the broadsheets got to work intellectualising the whole affair. It was just what radio needed, a real shot in the arm and we, along with our polar opposite employers, were the couple to do it. The geeky, ginger, working-class radio pro up against the beautiful, blonde, middle-class television presenter rookie – it couldn't have been more mouthwatering. There was something in there for everyone and with a bit of luck we would all come out winners.

Zoe played her part exquisitely, quietly smiling along while I declared all kinds of campaigns against her.

ME: 'It's war!'

ZOE: 'Well, you know how Chris is – he has his way of doing things and I have my audience and I'm sure the listeners will make their own choices.'

I was the crazed dog, she the cool cat, but we were both in a no-lose situation.

Zoe was probably going to be there for several years with a shiny new contract enjoying a crystal clear national FM signal, whereas I was only going to be around for a ten-week scrap on fuzzy old medium wave. Zoe was always going to slaughter me in the ratings, that was a given, but it didn't matter – before the first set of audience figures were through I would be out in the wilderness once again and Capital and their millions would be in. At least that's what we all thought.

In fact I was already preparing what I would say for the final link on my last show in ten weeks' time, something like:

'It's obvious to me what has happened here – Zoe's father has paid everyone in Britain to listen to her. Of nothing else am I more certain. I saw her dad Johnny at the bank every day last week. 'Think of a number,' he said to the cashpoint machine whereupon out poured zillions of pounds, and who am I to come between a father's love for his daughter? Good luck Zoe and farewell.'

As the countdown to our duel continued, radio was back on the agenda and back on the front pages. Zoe was making it sexy and cool, while I was making it controversial and exciting – and we hadn't even gone on the air yet!

When D-day was finally upon us, the frenzy of coverage reached fever pitch. Everyone chipped in and had their say. When it came to the review it was generally accepted that Zoe sounded a little nervous, but what she lacked in experience she was already making up for in warmth and enthusiasm. The general take on my efforts was that I was a little more self-assured. Self-assured? You're not kidding, I couldn't wait to get back behind the mic, and from 6 a.m. that day I soaked up every second for all it was worth and it felt better than ever.

After no more than a week Zoe was sounding infinitely more at home with her new medium. After no more than an hour I began to think that ten weeks just wasn't going to be enough.

top
10 Mantras

10 When opportunity knocks, make sure you're ready to answer the door
9 The best way to beat the system is to invent a new one
8 Ask not why – rather why not?
7 It's easier to chase than be chased
6 Every no brings you closer to a yes
5 Imagination is more important than knowledge
4 It's not money that's the root of all evil, it's the love of money
3 It's not about the size of your gun, it's about when you pull the trigger
2 First profit – best profit; first loss – best loss
1 Never negotiate out of fear but never fear to negotiate

After another tip-off from John Revell re: the current state of affairs between Capital and the Virgin Group, Michael had now begun to dig around to see what he could find with regards to the sale of Virgin Radio and whether or not there was any chance we could become involved. Wherever he went and whoever he spoke to, he kept hearing the same thing – specifically that the deal was done and that was that.

'Fucking bullshit,' he told me. 'Until the signature is on the paper, a deal is never done, every agent knows that. Capital think they've got it in the bag but they haven't – as far as I can see this thing is still wide open. All we have to do is wait till midnight on the day their exclusivity clause runs out and hope to fuck they don't realise. If we can then come up with the cash, we slip in and buy it straight out from under their noses. Simple, eh?'

Michael was absolutely right except for the last bit. The last thing it was going to be was simple but, hey, when had that ever stopped us?

Branson would have to be convinced that any alternative approach was genuine but we knew he wanted the money from the sale to fund his new European airline, so at the very least he would probably be willing to listen to an alternative offer. Especially if there continued to be an ongoing delay with the Monopolies and Mergers Commission who were turning out to be in no mood to be rushed.

As a result of our first few attempts to raise support for our scheme, we weren't surprised to discover that the majority of people we talked to thought we were insane to even think we might have a chance of pulling something like this off. But as an old pal of mine says, 'Every time you hear a no, it just means you are closer to a yes. It's all about the guy who is willing to knock on the most doors.'

Michael was happy to knock on as many doors as it was going to take and in the meantime we decided it was also the right moment to talk to the big cuddly Guinness-drinking bear.

I organised to meet D.C. surreptitiously one night in my favourite pub, a little jewel by the name of the Nag's Head in Belgravia Village, right by Hyde Park. The 'Nag's' is in a mews street and was originally an old spit and sawdust bar in the early 1800s frequented by stable boys and stable girls who looked after the horses of the upper classes. Now it is mostly frequented by unstable boys and unstable girls who can sometimes barely look after themselves.

I urge you to seek it out if you're ever in London. It is very much a part of our history, although if you stay there too long there's a good chance you will be too. If you do ever go, also make sure you steer clear of using your mobile phone or requesting chips or ketchup with your food. Kevin the landlord – a former Welsh Guard – has an abhorrence of all three and has been known to vault the bar to eject those heinous enough to indulge in such evil indulgencies.

Over the years this wonderful little pub has seen many comings and goings involving all sorts of characters with much plotting abounding – one of the reasons I thought it the most fitting of venues to perhaps hatch a plan. We would drink and we would talk and we would see what came of it. When I arrived David was already 'installed' with a pint.

I informed him that Michael and I wanted to buy Virgin Radio and we were interested to know if he might help us do something.

'Brilliant, go for it, I'm in,' he said, without missing a beat. I paused to see if he was pulling my leg but not a bit of it. He was here to listen and would do all he could to assist us but not before he went on to very calmly tell me what his terms would be. He suffixed it with the fact that these terms were non-negotiable and he required an answer immediately.

What he had proposed seemed perfectly reasonable to me – David's help would be vital to the success of any potential new takeover. I accepted his terms unreservedly. He almost looked impressed. We both knew there was a much bigger play on the table and it would have been silly to be sidetracked by the odd percentage point here or there.

When it came down to the nitty gritty, if anything David was even more upbeat about our prospects than we were. In his opinion, there was no reason at all why a bank or venture capitalist would not lend us the money to buy what was already a cash-rich business, even more so if we could prove to them that things were only going to get better.

He firmly believed that my presence on the breakfast show, although never a realistic threat to Radio 1, could make a marked difference when it came to the fortunes of Virgin Radio. In fact he suggested revenues might easily double if not triple within the first twelve to eighteen months as a result of my high profile and improved listening figures. This, he believed, along with the predicted upturn in radio's share of advertising across the board, was enough of a tempting proposition to take to potential investors.

The one thing David was concerned about, however, was time and the exclusivity contract. He believed it was only a formality until Capital thought to extend it, as a consequence of which we needed to move very quickly. David next informed me of several investors who he knew might be sympathetic to our cause and who had been there at the beginning when he had set up the radio station.

D.C. was already earning his fair share of whatever we might have to end up paying him, but he hadn't finished yet.

'You need to call this man first thing tomorrow. His name is Kenneth Ibbett,' he said to me, while writing down a number on the back of a beer mat.

'Who's he?' I asked.

'He works for Richard – he is the man who will tell you whether or not they will sell you the radio station.'

'Stone the crows,' I thought. 'This is really happening.'

top
10 Things People Put Off

10 Cleaning out their pet's cage or fish tank
9 Homework
8 Doing their expenses
7 Getting out of bed
6 Going to the gym
5 Breaking up with a partner
4 Going to the doctors (mostly men, admittedly)
3 Wrapping Christmas presents (alright, men again)
2 Saying sorry ('hey look everyone – it's a hat trick for the guys!')
1 Making that awkward phone call …

The next day I was alone in my third-floor office at Ginger Productions in Great Titchfield Street. I was alternating between staring out of the window and staring down at the telephone number on the beer mat as if it were daring me to make the call. I looked out of the window one more time, after which I had promised myself I would pick up the receiver. After a few more hesitant moments I started to count from sixty to zero to give myself one more minute – something I do a lot though I have no idea why.

As I counted I began rehearsing what I wanted to say and how I wanted to say it before taking a deep breath and beginning to dial the number.

'This should be fun,' I said out loud, almost trying to convince myself that it might be. Obviously I was completely wrong.

I heard the ring tone and after no more than two rings the line cracked open.

KEN: 'Hello.'

ME: 'Hello, is this Kenneth Ibbett?'

KEN: 'Yes.'

With just three letters this response told me, 'I don't care who you are, I haven't got time for this phone call or anything you might have to say to me. In fact I already wish I hadn't picked up, now will you please get on with it – you're wasting my life.' And why is it that these people always have the most perfectly quiet offices to make their silence seem even louder? I decided I needed to throw my ace card in immediately.

293

ME: 'It's Chris Evans here.'

This is what I heard next:

Nothing.

Not a single word.

It was like the line had gone dead except I could tell it was still there by the deafening ambience humming in my ear. I was crushed. This guy Kenneth didn't give two shits who I was, or that I was the current host of the breakfast show on his radio station – or even that I had just bagged a whole month of national free publicity for him and his boss, Mr Branson.

Oh come on you ungrateful bastard say something to me.

Still nothing.

ME: 'I was phoning about the radio station.'

Still nothing – not a word, not even a breath.

At this point I felt a swelling of anger. Now he was just being plain rude. 'I don't need this,' I thought. 'I'll just ask him what I want to know and either he'll tell me or he won't and that'll be that – apart from if I ever see him in a bar when I'll chin the miserable ****.'

This change of mindset was making me feel better, I'd only been in the corporate world for a few seconds and already I had learnt that real businessmen just get on with it. If you're the one with something for sale and somebody wants it then you're not the one who has to do most of the talking – or in Kenneth's case, any talking at all.

I was about to state my reason for bothering him when, just as I went to speak, another thought simultaneously shot into my head. I realised that this man, this living and breathing sponsored silence, had no idea that I was calling about the potential purchase of his radio station – why would he?

ME: 'Er ...' (*er ... fucking er ... what the fuck was that ... er – no more 'er's', mental note: do not say 'er' – for the rest of your life*) '... I was calling about the radio station?'

Now as you can see I have placed a question mark on the end of that sentence because in my mind I was desperately hoping that in some way this would constitute a question and that Kenneth might now somehow respond.

KEN: *Nothing.*

ME: (*Shit, fuck, wank, bastard, bastard, bastard.*) 'Er ...' (*No, God, please not another er ... What am I – Er-man all of a sudden?*)

But worse was to come ...

Now let's just take a time out here for a moment. Let's get one thing straight. The only other thing I'd ever bought over the phone of any real value was a car. So it was obviously to this 'model' that my stupid ginger brain was applying itself when it caused my mouth to utter these next five words.

ME: (*whispering*) 'Is it still for sale?'

What in God's name was I thinking? I sounded like a no life who was sat at home with nothing better to do than flicking through the small ads of the local paper and making a few random phone calls to see if I could pick up a bargain – *and why was I whispering?*

I was also by now, I might add, literally pouring with sweat. I felt so out of my depth. What was I doing phoning this man up as if I were Donald Trump or J.R. bloody Ewing and asking him if his radio station was 'still for sale'? It was *£90 million* for crying out loud and I didn't have *any* of the money or the first idea how to get *any* of the money.

I was about to pass out when Kenneth spoke his next words to me.

KEN: 'Yes it is.'

Result! Kenneth had spoken to me for a second time – I could have danced, I really could – and moreover, in what was now the most focused conversation I had ever been involved with in my life, I was almost certain I could hear the faintest suggestion of warmth in his voice. My whole being jerked back into action. I decided to go for it, what did I have to lose? It was time to talk turkey.

ME: 'So, if I had to write you a cheque out today – to buy the radio station, how much would that cheque have to be for?'

KEN: 'Eighty-seven million pounds and that would be without paper.'

I had no idea what this last phrase 'without paper' meant. I had never heard the expression before in my life but no matter, I was on a roll.

ME: 'Of course Kenneth, paper was never in my thinking. Thank you for your time.'

KEN: 'Not at all.'

And with those three brief final words Ken was gone, as concisely and efficiently as he had appeared.

Word score for the conversation: KEN 17 – CHRIS 66 – with two 'ers' – but no passes. It was several hours before I began to feel normal again.

I had made the call but I had no idea what to do next, so I did what I always do in such circumstances – I called my agent Michael.

I told him about the exchange I had just had with Kenneth and he began to laugh – a lot. Michael doesn't laugh very often so he must have found the idea of me trying to cut it with one of the big boys absolutely rib-tickling.

'Well, at least you discovered one thing,' he sympathised. 'We only have to find £87 million – not ninety – ha ha.' He was right – discount for cash, I had forgotten about that bit.

The £90 million price tag, it transpired, was the price that Capital had agreed to pay for Virgin but that included the aforementioned mysterious 'paper'. This, Michael informed me, was a term referring to Capital paying partly with cash and partly by giving Branson some shares in their own company – it was these shares that were the 'paper'. Virgin were not prepared to take paper off anyone other than Capital as part of the deal but they were willing to give a £3 million discount to anyone prepared to write out a cheque – bargain eh?

'I'll make a few calls,' Michael went on. He always says this phrase – it sounds so cool, like he's in a movie. I've never had cause to use such a phrase. It is my ambition that one day someone will ask me about something and I too will say, 'I'll make a few calls.'

After I put the phone down to Michael I went back to staring out of the window. Things looked exactly as they had done just a few moments before, but the call to Kenneth had set off a chain of events that would catapult me into a whole new world.

Preparation, preparation, preparation.

We had six weeks to get the deal done – that was it, that was when the Monopolies and Mergers Commission were due to clear the way for Capital to proceed with their purchase.

David got to work on the money men – the banks and venture capitalists – whilst Michael concentrated on hiring a team of lawyers.

If you're going to hire a lawyer, hire the best because if you don't and the other guys do, then you are sunk. This is exactly what Michael did: he signed up the services of a wise old goat called Simon Olswang. He was cool, very experienced, smooth as silk and very Jewish. He would eventually head our team of twenty-four solicitors!

Meanwhile D.C. had gone back to a company by the name of Apax Partners who were very much involved in the setting up of Virgin Radio at its inception. During this period David had the good fortune to work with a charming American lady by the name of Barbara Manfrey. Barbara was very attractive, tall with that classic combination of dark hair and pale skin. She was slim, almost always wore red lipstick and had a penchant for pearls. She always dressed immaculately and was a very influential member of the senior management there.

Barbara's belief in David and Michael and her readiness to take me at face value would prove to be the glue that would stick our deal together. In the course of the next month and a half, she would shed tears, take risks, suffer unnecessary abuse and put her reputation on the line, all to help us achieve our goal.

I think it was very much to do with Barbara's presence and the fact that she was a woman that we were able to accomplish our task within such a limited time frame. Barbara's ego was far smaller than those of any of the men involved and you may not be surprised to learn that it is the existence of such huge male egos that often stops some of the best things in life happening. When Barbara was in the room, however, the boys knew they had to behave.

Each conscript to our cause brought their own set of tools and skills to the table but Barbara brought a whole workshop full. Her practical approach to getting things done, her skill in the financial world, her powers of persuasion along with her talent and patience when it came to sensitive negotiation, and her all-round diplomacy were absolutely essential in pulling together what was quickly becoming a delicate web of personalities and priorities. Within only a matter of days Barbara agreed we had a strong enough proposal to make a formal request to her superiors for a loan of £20 million. She set up a meeting with her boss – what a guy.

When he arrived in the boardroom to see us he looked like a movie star from the fifties. He was taller than me at well over six foot two, broad shouldered, chiselled good looks with tanned skin and silver hair swept back. He was dressed in a sharp pin-striped suit that looked like it had never been sat down in. He hadn't said a word yet but he was already my hero.

This was just one of the many meetings I would attend that I considered it an entire privilege to be at. I had stumbled into this exciting world of high finance and was now witnessing these guys at the top of their game and all in the name of helping make my dream come true.

The film-star guy was called Ronald, and as a venture capitalist it was his brief to provide his clients with at least a 33 per cent return on their capital within three years. If you wanted him to invest in you – you had to prove you could deliver.

Our business plan required total funding of £87 million, which we then predicted would be worth between £175 million and £300 million within five years. We explained to Ronald that we were confident that should he want to exit after the usual three years, he would indeed be able to expect his usual required return – if not more.

He listened intently, thanked us when we had finished, wished us good luck and said he'd be in touch.

The next day I received a call from Michael.

'Ronald says he's in!' he screamed down the phone.

'You are joking me!' I screamed back, but Ronald was not joking, Ronald does not joke. That's why Ronald is Ronald.

Ronald was one of the biggest players in town and he had now agreed to be on our team.

With Ronald and his £20 million in the bank, we were still £67 million shy of what we needed to buy the radio station but we now had a real big grown-up financial firm that believed in us which could only serve to further our cause. With the help of Apax we began to find people more willing to take us seriously. This was further aided by the fact that Barbara had now joined forces with Michael and David full time on the fund-raising front.

It was only a few days later when their funding trail led them to an extremely ornate private dining room in Paris, where a highly secretive meeting was to take place.

There was a bank, you see, a very nice French bank, who favoured investment in media businesses. They had heard of our plans and were keen to talk. We were running out of time so decided to gamble on asking them for a sizable chunk of the rest of the money – £45 million was the figure we would propose.

At this point I suppose I should explain what it was we were saying to these people.

It was simple really. David and Michael explained where radio as a business was now and where they believed it was going whilst I explained how I might make the audience grow. The key to the financial argument was that Capital were paying a fair price for what the radio station was worth today but with a more dynamic and exciting breakfast show driving the ratings it could easily be worth double that almost overnight.

Their one main concern was my reliability. How did they know I was going to stick around and put the hours in for the number of years required to make a real difference to the value of the station after my disastrous ego-fuelled exit from Radio 1?

I spared no pains to assure them that I privately considered this the biggest mistake of my career thus far and one that I did not want to repeat any time soon. Furthermore, I went on that it was in fact the righting of this wrong that was now driving me to buy my own radio station so I could get back to doing what I loved.

'Alright,' they said, 'if you really mean that – and we think you do, otherwise we wouldn't be here – we need you to tell us how much money you have in your personal bank account and we then want you to withdraw every penny of that money and put it into the deal.'

'So, how much money do you have?' At this point there was a pause, it was bordering on comical. I had only paused, however, not because of the nature of the question but simply because I wasn't entirely sure how much money I did have in my bank account. The thought of putting whatever that amount was into the deal didn't bother me for a second – after all I was totally convinced we were going to make this thing work.

'I think it's about two million pounds,' I said unconvincingly, but thinking it may be somewhere around that figure.

'Actually it's a bit more than that,' one of them said – they had done their homework, 'but two million will do. Two million is the figure we would require you to put into the pot.'

None of this was a problem for me and I wasted no time in telling them so. This was the final tick in the box they needed as I was now committed both emotionally, professionally, energetically and financially. In short they had my balls on a plate but if it meant us getting our radio station then they could sprinkle them with salt and pepper and serve them up for dinner for all I cared – we were in France after all.

The message came back from Paris:

'The French are in!' Michael was screaming with delight again.

'*Mon dieu, zut alors, vive la France!*' I screamed back – or something like that.

What Michael didn't tell me was that after I had left the meeting they demanded a similar financial commitment from him. We were now both in this together and deeper than ever. We had both committed to putting everything on the line in the pursuit of our goal. The heat was being turned up. This was becoming no place for the faint-hearted.

We were now up to £67 million of guaranteed funding, all signed off and ready to be handed over, but as the days rolled by Capital were edging ever closer to a ruling in their favour from the MMC and would be in a position to exchange contracts the instant the decision came through. Incredibly though, they still had not woken up to the fact that they could extend their exclusivity option or that they might need to. This continued to leave the door open for us for now at least. We still had to get our hands on another £20 million and we had to do it fast.

top
10
Reasons Why I Presume
Capital Never Took Us Seriously

10 They were a 500 million pound company
9 I was a 'wacky DJ'
8 They thought the deal was in the bag
7 We knew it wasn't
6 They saw it as part of their corporate master plan
5 We saw it as beyond our wildest dreams
4 They did not want it enough
3 We could not have wanted it more
2 For them the heat had gone out of the deal
1 For us the heat was becoming unbearable

By now I had taken our quest to buy the radio station onto the air, declaring my intent to the audience. The management at Capital must simply have taken this as a bit of fun – purely for the benefit of entertainment – but the irony of it all was that everything I was saying was true.

I suppose they may have thought that no one in their right mind who was trying to steal a highly profitable business close to the value of £100 million from under their nose would choose to advertise that very fact every morning on the radio, but this is exactly what I was doing.

The more I talked about our efforts, the more we realised they might sound too fantastic to possibly be true. If it was a ploy to put our rivals off the scent of what was really going on then it was one that seemed to be working. I decided to ramp up the soap opera and make things so ridiculously transparent. I even went as far as where we were in the process, with daily updates. So far so good, but the clock was now ticking very loudly and we still needed to find the final chunk of our funding in what was now literally days.

This is where David's prior experience with Branson proved to be priceless. He explained that if Richard sold a company and in doing so had already realised a hefty profit, he had been known to leave a slice of the cash behind for another roll of the dice. David thought that this could be one of those occasions where he might be persuaded to do such a thing.

We had no choice but for someone to pitch our business plan to Branson himself.

It was decided that I was the principal so it was down to me.

The pitch had to be strong and confident. It had to have a story that would build layer upon layer as to why R.B. should sell to us as well as leaving some money in the pot, rather than get out clean by selling to Capital – and at a higher price.

We started to construct the call.

There was one massive consideration that we figured might swing things our way: Branson was fiercely protective of the Virgin name and brand – the very identity that he had worked for years to create and nurture and one that had become very much unique in the business world. Virgin was a mysterious mix of being corporate yet not too corporate, respected whilst still exciting, and now established but still at the cutting edge. Anything bearing the Virgin name had to reinforce that image and we figured it wouldn't be difficult to argue that the Capital group were unlikely to be suited to such a task. They were notoriously dreary and old school in comparison to Branson and his maverick ways.

David, who knew Richard better than most, said that this could be the Achilles heel of the Capital deal. In direct contradiction to what everybody else had been telling us, David said Branson might even 'prefer' to sell to someone else other than Capital, especially if that someone promised to remain more faithful to the Virgin philosophy. David was sure that if we could get this across to R.B. it could be the key to not only persuading him to consider selling to us but also to him maybe investing himself and leaving in the £20 million we needed to take us up to the magical £87,000,000.

The financial sell was, of course, also vital and would go something like: R.B.'s £20 million, if he chose to take us up on our offer, would to all intents and purposes be a loan but would also entitle him to close to an outright quarter share of the new company. If and when we sold, he would get all his money back plus the added booty of whatever the new company was worth on top. Meanwhile he would also receive full interest on his loan.

It was a very good deal. All I had to do now was pitch it to the great man.

The time for the call was set – the message came back that Richard would be available for a telephone conversation at 7 p.m. the following Friday.

Now I don't know if this was some kind of cruel joke or not but 7 p.m. on a Friday night was precisely the time *TFI* came off the air.

'You are not serious,' I said to Michael when he informed me of the news.

'That's the only time he has offered this week and if we leave it till after the weekend it may be too late – it's take it or leave it.'

Of course we had to take it.

'Oh and there's another thing,' Michael added.

'What's that?' I asked tentatively.

'He will be on Necker, his private island. He will have just finished playing tennis and will be waiting to start lunch, so he'll be in no mood to be messed around.'

'Fabulous,' I thought to myself. 'Not exactly the perfect time to ask a bloke to sell you his radio station and lend you twenty million quid into the bargain.' Still, always concentrate on the positives and you never know what might happen. 'Please God let him have won at tennis,' I thought to myself.

When it came to *the* Friday, the day was a confusion of preparing for the show and preparing for the phone call. I have to be honest and say the phone call was very much taking precedence in my mind. After all, I had hosted *TFI* dozens of times before whereas I had never made a phone call like the one I was about to make to Branson, the prospect of which made my previous phone call to Kenneth a couple of weeks ago seem like a walk in the park.

I knew that when it came to the pitch I had to go in hard and not waver for a second – to get Branson to take me seriously at all would be a minor miracle. If I stumbled or appeared unconfident or disorganised, particularly at the beginning, I would be toast for sure. Technically of course I still had nothing to lose – except now we were only one short conversation away from maybe making this once impossible dream a reality. I had to be on the form of my life. The principal of the piece had agreed to talk to us – the man who could say yes – and it was my job to convince him to do exactly that.

Whenever I'm in a situation similar to this, i.e. pooing my pants, I always think about twenty-four hours hence when it will all be over. We will all still be here and, sure, some things may have changed but basically life is never as dramatic in reality as we tend to make it in our heads. This would be one man talking to another, the first man offering the second man a completely respectable, well thought out, considered, not to mention very attractive, proposal – the second man able to accommodate the first man if he so wished. One way or another we would know the outcome soon enough.

My main priority as far as the preparation for the phone call was concerned was to retain enough energy to be able to concentrate come seven o'clock and so I consciously spent the whole day pacing myself. I'd been up since five, I had done a radio show, I had sat through three hours of briefings with the investors and the team, I'd been to the gym, I'd rehearsed the television show – twice, I was now actually hosting the show and yet the most important part of my day was still to come.

I had to make sure I had the mental wherewithal to get my pitch across – concisely, energetically, positively and convincingly. I had one shot at this speech, that's all, and I knew that if I blew it, a chance like this would probably never come around again.

That night *TFI* had the habitual three guests and three bands plus the usual bunch of jokes and sketches but all I could think about throughout the whole show was the damned phone call. Everywhere I looked I could see Richard's face – he was the lead singer in all the bands, he was all my guests, even the audience just looked like one huge set of dazzling white teeth staring right back at me.

After what seemed like forever, I introduced the last band and was immediately ushered off the set and into a room which had been prepared specifically for the phone call. A few senior members of the production team had been made aware of what was going on and had been briefed to get me in position as swiftly and efficiently as possible. The allocated room was the smallest of four dressing rooms, being not much bigger than a broom cupboard, I suddenly felt sorry for all the guests that we had forced to make do with such a claustrophobic space. No wonder Keith Allen was in such a bad mood after we'd put him in there! All that was in Dressing Room No. 4 for my tenure was: a chair, a bottle of water, a monitor so I could watch the end of the show and the dreaded telephone – just looking at it made my stomach disappear.

As the final band was still playing I dialled the international number which had been guarded by one of the producers all day. As I did so, I could see the end credits of the show beginning to crawl across the screen. I pressed each digit on the keypad extra firmly to ensure it registered, the whole dialling process seeming to take an achingly long time. A few moments later and the band had finished, the audience were applauding but there was still no connection. My palms were sweating and my right leg was shaking ten to the dozen as I continued to await the loud, clumsy click that would tell me I was finally through. A few seconds more and there it was, followed by the lazy ring of a telephone line somewhere thousands of miles away that tells you wherever it is you're calling, it's nowhere near anywhere else. After three or four rings somebody picked up – it was a lady's voice, bright and friendly and, judging from the ambience, she was outside.

'Hello, Necker Island.'

So far so good.

'Ah, hello,' I tried to sound as calm as I possibly could. 'It's Chris Evans for Richard. He should be expecting my call.'

'Oh yes, Chris, that's right, he is. I'll just get him for you.'

I can't tell you how much better that nice lady and her one fabulous sentence made me feel.

As I waited for Richard to come to the phone I could hear the distinct clink of cutlery piercing the air and people having fun laughing in the background as the breeze caused the line to crackle. I began to picture the scene there as opposed to where I was – holed up in a clammy little cupboard with chaos outside the door and sweat now dripping down my back. As the irony of the situation sank in, I could feel myself about to laugh.

'Hello, it's Richard,' said a recognisable voice on the other end of the line, instantly snapping me back to attention.

Shit, focus you prick, I chided myself.

'Oh, hello, Richard, thanks for taking my call. It's about your radio station.'

'Right, I see, what about it ...?'

'I want you to think about selling it to me.'

There. That was the plan. It couldn't have been any more concise than that now, could it? The perfect start.

'Ah, really, now I heard about this – tell me why.'

He sounded both amused and intrigued and, more importantly, he'd given me the green light to make my speech. This was all I needed. I launched straight in. I was suddenly totally in the moment. I didn't miss a beat.

I started off by explaining to him how I knew the importance of the Virgin brand as far as he personally was concerned, the spirit of where it came from, what it stood for and what people had come to expect of it. I then explained that Capital had little if anything in common with the aforementioned qualities and would ultimately only be interested in pushing their own brand and not that of another company. I ventured that it was even conceivable they might look to rename the station altogether.

Next I moved on to the workforce that was still employed at his radio station and how I had seen them operate over the last few weeks and how much pride they took in what they had created. He also needed to know how much they valued the fact that they worked for him and how downhearted they all were at the prospect of being sold to the men in grey suits from the Capital group. Virgin Radio was different because they were different and they were different because he was different.

All the while he just listened. It was going as well as I could have hoped for.

Having set up the downside of him selling to Capital, it was time for me to pitch the upside of him selling to us.

I urged him to consider that whatever he thought Virgin Radio was worth today, it had nowhere near reached its full potential. I did this by going through the financial arguments which by now I knew as well as anyone, having heard them time and time again in our meetings with the banks and our various investors.

I then went on to describe my own position and how, not unlike himself when he had started, I found myself somewhat of a square peg in a round hole. He was the maverick businessman, I was the maverick broadcaster and we both shared a comprehensive understanding, knowledge and passion for what we did for a living.

I explained that although this conversation was ultimately a money conversation, for me this was not a money deal but something much more, something I had to do in order to continue to broadcast. Obviously I realised the figures had to stack up as well, which is why I had surrounded myself with a grown-up, experienced business wall of steel, including David Campbell whom I knew he trusted; Barbara, whose company had helped Virgin Radio get on air in the first place, and my agent Michael Foster, who was the best playmaker in town.

I assured him that whatever Capital was lacking, I was confident we could deliver and not only that but there was also a real possibility he could end up making much more money. It was at this point I took a deep breath as it was time to inform him that if he were to go with us we needed him to leave £20 million behind to bridge the gap in our funding.

This is what I said:

'Richard, as it stands now, you will make £83 million profit if you sign with Capital. If you sign with us you will make £61 million today, and I can almost guarantee you will make at least another £40 million within three years – probably considerably more.'

I then went on to explain briefly our revenue and profit projections which were based on a three- to five-year exit plan.

The key to the whole pitch was that everything I was saying I believed to be true, something I hoped he would be able to perceive.

'And do you have the rest of the money?' he asked.

'Yes sir, we do, every penny, we are 100 per cent ready to go.'

This bit was 99.9 per cent true as we didn't physically have the money, but Michael, David and Barbara had 'funds in place', as they say.

'Our lawyers, all twenty of them,' I laughed, 'have the contracts and loan agreements waiting at their offices ready to be signed. If you say yes, we can do the deal today.'

And with that I was done. I had said all there was to say.

'Alright, thank you, that's very interesting. May I think about it?'

This last question took me by surprise.

'Er, yes of course.' For the first time I stumbled, but it didn't matter. I had done what I had to do.

'Good, very good, OK, I will let you know. Thanks for the call, goodbye.'

'Goodbye and thank you,' I said now speaking from somewhere on the floor, having gradually slipped off my chair onto my knees in some kind of subconscious display of gratitude.

'Alright Chris,' said Richard with a smile in his voice. I think he could sense my relief that this ordeal was coming to an end.

The line clicked dead. I needed a drink.

David and Michael had been outside the room, guarding the door for the duration of the call, and were both equally excited as well as anxious to find out how the conversation had gone. They also had thought to supply me with one beautiful ice-cold beer.

I informed them that although I had no previous experience of such matters to compare it to, as far as I could tell it couldn't have gone any better. I reassured them that I had managed to get in most, if not all, of the points we had rehearsed and that Richard had listened attentively before asking a couple of questions and telling me he would let us know. Satisfied with our combined efforts we rewarded ourselves with a trip back to the bar for more beers.

Nothing further happened over the weekend. Once again, we had done all we could, all that was now left to do was wait. We had batted our ball over to Branson's side of the court, what he did with it next was up to him.

It was four days later on the Tuesday of the following week when we received a response. It came in the form of a phone call from my old pal Kenneth Ibbett.

'Richard says if you want the radio station, it's yours.'

We could not believe it.

We had done it.

Well, we'd *almost* done it.

top
10
Human Responses I Experienced Leading Up To the Deal

10 Excitement
9 Frustration
8 Anxiety
7 Sleeplessness
6 Patience
5 Focus
4 Doggedness
3 Fastidiousness
2 Fear
1 Acceptance

The next week was absolute mayhem as we raced to tie up all the loose ends and push the deal through. Although Richard had agreed to sell to us, he had not agreed *not* to sell to Capital – it was still us and them, not us instead of them. If Capital for one second woke up to the fact that we were a serious threat, all they had to do was get their pen out, extend their exclusivity period and they could have put an end to our fantastic adventure. We prayed they wouldn't and decided to wise up a little.

I abruptly ceased all on-air mentions of anything to do with what might be going on, I quietly let the subject fade away. I also arranged to stay in a central London hotel for the next few days in case I was needed at short notice for one reason or another. I even stopped going out at night just in case I might get caught up in any 'unfavourable' circumstances. We really were so close now, it wasn't worth risking anything that might jeopardise the deal of a lifetime.

With all our team working around the clock it was only two days later when we informed Richard's office we were ready to sign. No more than ten minutes later the message came back:

'Richard wants to see Chris at his house in Holland Park within the hour – alone.'

I told the guys.

'There is no way you are going alone,' was the resounding response.

'But that's what he says he wants,' I protested.

Michael wasted no time in giving me both barrels.

'Look, Chris, I was with you on the plane when you almost signed a contract on the back of a menu for a show you didn't even know about. That was the last time I left you on your own with Mr Branson – remember?'

Of course I had no defence. Michael was absolutely right.

'There is no way you are going to his house without me and that's the end of it.' The little man was adamant.

'Or me,' said David. The big man was adamant too.

'Or me,' said Barbara.

'Or me!' said Kirit, my accountant, who now joined our merry band.

It was difficult for me to argue with the team. They were all older, wiser and much more sensible than I was, although I couldn't help feeling that whatever Richard wanted to see me for couldn't possibly be nearly as sinister as maybe they suspected. Moreover – at some point in every transaction there has to be an element of trust. No matter how much the 'legals' get involved there has to be a willingness on both sides to make things happen. I had no reason to doubt Richard as he had no reason to doubt me, and furthermore Richard had specifically asked me to go see him on my own. To turn up mob-handed would be a flagrant rebuff of his request.

'Are you sure about this, gang?' I said. 'Is all of us going really a wise thing to do?'

They were having none of it and were adamant I was not leaving without them. A few moments later we were huddled together in the back of a black taxi – destination Holland Park, West London, the home of Richard Branson and the Virgin Group.

The atmosphere during the taxi ride was strained to say the least – it was a mixture of nervous apprehension and abject fear with no one really knowing quite what to say. This was another make or break moment and certainly the most important in a recent list of many, but the difference this time was that none of us had any idea what was going on and why Richard wanted to see me 'on my own'. Anything could happen in the next half an hour, all we could do was wait to find out what. After some tentative attempts at small talk the cab fell silent and we each took to staring out of the window with only our thoughts for company.

This was another of those moments when time seems to stand still. Suddenly from being thirty-one, I was back to being thirteen staring at the wall in the playground, wondering if Tina would ever speak to me again. Everything is real, yet it is not real. You are there; yet you're not there. I could see the busy London streets with commuters marching onwards, head down, on the home straight of that day's rat race. I could see all the cars on the road jostling for position but not really knowing why. I could see the meter inside the taxi clocking up the fare that I used to be so wary of when I first moved down South, wondering if it would reach the amount I had in my pocket before I reached my destination.

As we drew closer to our drop-off point and I realised where we were, I found myself having to take deeper and deeper breaths to calm myself down. Our cab trundled past the big black iron gates that lead to Kensington Palace opposite a cafe called Diana's which proudly displayed huge pictures of the late princess in its window alongside the sandwich menu. We were now no more than a couple of minutes away – maybe less if the last set of traffic lights went our way.

I could feel my palms beginning to clam up, but now more with excitement than nerves. I reminded myself there are few opportunities in life to feel like this, and I should remember to enjoy it. Once again I told myself: I had nothing to fear – I had done nothing wrong and the worst that could happen was that in a few minutes' time we would all be going home with our tails between our legs.

I concentrated on trying to stay in the now and it was working. I knew that what we were doing was a good thing and that we were doing it for all the right reasons. As I repeated this mantra to myself over and over I began to feel an amazing sense of renewed optimism.

All the long hours of the last two months combined with all those years, right back from the lonely nights at Piccadilly Radio through to my early days in London up until where we were now, were coming together in one stellar moment. The kind of alignment that is often necessary to enable extraordinary things to happen. Suddenly I had this overwhelming feeling that it was all going to be alright.

top
10

Houses I Have Found Myself In
For One Reason Or Another

10 Chris Lowe's apartment – a wild party with the Pet Shop Boys

 9 Downing Street – drinks with the PM

 8 Chequers – dinner and a tour

 7 Bono and Edge's house in France – pizza, wine and brandy

 6 Lord Lloyd Webber's house, Belgravia – dinner and wine

 5 Lord Lloyd Webber's house, France – dinner and amazing wine

 4 Elton John's house, Holland Park – meeting with the great man

 3 Elton's house, Windsor – charity dinner with Bill Clinton

 2 Damon Albarn's house with Gazza, Damon wasn't home – long story, maybe for the next book

 1 Richard Branson's house, Holland Park – the night we sealed the deal

Richard owned two of the huge, white stucco-fronted period houses that made up this most majestic of roads.

Both his houses were next to each other and were entered via a set of white stone steps sheltered by a canopied walkway. One of the houses was his London home, the other his Virgin HQ. Ever since Richard had set up in business he had always done things differently, especially when it came to his offices. His first ever office was on a houseboat in Little Venice – all very cool, very cool indeed. As our cab pulled up outside, and we all bundled out I couldn't help thinking how uncool we must have looked, very uncool indeed.

David had visited here many times before and suggested that we were probably expected at the house that was the HQ, as opposed to Richard's private residence. This is how it normally worked, he said. After approaching the door, David very calmly stepped forward to ring the bell. He had assumed the position of team leader, something that was fine by the rest of us.

After a brief period of doorstep shuffling and more awkward silence, the grand entrance to this fine house swung open to reveal a glamorous lady dressed as a Virgin stewardess. He has stewardesses as private staff! This man really was living the dream.

'Hello gentlemen,' she pronounced courteously. 'Madam,' she added, nodding to Barbara respectfully. 'How may I help you?'

'Hi,' said Michael smiling, overly anxiously, keen to make a good impression. 'It's Chris Evans to see Richard.'

Plainly this was an inaccurate statement – it was Chris Evans plus four to see Richard.

'Sure,' said the lady, understandably a little confused. 'Please, do come in.'

We entered the hallway of the house and were requested to wait at the bottom of the stairs as the 'ground stewardess' daintily trotted up them – all four of us boys attempted to avert our gaze so as not to be seen taking a peek at her almost perfect bottom, which of course we all wanted to. Isn't it good to know that no moment is too powerful to conquer the hold the female form has over the simple male?

Barbara, for her part, looked 'professionally' down at her shoes, aware of how pathetically predictable we were being.

'Is she really a stewardess?' I whispered to David.

'Kind of,' he replied.

I was about to press him further on this subject when the pretty lady trotted back down the stairs.

'Richard will be with you in a moment,' she smiled, before quietly adding in almost a whisper, 'but I think he only wants to see Chris,' and with that she brushed past our group and disappeared off down the hallway.

This last piece of information, *'But I think he only wants to see Chris,'* although communicated to us more as a piece of friendly advice than as a stern warning, was nevertheless designed to leave us in no doubt as to its meaning.

So there we were, now feeling more awkward than ever, knowing for sure we had goofed. We were at the bottom of Mr Branson's stairs in the full knowledge that we were five, which was currently three men and one woman surplus to requirements. 'Told you!' I wanted to say triumphantly, and I would have done had it not been for the sound of galloping footsteps thundering down the stairs.

Seconds later, as if by magic, there he was, larger than life for all to see. Dressed in jeans and one of his upbeat stripy sweaters – Ricky B, rock and roll king of the corporate world, here to say hello.

Richard stopped short of coming all the way to the bottom, electing instead to halt and lean over the banister where, like a swashbuckling hero ready for a duel, he declared, 'Ah, Mr Evans, I see you have come with many men ... and one fair maiden. Well, I must ask you to tell these others their presence is not welcome here,' he exclaimed jokingly. 'They may go and help themselves to a drink in the kitchen. This is just about you and me, sonny,' and with that he cackled like a pantomime villain.

He was clearly playing with our collective paranoia but we were all so frozen with apprehension that we forgot to laugh.

Sensing the urgent need for us to be rescued from ourselves, Richard thought it best to promptly break into one of his trademark smiles.

'Seriously guys, relax,' he said almost apologetically, 'there's nothing to worry about – none of the stories are true,' he then laughed again, even more mischievously this time, he couldn't help himself, we were rabbits caught in the headlights although this time we did remember to laugh – sort of. Richard continued his reassurance, 'You guys go through to the back and grab yourselves a refreshment while Chris and I nip upstairs for a quick chat. Is that alright with you, Chris?'

'Sure,' I said, suddenly remembering to be excited again.

'Good, come on then, let's go,' Richard enthused.

Without looking back, I went to bound up the stairs after him when I felt the all too familiar grip of a small but firm hand on my arm preventing me from moving anywhere – it was the same impressive hold I'd felt on Concorde a few months before – the right hand of Michael, my trusty and loyal agent. He was in full-on protection mode again.

'*Don't – sign – anything,*' he mouthed.

'*Don't – worry – I – won't,*' I mouthed back but I couldn't get up those stairs fast enough.

Richard and I entered his office and there I was alone with the main man in his inner sanctum. It was so like I had wanted it to be – a very laid-back affair, much more New York loft than shiny big business. The furniture had that chic beaten up look to it, like it could have been from the set of an Eighties Mickey Rourke movie. There were a couple of funky pictures on the wall, an old rug thrown in the middle of the floor, several lamps with wonky shades, a small collection of books upon a shelf, and a fabulous globe in the corner – but best of all were the four objects sat on the window sill behind his desk.

They were: a model Virgin plane, a model Virgin train, a model Virgin balloon and a model Virgin speedboat.

I couldn't help smiling – it was perfect.

Richard invited me to sit while he plumped down in his own chair.

'Can I get you anything – tea, coffee, some water perhaps?' he asked kindly.

'No thanks, I'm OK,' I replied.

As we both settled, there was a brief moment of quiet as Richard looked at me and just beamed. It was a 'don't worry it's all going to be alright' kind of look.

He then spoke.

'Alright, so young man, how are you?' he asked sincerely.

'I'm fine thanks,' I replied. It was true, I couldn't remember ever feeling better in my life.

Richard was now tapping the tips of his fingers together under his nose like a contemplative professor.

'Well, it appears … from what I have heard at least … that we are ready to go … that we are ready to do this thing – as they say.'

I replied, sounding like a member of the CIA responding to the President, 'That's right, sir, I believe we are.' I felt an official response was called for and this was as official as I could sound.

'Wow, that's pretty impressive,' Richard offered, I presumed he was referring to my statement and not my newly officious tone.

'Thank you, thank you very much,' I replied, I was genuinely humbled by his compliment and didn't really know what else to say.

What followed was another pause – this one longer than the last. Richard was now looking ever so slightly more serious. He was staring straight into my eyes. His hands now clasped together under his chin.

I couldn't imagine for one second what he was thinking – not that I was trying. He was bound to tell me when he was ready. All I had to do was hold his gaze, that's what I was focused on. He was plainly looking for something, some sign to tell him what he wanted to know. He looked at me a little while longer and then after a few moments, as if satisfied, looked down at his desk to break the connection. Whatever it was he was looking for had either happened or not. I presumed I was about to find out.

'Alright now,' he said, 'I want you to know that I am fully prepared to sell you the radio station here and now, but before I do so, there is one thing I have to ask you and you must promise to tell me the truth, OK?'

Wow wee, had he really just said that he would sell me the radio station? Well, yes he had, but he had also stated quite categorically that I was still one question and answer away from that actually happening. Now, what the blazes was the question?

'I know,' he said, 'that you have put almost all the money you have in the world into this deal – just over two million pounds, is that correct?'

'Yes,' I replied.

'Very well, I now need you to tell me that you understand that if you buy this radio station and for one reason or another things don't work out, that you will more than likely lose everything – that is to say that your money been designated as the least senior debt and will be the last to get paid back – if at all. Therefore it is the most 'at risk'. Now bearing in mind you have less money than everyone else involved in this deal and even though I know this is your dream, based on those facts – are you absolutely, one hundred per cent sure you want to go forward and proceed with this, because nobody is saying you have to and you don't have to, but once we have both signed, there's no turning back?'

And that ladies and gentlemen, boys and girls, is all he wanted to tell me. He simply wanted to make sure that I knew exactly what I was getting myself into and that I also knew that nobody was holding a gun to my head telling me I had to go through with this.

I was blown away by his consideration. Never in a month of Sundays would I have guessed this is what he wanted. In the middle of all the madness, Richard had slowed the train right down to make sure I didn't want to get off and to tell me that I could if I wanted to. To show that level of concern for my personal well-being and to show me that, in the end, no matter how big the deal, nothing is more important than people is a sentiment that will stay with me forever – what an absolutely top man.

With a sigh of relief and a heart about to burst, I gave him his answer.

'You have my word, Richard,' I assured him, breaking out into as wide a smile as I could manage, 'I know my position and I definitely want to do this.'

I had never been more certain of anything in my life.

'Alright then,' he said, the big Branson smile instantly returning. 'Let's do it.'

Thirty-six hours, thousands of pages, and over one hundred signatures later, I would become the proprietor of Virgin Radio, the jewel in the crown of the soon to be formed Ginger Media Group.

What could possibly go wrong?

Congratulations and celebrations … from my old boss Michael Grade, my bank and some bloke called Jonathan Ross.

BARCLAYS

BARCLAYS BANK PLC
Hanover Square Corporate Banking Centre
8/9 Hanover Square, London W1A 4ZW

C Evans Esq
Ginger Television Productions Ltd
3rd Floor
The Media Centre
131-151 Great Titchfield
London W1P 8DB

Your Ref:
Our Ref:
Direct Dial: (0171) 445 2421
Facsimile: (0171) 445

9th December 1997

Dear Chris

I am delighted that you have been successful in your negotiations for

Many congratulations on achieving this major step in the ultimate flo

We are very proud to be the Group's bankers.

Yours sincerely

CHRIS MCENTYRE
SENIOR CORPORATE MANAGER

Chris –

Congratulations on the Virginger deal – it's incredible.

I think you are a huge talent etc. etc.

well done, again

Cheers – Jonathan

PS ~~Your~~ Asian Newsagents Perfect Day was the _best_ thing I have ever heard on Radio

---

1 FIRST LEISURE CORPORATION

FIRST LEISURE CORPORATION P
7 Soho Street London W1V 5FA
Telephone 0171-439 3775 Telefax 0171-2
DX 44730 Soho Square

MICHAEL GRADE CHAIRMAN

FAX all
Hi Chris EVANS
% GINGER PRODS

Dear Chris,

Congratulations and welcome to the wonderful world of real business. As ever, you have made a brilliant move for your career. Ownership is much more fun. I am always here if you ever need any help or advice.

Good luck.

Yours,

FIRST LEISURE CORPORATION PLC

preview prologue
of the next book

top
10 Stories Still
to Come …

10 How much is that chat-show host in the window?

9 How not to buy a national newspaper

8 The management have walked out – what do I do now?

7 Let's give away a million pounds – hey, I've got an even better idea: let's give away two

6 Macca and the maddest *TFI* moment of all

5 The £30,000 carrier bag

4 Gazza, the tour bus and a 'convenient' substitution

3 Quick, wake up – you're 300 and something in the *Sunday Times* rich list

2 The £24-million cappuccino

1 Billie, the Doctor and a golfer named Natasha

appendix

it is what you think ... notes from the cast

NAME: Zig and Zag

The first time we met, Chris Evans was shooting the pilot for *The Big Breakfast* in 1992. Coming from the Planet Zog, we had never heard of Chris Evans, we presumed he was there to make the tea or put the bins out. But his 'Way Hey' personality soon made us realise he was the star of the show.

Our slot, 'The Crunch', was supposed to be 'our' slot, but Chris became the third alien in the bathroom. We used to have such a laugh together; sometimes we continued to crack up even after the cameras had stopped rolling! He became our Earth Dad and we even had tea in his real house with his real wife Carol, who then kicked him out when he became the Ginger Whinger and got all showbiz. Mind you, he was still our Dad, so we let him move in with us in our swanky apartment in Limehouse E14. He said he was only going to stay for a couple of weeks until the press stopped hassling him. Six months later he was still there nicking our cornflakes, wearing our socks and staying up late with his new girlfriend Kim Wilde.

We ended up having to kick him out, but the thing about Chris is you can't help but like him! When he left *The Big Breakfast* it was never the same again. We met Chris a few times after that when he invited us on to his cool show *TFI Friday* and then he starred in an episode of our series, *Dirty Deeds*, where we wrote a musical about his life called 'Gingerella'.

And even though he's become a multimillionaire superstar DJ, he'll always be our ginger dad from Planet Earth, who sadly doesn't call us anymore ... or send us presents on our birthday ... or even give us a free copy of this book ...

NAME: Charlie Parsons

Chris isn't just the icing on the cake guy, he's the cherry on the icing on the cake.

Always the most stunningly entertaining guy to watch and listen to, his particular strength is turning a good idea into a brilliant idea.

When we at Planet 24 first came up with *The Big Breakfast*, the Channel 4 stand-up show *Whose Line is it Anyway?* was big and we thought, hey, our show is set in a real house, let's call our competition 'Whose *Washing* Line is it Anyway?' and put up a washing line in the garden.

Chris comes in as presenter and takes the whole thing further by using props for the phone – only Chris would have picked up a banana and used it to receive viewers' calls. A banana! Comedy genius! So Chris was the first person on British television to talk to viewers using a banana.

He has the ability and the charisma to inspire a team – to make everyone work towards the same goals – because it was always amazing fun. This was often driven by things he is passionately interested in – like helicopters and cars and engines and dogs – and, err, pretty women! He makes everyone want to do really well – and it isn't just the fear of being shouted at. On *The Big Breakfast* when he made people change something at the 5 a.m. meeting he was always right, despite the tears due to exhaustion or the fear of having to start all over again in order to make his changes. He was such a perfectionist he used to refuse to read scripts if they had spelling mistakes. He used to watch the shows back immediately after they went out so that he could see how and what things worked and what didn't – so the same mistakes would never be repeated.

The improvements were made with such energy you knew they were right. I think he was fuelled by a special kind of adrenalin. Perhaps that's why after his morning bath he'd wander round *The Big Breakfast* house naked.

Years later he put the icing on the cake for me again when I produced *Never Forget*, a musical with the songs of Take That. He came to see it and he loved it, but gave three very sharp and clever script suggestions. All of them made it better. He's changed a bit though – as far as I know he didn't walk round naked afterwards. Shame!

NAME: Gaby Roslin

Chris Evans and I never slept together! It's still the one question I'm asked even after all this time.

1992 was when we first worked together to launch *The Big Breakfast*. After our first day on air one of our bosses walked us to our cars and said, 'You do realise your lives are never going to be the same again!' I didn't realise that he actually meant that 17 years later people would still want to know if we'd ever had sex!

Chris was always the BEST in my eyes, even when he was hit in the eye by a low-flying snowball one freezing morning and he lost his temper live on air; or the time he sneezed into his mug of tea and we both giggled for far too long; or even the time when we both became hysterical when he fell over his chair.

Chris is an incredibly loyal man. He loves his mum and loves life (even though back when I first knew him he would never have admitted to loving life). He cries openly when he really feels something and laughs uncontrollably. He's a bugger to get hold of but when you do get together he listens and then he pours out far too much alcohol.

Bizarrely the one abiding memory I have of our time together on the *BB* is his last show. We were both heartbroken and cried ridiculously throughout the two hours, but as the show came to an end and as he walked off silently into the distance, dressed in a brown raincoat, just like the wonderful Eric Morecambe had done many years earlier, we both stopped crying and smiled.

He's a generous, good man. I'm proud to say we have never, ever fallen out over anything ... and we never will.

Every time anyone asks me about Chris (apart from the 'no we didn't' line) I always say the same thing.

He's a decent good man and I love him!

NAME: Kim Wilde

C of E

Chris Evans first came into my life in 1990 as I sat in the bath in Primrose Hill where I was living at the time. I had never met him but loved his radio show, *The Greenhouse*, on GLR, and I would tune in whilst having a soak; he really made me laugh with his innocent and very silly but clever humour. I soon became a fan and shortly afterwards was pleased to accept an invitation to pop into the studio one day to say 'Hello'.

I didn't realise it at the time, but he was my fan too.

Then a call from *The Big Breakfast*: 'Did I want to step in for Gaby Roslin for a week with Chris?' In truth, the thought terrified me. I was a big fan of the show ... everyone was, but I didn't have any presenting experience so it was a challenge for me. However, encouraged by my mum, I took the plunge and before I knew it I was right in the heart of an extremely mad but fun-filled world. I knew this coveted offer was out to several high-profile female presenters at the time, but Chris made sure I got the job and gave me total support. It was a week I'll never forget.

Subsequently I appeared on *Don't Forget Your Toothbrush* where Chris and I were pitched against each other in a competition to see who knew more about me and my career ... needless to say, Chris won!

Chris's incredible energy and ambition were always countered by his genuine love of people, whether they were 'A listers' or someone making the coffee backstage. He effortlessly gained people's respect and devotion by treading his own path, his own way, whilst irresistibly inviting you to come along and share it all with him.

When I think of Chris I always smile and I am glad he found what he was looking for, just as I know he is glad that I did too.

NAME: Matthew Bannister

Dear Sir,
Re: Your request for a reference for Christopher Evans

Whilst he has many strong points, of which I'm sure you are aware, there are a number of issues which prevent me from endorsing him unreservedly. Although there appears to have been a miraculous transformation recently, in the past he has suffered from the following problems:

- A tendency to skateboard down the corridor at work in his boxer shorts.
- An insistence on using his own toaster in the office which repeatedly set off the fire alarm.
- A determination to fly his own flag from a BBC building, which led to endless meetings with angry people from the premises department.
- An insubordinate attitude to authority, tending to refer to his boss as 'the Fat Controller'.
- An impeccable sense of timing which led to him telling a joke about oral sex and Brussels sprouts on the day I was due to defend him to the BBC Board of Governors.
- An unreliable attendance record which culminated in him taking the day after the Christmas Party as a 'sickie'.
- A tendency to flounce out if not given Fridays off.

Apart from these minor defects he is, of course, a brilliant broadcaster who has single handedly changed the face of British radio and an all round good egg. I'm very proud to have been associated with bits of his career.

NAME: Michael Grade

My first sight of Chris Evans was that day at Channel 4 when we ran two parallel live pilots of potential shows to fill the breakfast slot. I had two TVs on in my office, one showing *The Big Breakfast* effort, the other another pilot from an established broadcaster. Within ten minutes of the two-hour show, I had abandoned watching the other pilot, and became glued, if not transfixed by the carroty haired, smiley voiced unknown co-presenter Chris Evans. The rest is history. From *Big Breakfast*, to *Don't Forget Your Toothbrush* (who COULD forget that classic?) through to *TFI Friday*, he became a part of Channel 4 legend, a regular visitor to my office to offer advice and to receive advice.

Despite his occasional public notoriety, I would have to say I never had a moment's aggravation with Chris. I found him always professional, always intelligent about his career, his shows, his views about TV. In fact, I often thought he would make a top-notch TV channel controller. I became, and still am, very fond of him, and still a fan. He is a natural broadcaster, at home on TV or radio. He is one of a kind, like the late Kenny Everett or Jimmy Saville, and I am certain his career will continue to flourish. He is certainly a man for these times – he never fails to brighten your viewing or listening with that infectious, irreverent, anarchic and fantastical imagination. He has the gift of the gob, and deserves all the success he has worked so hard for.

NAME: Timmy Mallett

I'm very fond of Nobby. He was a tall, gangly teenager, very red headed with an infectious nervous enthusiasm. Saying he was from hospital radio, Nobby hadn't a clue how to work the old tape recorder he'd borrowed from his brother but his questions were very memorable – '*How many cars have you got?*' '*Which are better – tadpoles or newts?*' As he packed up, he overheard we needed a new keenie. Nobby's letter landed next day asking for a job. It would have been rude to refuse ...

So I gave him an on-air persona – Nobby No-Level – with a catchphrase '*what I don't know – I don't know!*' and he lapped up every tip, every opportunity, every chance to try something. He was like blotting paper absorbing the magic of radio and the work that goes into getting it right. He leaped around on Roadshows chucking buckets of water, and came to watch and learn how to perform onstage at gigs. Out in the radio car with no-one to interview, he did an hilarious one-way chat with a grid in the road; talked his way into Tina Turner's dressing room to do a live interview with her in her underwear; and helped make *Timmy on the Tranny* the number one radio show in the national Sony and *Smash Hits* polls.

Nobby has a charm that is very appealing. Like the crack of dawn he surprised me in his dressing gown with a bottle of champagne and a big grin to celebrate 'Itsy Bitsy' going to No.1!

He likes a bit of mischief too and offered to partner my dad in the treasure hunt at my wedding – they collected half the stone statues together from the castle grounds. I always thought that the death of his own father when he was 15 was the catalyst for Nobby to embrace life and all the opportunities that came his way. So it was lovely to share a special moment on holiday with him and friends in the summer of 1992 – I was signing autographs for a crowd of 'Itsy Bitsy' and *Wacaday* fans in a pub and over my shoulder was someone waiting his turn ... '*this'll be you in a couple of months, Nobby, when the Big Breakfast starts ...*'

Carpe diem – seize the day and make it happen!

NAME: Tina Yardley

It's not what you'd think – first love and romance, well not so much romance really! My memories start with Chris playing a soldier in an Old Time Music Hall, I was the young lady who had to take his arm on stage, singing and dancing whilst trying to make him think I was coy and vulnerable! That would be very difficult now, but at the time we were ridiculously innocent, both wanting to be adored. It didn't take long to move from 'going out' to complete adoration and first love but I remember silly things like a Beatles song book, his green quilted coat, never the style icon; walking dogs, sitting and watching the telly with Minnie and Diane. Being buried in the snow and actually being furious but not having the courage to walk off in a huff. Chris being chased out of the house by my Mum wielding a log because he implied that she resembled a witch! Always walking me to 'Holbrooks' before turning round to go back home.

We would spend hours in each other's company doing absolutely nothing, listening to the King's Singers (you may well look puzzled), walking through the park; it's hard to remember what else we did in those early days because we had no money and we were too young to drive.

When we were older Chris was always the risk-taker, entrepreneurial and looking for new challenges; at Piccadilly his talent and creativity shone through, much to the annoyance of the established DJs! I was happier to be the anchor, too scared to really embrace all that was happening around us.

We complimented each other well and even though time has passed and we are so very different as people, we can both count on unquestionable friendship and loyalty if needed.

NAME: Rachel Tatton Brown

Dear Chris

What to write? You know me, I was never great at expressing myself. Why you put me on camera I'll never know. And how you got me to wear those hideous suits – it must have been love.

I don't think what I write will make the book but I wanted you to know that I loved every minute of our time together and wouldn't trade any of it, even the bad times (of which there were a few, although not as many as people would like to think).

Time has made the memories a bit hazy but generally I remember it all being about the fun of the small things in life. It was never the showbiz life with you, I remember being dressed and in the lift on the way to a premiere when we both decided not to go. Instead we sat on the double deck chair on the roof of the flat watching fireworks. I remember the joy you felt when you bought your first Ferrari but you were still willing to let my friend Gill drive it on Christmas Day in her apron.

That's not to say you didn't mind the grand gesture occasionally, buying me a car for my birthday when we'd only been going out 2 weeks, or flying my sister from New Zealand to surprise me live on *Don't Forget Your Toothbrush*.

I've only ever wanted the best for you in life and will consider you a friend always. You have a good heart and deserve all the happiness that life can bring.

I just wanted to say thanks for making a great chapter in my life and I'm touched to be a couple of lines in yours.

Love
Rachel x

NAME: Will

The one question I get asked by London cab drivers more than 'Where to guv?' and 'Hasn't political correctness gone mad?' is: 'What's that Chris Evans like?'

Well, to paraphrase the transcendentalist (try saying that after a night out in 1998) Ralph Waldo Emerson, there are two types of TV genius – those that think and those that inspire others to think. And to me Chris's greatest quality has been to make me think.

In a world where taking no for an answer is a short cut to an easy life and a bland television programme, his stubbornness and 'road less travelled' attitude has wound a few people up, but it certainly has inspired me into pushing a little harder.

My first experience of this: Bumwrestling.

Very late one night in 1992, only a few hours before the dawn breaks on another two hours of live television by the side of East London's scariest effluent-ridden canal, and my main *Big Breakfast* item, a 10-minute set-piece involving 15 sheepdogs which I've spent a week preparing has fallen apart. So it is somewhat nervously that I phone Chris to run through a makeshift, that'll-do, thrown-together piece for the morning with a man who collects Take That stickers.

His response? We can do better Will.

I don't get it. It's only a few minutes of meaningless TV, and more importantly it's on air in about six hours. Who cares? Certainly not the comatose students and Sugar Puff-filled pre-schoolers watching. Let's get through it and go home. But I'd reckoned without that Evans determination to push.

Twenty minutes later, and we'd invented a new sport. And not just a vague thought for a sport. This one had its own rules, and its own federation. So detailed were its codes and the history we contrived that we were able to convince the Series Editor of its existence and that we should spend a chunk of national network television telling Britain about it. I spent the rest of the night writing the sport's legislation and trying to find a celebrity to endorse it.

And so, at 7.23 that morning we unveiled to the world the historic underground sport of Bumwrestling. A sporting, er, ring had been built outside, competitors and a ref in bespoke outfits were ready. Chris explained the rules in hushed tones, and we brought out an expert in the sport, Olympic legend Tessa Sanderson, who in reality had been briefed in the car on the way to Bow. And then, a bout. The competitors bent over, derrière à derrière, and on the referee's whistle, pushed. A few minutes of straining thighs later, one bum athlete had been projected from the circle and it was over. Yes we had lied to the nation, but surely it was more entertaining than what was on *GMTV* at the same time.

So here's to Bumwrestling, the sport that taught me to think a bit more. And surely a sport Britain can win medals at in 2012.

Thanks Christopher. To cab drivers everywhere: he's a brilliant producer, a good friend, is inventive, funny, a true original and though he might drive you nuts, stick with it – it's worth it.

NAME: David Campbell

I first met Chris a rather scary two decades ago when he worked with Jonathan Ross at Radio Radio – a company we at Virgin owned (we nicked the name from CBS in the US, sorry, it was a totally original idea and just a coincidence). In any case, I got to know him a few years later when he started his stellar on-air radio career at GLR, and it was obvious from that point on the boy had talent, and lots of it.

Like any brilliant inventor and engineer, Chris has an insatiable appetite for understanding how things work and for creating. His interests are broad, but nowhere is his skill more apparent than in media, where his natural abilities are well documented. He just gets it ... so much more than almost anyone else.

Chris is my friend, and I'd like to think the feeling is mutual. However, no matter how many people come up to him on the streets (and there are always lots – many far more visually appealing than me), Chris has a great ability to make you feel special and as if you are the most important one. (I have only ever met one other person, (Sir) David Frost, who has this unique charm.)

It's always a temptation to go back and reinvent what you have done before, especially when it was so much fun – and I'd be first in line for a new edition of *TFI Friday* (loved that show) – but Chris certainly subscribes to the school of thought that is all about looking forward, and that is a great attitude. The best is (always) yet to come.

Mr Evans, you deserve everything. However, you are a lucky bastard to have such a lovely wife and son, fab car, etc ...!

NAME: Duncan Grey

I am a very lucky man. I have spent 20 years working in show business. I have had the most incredible experiences and as a result I met my gorgeously captivating wife Eve, the extraordinary mother of my three beautiful children.

And you, Chris Evans, are one of a handful of people (by my reckoning there are five) who made the life I enjoy possible, by showing me what happened if you reached down into the depths of yourself and settled for nothing else than giving your absolute all and bringing out the best of everybody around you each and every day.

I first met you in October 1989. A very nice man called Trevor Dann had helped me organise a debate entitled 'Rock and Roll Has Lost Its Balls' at The Oxford Union in the summer of 1988.

In October 1989 I called him out of the blue on the pretext of finding out how to get on record companies' white label mailing lists to help my job as a nightclub DJ. The banks and consultancy firms had stopped coming to universities to hire 21-year-olds like me that year because of Norman Lamont's Black Monday, and I had always kind of known that that kind of job wasn't for me anyway.

Trevor said, 'Come down to GLR. Have a look round and see what you think.' I did and during my tour he said, 'I want you to meet somebody. He's from up north.

He's Emma Freud's producer and I think he's going to become a huge star. He has his first show for us on air tonight and I need somebody to answer his phones.'

You looked up and said 'Hi'. That's all you said. Nothing else. I hung around slightly in awe of where I was and who we shared our office with (Janice Long, Johnnie Walker, Emma Freud and Nick Abbot). When you went on air that night at 7.30 I fell headlong in love. With you, with the idea you could do this thing for a living and with the adrenal pleasure hit of answering a phone, prepping a caller and hearing them on air 30 seconds later.

I had to go back to university nine months later and cram my degree in. You weren't too happy about that I know. And I got pretty fucked off with you when I couldn't get a job on *Power Up* in Heathman's Yard after my finals. But I had my life and you had yours and I always think that's why we were so good for each other.

Cut to January 1992 and I had just landed my first TV job at Planet 24 as development writer. Charlie Parsons passed by my desk, a whir of frenzied energy and said, 'Channel 4 are going to launch a breakfast show. You need to write one'.

So, like a 24-year-old chimpanzee with an Amstrad 9512, I did. It was the show we did on GLR mixed with Simon Mayo's brilliant breakfast show on Radio 1 and my favourite TV show as a kid, *Tiswas*. I told Charlie it was a bit like 'zoo radio': the Howard Stern Show I had listened to when I was visiting a friend in New York.

Charlie had thought of the house and Bob Geldof had thought of the title *The Big Breakfast*. And I always remember them looking at me as they read the first bits of paper and saying, 'But who on earth can do this?'

I said, 'Well there's a guy I answered phones for at GLR. He's called Chris Evans.' You know I didn't know anybody else then, it was just instinct. If they had said somebody else more famous I probably wouldn't have said much. I was very naïve. I figured everybody in this incredible world of television, radio and magazines was as excellent as you.

You met Charlie and although you were the hottest name in town (I subsequently discovered you were on pretty much every C4 breakfast slot proposal) you shook hands with him and said 'yes'.

Do you remember that summer of 1992 auditioning for your co-host? Endless run throughs whilst that house was being built? The noise of saws and stuff drowning the shows we were shooting on little hi-8 cams? The final three were the gorgeous Joanna Kaye, Gaby Roslin and the then unheard of model booker and party organiser, our friend Davina McCall.

When the *Big Breakfast* team was assembled I became the researcher on Friday's show. I sat at home and watched the very first show on the Monday the *BB* launched. I cried all the way through. Oh my God. We had all done it! And you could feel every day the country switching on to this thing. You heard it on the Tube and in the pub, and you saw it in the newspapers and then six weeks in you and Gaby were on *This Morning* being interviewed by Richard and Judy and we all knew we had arrived.

We parted again when you went upstairs to do *Toothbrush*. I didn't feel that mad I wasn't part of that gang – simply because I knew we were different and had separate lives.

And I am so sorry for standing on my dignity for too long. The Saturday I brought my first born, Louie, home from the hospital in November 1997 I sprinted to the 7/11 on the corner of Chepstow Road and Westbourne Grove to buy a lottery ticket (I realised I was the luckiest man in the world and tonight was my night) and we ran smack into each other, knocked each over and picked ourselves up, turned away and said nothing.

Sorry. That still shames me.

You know what? I've been really lucky. I've had the most incredible time working with some of the most talented people in the world of television, but it all started with you. And that silly little show *The Greenhouse* on GLR. That's where you taught me how to do it.

And when we saw each other last week and you asked me to write this bit for your book, I was glad. Truly, truly glad. To be able to say thank you. For the record. Thank you Chris Evans, for everything.

NAME: Suzi Aplin

10 things you may not know about Chris Evans

1. He is the only person I know who can make a Ramsay-standard concoction with the following five ingredients: one tub (yes, a whole tub) of Philadelphia (and, crucially, not the Light alternative), one can of tomatoes, one lemon, one onion and one clove of garlic – all thrown together with penne cooked *al dente*. Oh, and heaps of black pepper. It's delicious. Trust me, I've challenged many a supreme cook to try their hand at this and they have, without exception, failed.
2. Bono's nickname for him is Elvis.
3. He is an annoyingly gifted games supremo – I've never known him be defeated by a crossword, he's dynamite at Boggle, fearsome at Trivial Pursuit and legendary at Articulate. Though when it came to Scrabble, I trounced him every time.
4. He is more at ease naked than any man or woman I know – without question, his best ideas come when he is free from the constraints of clothes. In fact, nudity often leads to more nudity – the infamous Naked Parade that ran for a long spell on *TFI Friday* came about when, locked in the bathroom for an hour after some heated discussion or other, he emerged steaming from the room, proud and bare, with a lampshade propped upside down on top of his head.
5. He pretty much accomplishes anything he turns his hand to ... perhaps failure is not an option. Three alternative careers I think could have been his if he'd set his heart on it: 1. Concert pianist. 2. Michelin-starred chef. 3. Golf pro.
6. On the flipside, he is a totally rubbish swimmer.
7. He is extraordinarily, wonderfully, sometimes stupidly, generous – with sharing, with embracing, with loving. He seizes the moment and all it encompasses – lost souls, dangerous strangers, mad adventures, ridiculous challenges – like no one I've ever known. If you've not yet been

bought a drink by him, your time will come. He will find you eventually. And you will have a wonderful night.

8. He never washes his hair but it is *always* clean. In six years I never saw a drop of shampoo get within a mile of him. Is that weird? Is he onto something he should be bottling?

9. His initial attempts at a rendition of 'Sympathy for the Devil' for *Don't Forget Your Toothbrush* were so painful they would have prompted tears from Mick Jagger. Jools Holland had to momentarily leave the rehearsal room. He got there in the end, of course, and pulled it off proudly on the actual night, but the rehearsal tape remains safely locked up in a TV vault somewhere – I'm not sure the time would ever be right for public consumption. He later went on to make a *TFI Friday* special with The Rolling Stones – it was a huge coup and I was never sure if word had reached Mick of Chris's passionate homage.

10. This list could go on forever – it's impossible to narrow it down to ten. So instead, I'll just sum up by saying that when you are sharing his air space – be it as friend, partner, colleague or fleeting, passing stranger – you absolutely believe that *anything* is possible. Growing old is mandatory but growing up is optional. Chris's mantra is that life is incredibly short and an absolute gift, and as such must be grasped tightly because every single second counts. With this comes inevitable risk and danger, but wow, it's always an adventure. With him I experienced some of the most outrageous, insane, bizarre, scary and occasionally dark moments. But I also had the most fun, exciting, blissful, loving, funny and unbelievably happy times with this fireball of a human, and I wouldn't swap any of it for a moment. A lifetime of amazing memories – and who could ever wish for more than that?

NAME: Michael Gates

What are days for?
Days are where we live.
They come, they wake us
Time and time over.

They are to be happy in.
Where can we live but days?

Ah, solving that question
Brings the priest and the doctor
In their long coats
Running over the fields.

Philip Larkin

Summer 1987. Ainsworth, near Bolton, Lancashire. Chris, 21, and living in a tent in our back garden, has hired a video camera for the day and got me to film him in a demo for the BBC. It's the first time he has ever appeared on screen. Listening to his running order in my tiny bedroom at The Old Vicarage I realise for the first time that he is a genius, but somehow cannot bring myself to tell him.

I have known him since Tony Ingham, Programme Controller at Piccadilly Radio, asked me to show 'some 16-year-old kid from hospital radio' (not true – he had never set foot in a studio) how the station worked. I still see him clearly sitting on the sofa outside the control room with wiry dark red hair, set off by a white and turquoise DJ-style jacket. Goggly eyes. Specs. I discover he has never eaten rice.

Our demo starts with a wobbly hand-held close-up of an alarm clock ringing (*Big Breakfast*?), then cuts to his sleeping wedge-shaped head: my Anglo-Saxon tutor at Oxford believed that such heads are always the most intelligent. He opens his eyes, and a new day dawns.

I am now filming him driving his old white Ford Escort as he talks straight to camera about why he should be on TV. 'Let's see what's on the radio,' he says, pressing the button with a flourish. Supernaturally on cue 'There's no business like show business' blurts out of the tinny loudspeaker.

Accidents always seem to happen around Chris. Twists of fate – both lucky and unlucky. He believes in karma. The unlucky twists are easiest to remember: the gas explosion next to his car; the woman pouring a cup of tea over his head before the lights had changed as he sat in his MG; the swarm of flies buzzing out of his maggot box when we went fishing; the botulism from a tin of tuna that nearly killed him on-air; the Bob Geldof interview he recorded over; Bryce Cook's taped Sunday religious show spiralling onto the studio floor seconds before it was due to be broadcast ...

And the video? Does this historic piece of film hold pride of place on his bookshelf? Can you find it on YouTube? Is it in the 'Don't-Call-Us-We'll-Call-You' file, gathering dust in Broadcasting House?

No. None of these. 'Someone nicked it from the back-seat of the car,' he told me a few days after we made it, with a shrug and a laugh.

There were even louder laughs when, not long after, another Piccadilly Programme Controller, Mike Briscoe, halved his modest salary. Partly my fault, so I was feeling pretty guilty. 'He must have been really really angry,' Chris explained as he held Mike's letter up to the window. 'You can see the light through the holes where he typed the full-stops.'

Summer 1990. Oxford town centre. A man slumped on the street asks us for money and claims to be P.J. Proby, the trouser-splitting 60s pop star, fallen on hard times. Chris gives him some and muses on fame and fortune, as is his wont. The downs stimulate him as much as the ups. Particularly the slender twists of fate that separate one from the other.

Strange. DJ-ing can be a frothy, shallow, brainless business. But the unknown Christopher James Evans is as deep as they come. The big philosophical questions are what, at heart, drive him. 'What are days for?' Larkin asks. Chris, I think you know better than most.

NAME: Jade, Chris Evans's daughter

What was it like having Chris Evans as your dad?

It's hard to explain. I used to get asked that question all the time, amongst other things such as, do you hate him? Does he send you millions of pounds for your birthday? Which I'd then reply with no, why would I hate somebody I didn't know?

Some people say I've missed out on having a dad but what would they know? How could I miss something I've never had?

The first time I met my dad I had mixed emotions. I was obviously nervous. Would we get on? Would he like me? Would he want to see me again? But as soon as I met him he put me at ease. He is so easy to get on with and there weren't any awkward silences that I'd imagined there may have been.

My dad is one of the nicest, most caring and generous people I have ever met. He can make a conversation with anybody and never fails to make people smile. I couldn't be happier that we have made contact and are now building on our father–daughter relationship.

Not only have I gained a great dad but I've also gained an amazing family too, who have made me feel welcome and loved like I've always been a part of it.

Things happen the way they do for a reason and it doesn't matter if it's taken my dad and I a bit longer to get to know one another than it maybe should have, at least we've got there.

NAME: Danny Baker

It's incredible to imagine now but when I first met Chris he was barely nine years old. No, hang on, I just looked it up and he was actually twenty-one. Indeed, now I think about it, 'nine' was a lazy and ridiculous guess at his age in 1988. I apologise for that and promise you I will give more thought to the rest of this entry. Still, wouldn't that have been something, eh? Me, at thirty-one, hanging out with a nine-year-old radio producer? People would say, 'Is *that kid* producing your hit radio show?' And I'd say, 'Yep.' And they'd say, 'Well, how old is he?' And I'd go, like, 'Nine.' And there he'd be, all concentration and tongue sticking out the corner of his mouth, cueing up terrible records and shouting at the phone answerers.

No, Chris, as I'm sure you've already read, was born in 1966. What he may have been too abashed to tell you is that at just three days old he was already all set to make national headlines when, after briefly going missing, he was found behind a hedge by Pickles the dog. Sadly this story was knocked off the front pages when, just half an hour later, Pickles also found the recently stolen World Cup and nobody cared about the red-headed baby angle any more. But his time would come.

So, back to 1988 when our combined ages were just forty. I had never been in a radio studio before and was asked if I was OK with handling the phalanx of dials, knobs and levers that would somehow give my audio creature life. Swallowing something hard and jagged, I told them that I was from TV and all you had to do there was stare at a glass rectangle and yodel. A muted internal phone call was made in which, I believe, the phrases 'milquetoast' and 'big Jesse' were used.

Within minutes help had arrived, as in bounded a long streak of electricity wearing Buddy Holly's glasses and Rufus the Red's spare toupee.

'Hello!' he boomed in a strangulated screech, 'I'm Chris Evans. Look, working this desk is simple – you just ...' And then he proceeded to morph into Squiddly Diddly the cartoon octopus as he simultaneously tweaked, faded, balanced, equalised and cued about eighty things at once. Two minutes later he stopped. 'Got that?' he said. I whimpered that I might need him to 'stick around during the first show ...'

For the next few months we had a completely magnificent time inventing each other and tearing jagged, boss-eyed raucous radio straight out of the ether.

At the time of my debut on GLR I had already been on TV in London for about eight years. After about our third show, Chris and I decamped across to The Rising Sun pub and as we stood at the bar, holding a five-pound note aloft and bellowing that we were not leaving until we had spent it all up, a couple came across and asked if I was Danny Baker. After ascertaining that they weren't creditors I confirmed their suspicion. They then asked for my autograph which I, as is my style, proceeded to furnish in the most flamboyant script. Happy with this, they then backed away from us, complete with touches to imaginary forelocks.

Chris was absolutely astounded.

'Wow!' he said all flushed. 'Wow! What the fuck does that feel like?'

It turned out he had no idea that I was regionally, partially famous. He seemed knocked out to actually know someone, really know someone, who signed up to three autographs a month.

His eyes jangled in their sockets. A sort of heavenly choir played trombones inside his head. His mouth flooded with the ambrosia of ambition. I could see there and then that he wanted some of that. He threw back his head and howled a long laugh of excitement at the moon. This, he finally felt, was really going to happen.

The kicker part to this minor tale of self-regarding nonsense is that if you jump forward a decade from this incident you will see countless tabloid photographs of Chris leaving both murky dives as well as some of the smartest venues in the capital and there, lagging in the gloom behind him, is what at first glance appears to be a fat old tramp looking for a handout. In the countless captions and articles that accompanied these shots documenting Chris's daily adventures this individual was rarely given a name but usually contemptuously referred to as simply 'one of Chris Evans's bootlicking entourage looking to glean some reflected glory ...'

And that, my friends, is as good a guide to the giddy roulette wheel of show business as I can offer you.

We remain the nearest of hearts, the best of brothers.

NAME: Minnie Evans, Chris's mum

I remember the first time our Chrissie was ever on the radio.

Every Sunday morning as a family we used to listen to a show on Piccadilly Radio called *Tripe and Onions*. It was more for children than adults really but the kids liked it so we used to have to listen to it as well. It was quite good actually.

This particular week they ran a write-in competition following an item on size. There were three questions:

1. What is the tallest structure in the UK?
2. What is the tallest mountain in the UK?
3. What is the unit of measurement for measuring the height of horses?

As the rest of the family called out the various answers back at the radio Chris said nothing, we thought he wasn't listening but we were wrong.

Five minutes later he asked his dad if he could have a postcard. He had heard all the answers and wanted to enter the competition. He took a stamp from the top drawer and ran off to the post box to send in his entry.

The next week we received a phone call from a nice lady at the station asking to speak to our Chrissie. It turned out he had only gone and won the damn thing and they wanted him to appear on the show to accept the prize. They always invited all the kids who won onto the show to encourage other children listening to join in.

After I had gone back on the phone to confirm we could get him to Manchester for the programme the following weekend, a miniature scene broke as it was his sister and brother who had known the answers and they wanted to go as well. In the end it was decided we would all make the trip, including Dad.

The radio station were very good as they gave each of them a prize. Chrissie and Diane received a Spacehopper each and David received a pile of records.

Chrissie was also interviewed, during which he supplied the answers to the questions as well as telling the interviewer a few things about himself. These included him sharing the fact that his hobby was building model aeroplanes.

'And does your Mum let you hang them from your bedroom ceiling?' the lady asked.

'No, she throws them in the bin when I'm at school,' came his reply.

This was an out and out bare-faced lie but of course everybody believed the sweet ginger-haired little boy and not me, his hard-working mum who bought him the flippin' things.

Having said that he's not a bad lad really. I am very proud of him but no more than any of my other children or grandchildren.

P.S. The answers to the questions, by the way, were: The Post Office Tower, Ben Nevis, and 'hands'.

Plate section page 1, the answers to the questions:
1. Llandudno, North Wales, 1959.
2. The last boy in the line.